THE COVENANT AND THE SWORD

TO MY PARENTS

THE COVENANT AND THE SWORD

Arab–Israeli Relations
1948–56

by

EARL BERGER

LONDON: Routledge & Kegan Paul Ltd
TORONTO: University of Toronto Press
1965

*First published 1965
in Great Britain by
Routledge & Kegan Paul Limited
and in Canada by
University of Toronto Press*

*Printed in Great Britain
by Cox & Wyman Limited
London, Fakenham and Reading*

CONTENTS

ACKNOWLEDGEMENTS

THE Armistice Affairs Division of the Israel Foreign Ministry
kindly allowed me access to the Records of the Mixed Armistice Commissions on which much of this book is based. Walter
Eytan, then Director-General of the Ministry, and his officers
offered much information to a suspicious-looking Ph.D. student.
I take this opportunity to apologize to the security section of
the Ministry for the anxiety which I seemed to have caused
them.

The Reading Room at Chatham House offered considerable
assistance and the Press Library was my rod and my staff at all
times. I am profoundly grateful to its young ladies for the many
tedious hours they spent sorting clippings for me. The extent of
my debt to the journalists, the unsung chroniclers of contemporary history, is written on every page of this book. I would like
to thank Thomas Hamilton of the *New York Times* in particular
for sending me information on the Conciliation Commission for
Palestine. The library at the London School of Economics went
to great pains to locate UN documents for me. The Central
Zionist Archives in Jerusalem provided interesting material
on the Zionists' early plans for the economic development of
Palestine. The University of Ghana was kind enough to allow
me a short leave of absence to re-examine documents in
Jerusalem.

Elie Kedourie, lecturer in Politics and Public Administration
at the LSE, gave generously of his time and advice when it was
badly needed. I would like to thank Professor C. A. W. Manning, former chairman of the Department of International
Relations at the LSE for his encouragement and support, and
Brigadier Stephen Longrigg and Erskine Childers for their

suggestions. L. M. C. van der Hoeven Leonhard of the Netherlands Arab Institute kindly sent me an English translation of his article on the Arab refugees, published in *Libertas*.

Harry Arthurs, Carsten Holbraat, David Melnik and Evan Rotner suggested valuable improvements. Major Tom Finan read the manuscript with a fine military eye for detail, and Norman Franklin of Routledge and Kegan Paul and Richard Davidson of the University of Toronto Press greatly assisted me in bringing it up to publication standards.

To the many others who gave advice, information and encouragement, I offer my thanks, heartfelt even if inadequate to meet my debt. In particular, I want to mention Harvey and Ida Weiner whose friendship was gratefully received, and my wife who patiently bore up under the complaints and tribulations of the writer in labour.

MAPS

vii

ABBREVIATIONS

ADL	Armistice Demarcation Line
CCP	Conciliation Commission for Palestine
DZ	Demilitarized Zone
GAA	General Armistice Agreement
HKJ	Hashemite Kingdom of Jordan
JVA	Jordan Valley Authority
LCA	Local Commanders' Agreements
MAC	Mixed Armistice Commission
RIIA	Royal Institute of International Affairs (Chatham House)
UNRWA	United Nations Relief and Works Agency (for Palestine Refugees in the Near East)
UNTSO	United Nations Truce Supervision Organization
CSM	*Christian Science Monitor*
GAOR	*UN General Assembly Official Records*
JAD	*Jewish Agency Digest of Press and Events*
JOMER	*Jewish Observer and Middle East Review*
JP	*Jerusalem Post*
LaB. Egypt.	*La Bourse Egyptienne*
MEA	*Middle Eastern Affairs*
MEJ	*Middle East Journal*
MG	*Manchester Guardian*
NYHT	*New York Herald Tribune* (and the European Edition)
NYT	*New York Times*
SCOR	*UN Security Council Official Records*
Times	*The Times* of London

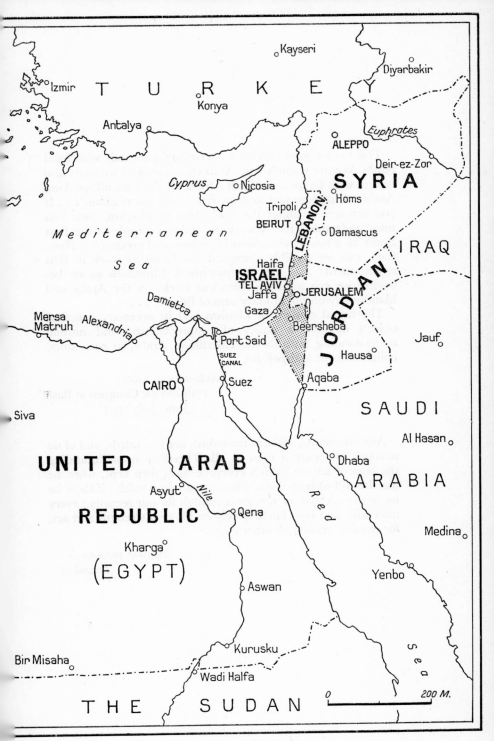

Israel in the Middle East

This too we were taught: we have to do not only with local Arabs. We are encircled by Arab countries, and we must also reckon with Egypt and North Africa, all Moslem, all speaking Arabic. I implore you to draw the deadly conclusions. . . . If you are serious about the realization of Zionism, then you must understand that we are becoming a people of the East again, in a new environment of politics and geography. How, then, can we possibly disregard the forces at work in that environment? . . . Yet our pinchbeck Churchills go on believing we can afford to turn our backs on the Arabs and blandly rely on the military arm of Britain. . . .

The moral content of Zionism and its necessary practical objects demand a policy of rapprochement and mutual understanding towards the Palestinian Arabs, in economics, enlightenment and politics.

DAVID BEN GURION
17th Zionist Congress at Basle
(June–July 1931)

And covenants, without the sword, are but words, and of no strength to secure a man at all. Therefore notwithstanding the laws of nature (which everyone hath then kept, when he has the will to keep them, when he can do it safely) if there be no power erected, or not great enough for our security; every man will, and may lawfully rely on his own strength and art, for caution against all other men.

THOMAS HOBBES
Leviathan

Chapter One

BACKGROUND TO THE
CONFLICT

IN January 1949 the first Arab–Israeli war ended. In October
1956 the second began with Israel's invasion of Egypt. What
happened in those intervening seven years to persuade the
Israelis to attack is the subject of this book.

Israel's relations with the Arab countries formed only a sub-
plot in a complex, many-layered drama. The main characters
were the Arabs and the Great Powers. The story moved in three
main themes: the argument amongst the Great Powers over
who would have what in the Middle East; the Arabs' struggle
against the West for independence and self-respect; and the dispute amongst the Arabs themselves over who should lead that
struggle. These themes were well developed long before the
Balfour Declaration was put in the mail and the Palestine
Question became an important issue.

Palestine itself is, or was, an unprepossessing land: small,
rocky, sandy, dusty, and mosquito-ridden, the milk and honey
long gone amidst the havoc of centuries of unending invasion
and war. It contains a narrow coastal plain, backed up by
rocky foothills and a range of eroded mountains. It lies across
the only land route connecting Egypt and Africa to the Arab
countries, Europe and Asia. Were it not the 'home' of three great
and quarrelsome religions it would merit hardly more concern
than does Lebanon. But home it is, and this makes it virtually

I

impossible to examine its history with anywhere near the same degree of dispassionate interest and punctilious objectivity which can be brought to bear so readily on the affairs of areas of comparable population like Lebanon, Guatemala, and Cleveland, Ohio.

In one form or another the struggle amongst the European Powers for domination of the Middle East stretches back for hundreds of years. The present conflict took its shape in the 1830's, during the First Syrian War, when Britain and France became alarmed at the sight of Russians moving to the Bosphorus to assist the Ottoman Sultan against the threats of the Egyptians led by Ibrahim Pasha, who had just conquered Syria with the help of the French, who had not counted on Russian intervention. Not a great deal has changed since then.

The exigencies of the First World War necessitated the partition of the Ottoman Empire. The British saw their chance to occupy it from the Persian Gulf to the Mediterranean: it was necessary only to exclude France. The Russians, occupied with their revolution, were no longer interested in the Middle East. The British encouraged the young Arab nationalists in an anti-Turkish revolt in 1916 in the hope that a liberated Arab world would cooperate with them—and with the Zionists. The rot set in before the peace treaties were signed. The following decades were marked by the steady, reluctant contraction of British influence in the face of burgeoning Arab and Zionist nationalism. They won neither friendship nor trust from either; only in Israel did they leave behind well-ordered, stable government.

The French never forgave the British for trying to oust them out of Syria and Lebanon. What little political influence they retained, as the two Arab countries moved into independence, was used to embarrass Britain and to prevent anyone else from replacing them in Syria and Lebanon. They assisted the Zionists against the British. They opposed plans for a Fertile Crescent union of Syria, Lebanon and Transjordan led by the British-sponsored Hashemite kings of Transjordan and Iraq. They interfered in the work of the Conciliation Commission for Palestine in order to frustrate a peace settlement which would benefit the Hashemites. In November 1956 they acted directly to prevent Egypt from bringing Syria into federation with her.

The Americans took no consistent interest in the Middle East until the late 1940's when Britain's decline forced them into an active role opposing the spread of Russian influence. The mainspring of Anglo–American tension in the Middle East, as elsewhere, was the powerful, anti-colonial feeling imbedded deep in the fabric of American thinking—official as well as public. The Americans, whose experiences of British rule were not always relevant, saw only its many defects and often failed to understand the nature of the eruptive and divisive forces which it held in check. Here there was ripe ground for Anglo–American dissension and dispute, not only over Palestine, but wherever the British were struggling to maintain the tattered remnants of control. The Americans' oil holdings in Saudi Arabia further complicated matters. Understandably they felt it expedient to support the Riyadh–Cairo axis against the Hashemites and their plans for Fertile Crescent unity.

Lack of experience left the Americans unprepared to cope with the nationalistic forces which their anti-colonial policy encouraged. They could not understand why the Arabs should class them as imperialists, in the same category as the British. American policy contained an inherent, fundamental tension. On the one hand it was anti-colonial and pro-nationalist; on the other it was anti-Russian and anti-communist. It was the latter which truly exercised the Americans. They could not accept that a nationalist movement would in all sincerity prefer the bear to the eagle or, more commonly, prefer not to have any preferences. To the Americans, their struggle with Russia was a moral one in which all right-thinking people would want to involve themselves. The corollary was that those who did not so involve themselves were not right-thinking. Experience has brought knowledge, but in the early 1950's the Americans and the Arabs had remarkably little to say to each other about the Cold War that the other understood.

The Russians did not leap into the Middle East. Until the death of Stalin they were reluctant even to work with the Arab nationalists whom they regarded as members of the *bourgeoisie*. Russian support for the Zionists in 1948, as a means of

3

embarrassing the British, indicates the then limited views of Soviet policy-makers. But, to the Arabs, the Russians could do no wrong. The Russians did not ask for military treaties, oil concessions, army bases or those ominous 'understandings freely negotiated on equal terms'. The Arabs needed the Russians. The wonder is not that the Russians carried off the great *coup* of the Czech arms deal in 1955, but that they did not seize the numerous opportunities offered earlier. It is a pattern with which we are now familiar, but, again, in the 1950's we had still much to learn about how the newly-independent countries regarded Western democracies.

How did Israel stand in relation to the Powers' quarrel with each other, and to their conflict with the Arab nationalists? It is easy to point to numerous examples of heightened tension and anger, but it is hard to see where Israel created any fundamental changes. Take the tension between the Arabs and the West, a commonly-held example of the difficulties which the creation of Israel engendered. To say that Israel is responsible for Britain's and America's difficulties with the Arabs is to mock the Arab nationalist movement and to ignore history. Tension between the Arabs and the Christian West has existed for centuries, and involves issues far more important than Israel. It is worth recalling the Crusades (as the Arabs do continually), the massacre of Christians at Jeddah in 1859 and in Damascus and Beirut in 1860, the plunder of Egypt in the early part of the nineteenth century and the circumstances surrounding the Arabi revolt and its suppression, the Iraqi Rebellion in 1920, and the shelling of Damascus. Obviously Israel forms a part of the Arabs' conception of Western oppression and imperialism, but only a part.

Taking more recent times, it is hard to see how Israel affected more than marginally the conflict arising out of the Arabs' desire for independence, sovereignty and self-assertion, and the Western powers' desire to maintain and protect their interests in the Middle East. Nasser and Dulles fell out over their differing conceptions of national interest, not over Israel. To say, as some do, that without Israel Egypt would have joined the Western-sponsored Middle East Defence Organization or allowed the British to remain in Suez, is to say that the Syrians should have joined the French Community because France did not turn Aleppo into a Greek city.

The British, the Americans, the French, all considered that they had interests in the Middle East which should be protected. The Arabs considered this to be incompatible with their ideas of national development. This was the watershed of the problems and difficulties the West faced, both in their relations with the Arab States and in the struggle against Russia. Arab–Israeli relations hastened developments, exacerbated feelings, complicated issues. It was the pepper in the stew, but the pot was already boiling.

Arab nationalism has always been Pan-Arab and Islamic. Like most nationalist movements, it looks back to earlier days of glory for its identity: the days of the Arab Empire. The Arab Empire was Islamic before it was Arab. It was the Muslims who gave to the Arab peoples their sense of unity and of common destiny. The Muslim Arabs came out of Arabia as crusaders, intent on spreading to all mankind the message of God as brought to them by Mohammed. The people they conquered in their expansion along the southern coast of the Mediterranean lived in small, discontinuous, diverse communities, loyal to their families and their tribes. With the Muslim invasion these peoples became Arabs and Muslim—at least the majority did. After the break-up and disintegration of the Empire the old particularist loyalties reasserted themselves. What remained of the racial concept was a vague feeling of Arabism expressed in the common use of Arabic, but with little political influence. Islam, however, lived on as a powerful, fundamental and all-embracing force in the life of the individual and of the community. Attempts to revive the concept of Arab unity would, of necessity, lay the greater stress upon religious sentiment—the only bond common to most Arabs.

Islam lies at the heart of Arab nationalism: without it there cannot be an 'Arab nation'. Arab nationalism is not merely a movement designed to rejuvenate Arab greatness: it is a vehicle for the reaffirmation of the validity of Islam. Islamic tradition is founded on the principle that destiny is in the hands of God, and that the Islamic community is His favourite. There is little distinction between Islam as a religion and Islam as a political entity. Political power is an essential ingredient of Islamic doctrine, for it is only in the power of the community that one can find the embodiment and justification of God's message. This conception reached its highest point of actuality —and confirmation—during the days of the Arab Empire. The subsequent decay and suppression of the Empire can be considered as a reflection of Islam's weakness, of its inability to meet the challenges of history.

In the course of recent history the Muslim world has been dominated by the Christian colonialists, and defeated by the Jewish Zionists. This is the crisis of Islam. Arab nationalism is the response: a concerted effort to redress history, not just to achieve independence in the various Arab countries, but to restore greatness, unity and respect to the 'Arab nation'.

Israel, of course, has an especial importance for the Arab nationalists. She did not create the crisis of Islam or its manifold effects. All these existed long before the Balfour Declaration and independently of Zionism. To this extent Israel is not fundamental to an explanation of the Arabs' situation. But by her very existence she illuminates the crisis and the weaknesses which engendered it as nothing else does now. The West can be driven out and humiliated, but Israel remains. Not only is she a remnant of Western imperialism, not only has she inflicted a great injustice on the Arabs, but also she is Jewish, by definition inferior to the Islamic world. Yet twice, in 1917 and 1947, the civilized world chose the claims of the Jews over those of the Arabs. In 1948-9 the Arabs found neither strength nor unity but only weakness and division, corruption and selfishness ending in humiliating defeat.

It is not surprising that they conceive of Israel as a problem involving their 'survival or extinction'.[1] The symbolic importance of the struggle is such that, to the Arabs' present thinking, only through Israel's defeat can Islam and Arabism be vindicated. In this sense the presence of Israel acts as a catalyst,

---

[1] N. A. Faris and M. T. Husayn, *Crescent in Crisis*, pp. 175-6; see also C. Malik in *Foreign Affairs*, January 1952:

Israel 'constitutes a virtual touchstone of Arab capacities for self-preservation and self-determination. . . . There is abroad a grim sense of destiny.'

hastening the process of disintegration endemic in developing countries, and quickening the growth of the new, more modern forces in the Arab World.

There is, of course, more to the Arabs' dislike of Israel than wounded pride and religious uncertainty. The Zionists came out of Europe armed with a piece of paper and the authority of the British Empire and deprived the inhabitants of Palestine of their land and of their political and economic future. It was, in Arab eyes, a 'premeditated, systematic and ruthless'[1] policy of expansion which might easily include all the Arab lands between the Nile and the Euphrates[2] and create how many more millions of refugees.

The Arabs see that the Israelis could not exist without the support of the Western countries, and so they believe that Israel is 'a bridgehead . . . for imperialism against the Arab States . . . capitalist domination in its cruellest form . . . behind which the ambitions of imperialism hide themselves'.[3] Largely ignorant of the peculiarities and history of the Judaeo–Christian symbiosis, the Arabs have never been able to understand the stark forces impelling Zionism, or the West's reluctance to stand in its way. It has been much easier for them to think of Zionism in terms of a great international plot directed against them personally.

These are the reasons for the Arabs' hatred of Israel: a 'pathological antipathy'[4] which goes to the very heart of Arab thought and sentiment, and which is, for the time being, beyond mending.

The character of Arab nationalism has also been shaped by the division, dissension and strife which have continually plagued the Arab world. In recent times the Arab world has suffered from all the social and economic tensions and upheavals to which rapidly developing, but still underdeveloped, societies are prone. Also, contrary to popular belief, the Arab world has always been divided, except for a brief time during the days of the Arab Empire. The divisions go back to the earliest

[1] *SCOR*, 511th mtg., 16th October 1950, pp. 6, 9.
[2] Nuri es-Said, *Mideast Mirror*, 7th April 1956, p. 13.
[3] Gamal Abdul Nasser, in R. K. Karanjia, *Arab Dawn* (Bombay 1958), pp. xiii–xv.
[4] Emile Bustani, *Doubts and Dynamite* (London 1958) p. 13.

days of civilization and correspond roughly to what we now call Iraq, Syria, Egypt, and Saudi Arabia (including Jordan). In 1948, as Israel was emerging into statehood, there were two Arab blocs. In the one, there were the Hashemite countries of Transjordan and Iraq led by the then Emir of Transjordan, Abdullah, who wanted to lead a union of Fertile Crescent States; in the other, Syria, Egypt and Saudi Arabia.

The Syrians with their long tradition of republican, nationalist sentiment were unwilling to be superseded in the Crescent by Jordan, or to accept the possibility of a Hashemite royal government, or to accept the extension of British influence in the guise of Hashemite rule. The Saudis' opposition to the Hashemites was based partly on tribal feuds and partly on Ibn Saud's desire to lead Arab unity himself. Lacking all the necessary resources except money, he had to content himself with supporting the Egyptians and other anti-Hashemite factions wherever they appeared. The Egyptians were comparative newcomers to the Arab world, even though Cairo had been a nationalist centre for years (some Arabs still regard the Egyptians as outsiders).[1] Their involvement in 1948 in Arab affairs was largely the result of their determination to squelch British influence represented by the ambitious Abdullah. King Farouk, of course, had his own ideas about who should lead the Arab world. The Lebanese, mindful of their delicate domestic compromise between the Christians and the Muslims, steered a wary course between the Hashemites and Syria.

After 1948, Hashemite influence in the Arab world declined rapidly, and Egypt's rose. This was paralleled by the growing strength of nationalist sentiment. The various leaders may have squabbled often and at length, but the general message of Arabism was permeating the masses. In the 1940's, Arab unity was the concern of a few intellectuals and a talking point for politicians. By the 1950's, it was a popular concern, one involving all articulate sections of the population. It is possible that Arab unity may never be achieved. Despite the pull of Islam and the growing sense of national identification, the divisive influences may prove too strong.

[1] In May 1956 Nasser was still making a clear distinction between Egyptian interests and those of the Arabs. *LaB. Egypt.* 31st May 1956, quoting *Al Gomhourya.*

For our purposes, however, the future of the movement is irrelevant. In 1948–50, the Arab States were badly divided in their attitudes towards Israel; peace by negotiations was possible. But in the 1950's, fostered vigorously by Egypt, Arab nationalism went from strength to strength. It and its attendant anti-Israel sentiment so saturated all sectors of the Arab world that by 1956 there was no hope for peace through negotiations or of limited co-operation, or even of peaceful coexistence. Arab nationalism was in full stride, and Israel was both a goal and an obstacle.

Zionism was a failure, until Hitler came to power. Outside of East European Jewry, few people were willing to go and actually live in Palestine. Between the 1880's and 1927 the Jewish population in Palestine rose from about 25,000 to just under 150,000, thereby forming about one-seventh of Palestine's total population. Impressive as this accomplishment was, Zionism was rapidly failing.

Theodore Herzl had said that there must be a majority of Jews in Palestine. But by 1927 the sources of immigration were almost dried up, and those who had immigrated were showing a distressing tendency to emigrate. If the Zionists were ever going to achieve a majority, they had to bring in tens of thousands of immigrants annually for decades. Between 1920 and 1932 the figure of 10,000 was surpassed only three times. Usually the net gain was less than half that. It was almost impossible for the Zionists to find sufficient immigration to offset the Arabs' high natural population increase just to maintain a ratio of six to one. It seemed inconceivable that a Jewish majority could ever be created.

This was accepted with equanimity by most Jews. We often forget that the Zionists formed only a small part of world Jewry. The vast majority of Jews, including many Zionists, were not really concerned with statehood. Men like Chaim Weizmann and David Ben Gurion were 'extremists', far ahead of their time and of their followers. Statehood was the official policy, but there was no sense of immediacy—or perhaps even of reality. Ahad Ha'am seems to have summed up prevailing opinion when he described Palestine as a 'safe refuge for all oppressed and persecuted Jews'. As long as there was a 'National Home' in Palestine, a *Yishuv*, for Jews who had no place else to go, the situation was regarded as more or less satisfactory. Despite the well-publicized militancy of some Zionists, most of world Jewry was opposed to Zionism, apathetic, or interested only to the extent of contributing money.

Nazism gave Zionism its impetus and the strength necessary to overcome the enormous obstacles in its way. Not only did immigration shoot up to over 60,000 in 1935, but membership in the various Zionist and pro-Zionist organizations doubled and trebled. Jews everywhere were made aware of their vulnerability. No European Jewish community had seemed safer or farther along the road to assimilation than that in Germany. Now, not only were Jews being slaughtered, but those who escaped found it difficult to obtain refuge in the 'liberal-democratic' countries only because, so it seemed, they were Jews.

Extremism and ruthlessness became the characteristics of Zionist policy from this time forward. It was not so much a case of the extremists taking over as of everyone becoming an extremist. Many calculated, unpleasant things were done which give to the Zionism of that time an air of conspiracy directed against sensible people of good intentions. But there seemed to be no room for moderation, no room for long-term development, no time to ship D.P.'s off to the United States or Brazil. The Jews were determined to have a place of their own. In their eyes Nazism was the culmination of centuries of persecution: the Gentile could not be trusted. It is misleading to dismiss Zionist propaganda of the time as nothing more than propaganda. It revealed a state of mind—a crisis of self-awareness—which had done with doubts, hesitations and qualifications. Hitler had made Jews everywhere aware of their Jewishness, of their vulnerability. That vulnerability had to be ended.

This then was the mainspring behind modern Zionism—and later, Israeli nationalism: the persecution, the insecurity, and the reaction against hate and murder. There grew up a desperate conviction that there had to be a state, that it had to work, that it would be unbearable to return to the old ways. After 1945, the mood of desperation was transferred to Palestine and latterly Israel. The Jews there found it difficult to forget that many Arabs had supported the Nazis, and it was easy for them to assume a similarity between Arab and Nazi propaganda and intentions: the pattern was all too familiar. It is unnecessary now to ask whether or not the Arabs really intended to 'exterminate' Israel. It is important only that they left little doubt in the minds of the Israelis and of Jews generally.

The peculiar circumstances in which the Israelis were forced to live caused them to extract from the great mass of widely varying Zionist 'philosophies' a distinctive nationalist doctrine, based on the concept of an *élite*, in which the influence of the Old Testament, not unnaturally, was strong.

This doctrine receives its fullest and most important expression in the speeches and writings of David Ben Gurion, long-time Zionist leader and premier of Israel. He speaks unambiguously of the 'messianic purpose' of the Jewish people, of his belief '. . . in our moral and intellectual superiority, in our capacity to serve as a model for the redemption of the human race. . .' 'We are sons of the Homeland, disciples of the Bible, and bearers of the vision of the great redemption of the Jewish people and of humanity. . . .' Israel, although small, is 'in ethics and intellect marvellous': 'it walks with the greatest among nations'. Ben Gurion places great emphasis upon the State, as distinct from the Nation: 'The State has become the main and keenest instrument to fulfil the vision of Zionism. . . . The [Zionist] Movement must bring itself . . . to recognize the State as prime and supreme among the bringers of redemption.'[1]

This kind of thinking is common to most nationalist movements. In Israel's case the circumstances surrounding her creation and survival fostered what some might regard as an undue and unhealthy emphasis upon the concept of an *élite*. (Although without this faith in themselves and their mission it is unlikely that Ben Gurion and his countrymen could have succeeded or even survived.) But it is difficult to say how much of it truly reflects a feeling of superiority, and how

[1] See the two speeches quoted in A. Hertzberg, *The Zionist Idea*, and Irving Miller's retort that the Israelis have forgotten the original principles of Zionism (p. 82).

much it is a defensive reaction to the inescapable threat of Arab invasion, and to Arab accusations and an Islamic philosophy of Jewish cowardice and inferiority (and to a European history of passivity).

Disregard for the Arabs was one of the Zionists' greatest strengths. Any objective study in 1917 of the difficulties to be faced would have convinced most Zionists that the venture was hopeless. In so far as they thought about cooperation it was in terms of a modern, developed community moving in to assist a backward, ignorant peasantry.[1] Talk of the two nations marching together toward enlightenment and socialism clearly indicated the Zionists' misunderstanding of the Palestine Arabs. There were Zionists who saw what was happening and tried hard to effect some sort of inter-communal cooperation. They were defeated by two unsurmountable obstacles. One was the absence of anyone on the other side to talk to. The other, and more important, was force of circumstance. Up until the early 1930's the likelihood that the Zionists would never form more than a small minority in Palestine provided a possible basis for cooperation and understanding. After Hitler came to power there was no scope for compromise with the Arabs on the question of Jewish immigration, and without agreement on this there could be no cooperation. The moderates had been squeezed out by circumstances.

The Zionists' relations, and latterly those of Israel, with the Great Powers have always been determined by factors beyond their control: specifically the state of the Powers' respective interests in the various parts of the Middle East. This, in part, explains why the Balfour Declaration in 1917 was such a vague, contradictory document. When they made it, the British were thinking less of the Jewish National Home and of the future

---

[1] At the time the Zionists believed that they had taken all the steps necessary for cooperation with the Arabs. Weizmann had made his 'agreement' with Feisal. Also the Zionists expected to settle on the land east of the Jordan River, in the Negev and in the north: all empty areas. But the British handed eastern Palestine (Transjordan) to Abdullah, and sold most of the large tracts of empty land in western Palestine to Arabs. The Zionists were forced to settle in well-populated areas where their presence and their activities were bound to cause friction. See Frischwasser-Ra'anan, *Frontiers of a Nation*, pp. 85 *et seq.*

I am grateful to Isaiah Friedman for providing me with much information on the subject of Arab–Jewish cooperation during this period.

relations between the Arabs and the Jews than they were of their own imperial position.[1] The Declaration was made for a peculiar combination of reasons having to do with Britain's assessment of the Middle Eastern situation—one reason, worth mentioning now because it reappeared in a slightly different form in 1956, was Britain's desire to obtain a landlink between Iraq with its oil fields and the Mediterranean—and it remained to be seen how long this combination would continue to favour the Zionists. The Arab Revolt in 1935–6 marked the turning point. Up until that time the Arabs were unable to sink their differences in pursuit of a common goal. Furthermore, the British did not have to take Arab complaints seriously, because there was no other Great Power in a position to exploit the situation. The benefits obtained from keeping the National Home alive seemed sufficient to offset the disadvantages.

There is a marked similarity between this period, 1918–35, and 1948–54. In both cases, the Arabs refused to cooperate with the Jews, and were unable to cooperate with each other against them. The Powers were occupied elsewhere and uninterested in exploiting the situation. The result was that both times the Jews had time to strengthen their position before the situation began to deteriorate. Both times the Arabs began to organize themselves for an effective campaign of violence against the Jews, while a rise in international tension resulted in the Powers seeking to support their position in the Arab world at the expense of the Jews. The Palestine question became enmeshed in the whole complex of inter-Arab, Arab-Western, and inter-Power struggles. And, in each case, it was the Jews' ability and determination to fight for their preservation which decided their success.

[1] According to one observer the Declaration was made because it was 'considered . . . clearly a British interest to do so'. Sir Charles Webster, *The Art and Practice of Diplomacy* (London 1961), p. 121, see also p. 119.

The text of the Declaration ran as follows:

'His Majesty's Government view with favour the establishment in Palestine of a national home for the Jewish people and will use their best endeavours to facilitate the achievement of this object, it being clearly understood that nothing shall be done which may prejudice the civil and religious rights of existing non-Jewish communities in Palestine, or the rights and political status enjoyed by Jews in any other country.'

Chapter Two

GENERAL COMMENTS ON THE ARMISTICE AND ARAB–ISRAELI RELATIONS

THERE are many ways to approach the tangle of Arab–Israeli relations. I have chosen to start with the General Armistice Agreements signed between Israel and each of her four Arab neighbours in 1949. The GAAs did not signify merely the end of the fighting. They were also set up 'to facilitate the transition from the present truce to permanent peace in Palestine'. Their primary, their long-term function, was to lay the groundwork, to provide the equipment necessary to bring Arab and Israeli together in political peace. If we want to understand why the Israelis acted as they did in 1956 we have to start with what was agreed upon in 1949, or at least what the Israelis thought was agreed upon in 1949.

They believed that the armistice would last for only a few months while the details of a final peace settlement were hammered out. We do not know whether or not the Arab leaders had any clear-cut ideas on the subject of peace while the armistice negotiations were still under way. Neither do we know by what process they decided later to work towards a 'second round' against Israel, or even if there actually was such a decision taken. But we do know that by their statements and their actions after the GAAs were signed they gave the Israelis the impression that they refused to make peace, that they would invade Israel again when the time was ripe, and that they were using the armistice only as a means to this end.

In politics what matters is not the truth but what people think is the truth. The Israelis were convinced that the Arabs did not want to make peace and would exploit every weakness and mistake of the Israelis so as to destroy them eventually. Consequently the Israelis approached the Arabs with the emphasis on strength rather than on conciliation, on the probability of war rather than of peace, and on the dangers of offering concessions to an enemy who would only come back and demand more until there was nothing left to give.

The Israelis may have been wrong in their assessment of Arab intentions—just as they may not have realized that it was partially fear of them which convinced the Arabs to speak and act as they did—but it was theirs and they acted accordingly. This meant that the 'activists'—Premier David Ben Gurion, the Ministry of Defence and the Army—inexorably took control of policy toward the Arabs away from the Foreign Ministry, stronghold of the 'moderates' led by Moshe Sharett. Since Israeli foreign policy was devoted largely to coping in one way or another with Arab hostility, this meant that the moderates were relegated to trying to justify to the outside world the policies of the activists.

So far as concessions for peace were concerned, on the whole the Israelis opposed large-scale territorial concessions or refugee repatriation. But they were agreeable to free ports, land-links, border adjustments and refugee compensation. When the Arabs turned these offers down, the Israelis tried a few unilateral concessions. The first was the 'reunion of families' scheme. Later, in 1952, at the suggestion of the Conciliation Commission for Palestine they released about a million pounds sterling of the refugees' blocked funds. The sum itself was small, but considering that Israel was then teetering on the verge of bankruptcy it was to the Israelis no small sacrifice. Later, in 1954, at the urging of Barclay's Bank and the Ottoman Bank,[1]

---

[1] Palestinian Arabs residing in Jordan successfully sued the two banks for their money blocked in the Israeli branches of the banks. The banks then offered Israel a loan to cover the cost of releasing the funds, and another to alleviate her pressing foreign currency shortage.

and in the hope of softening up Colonel Nasser, the remainder of the blocked funds were released. The Israelis also offered minor border adjustments to alleviate the plight of the refugees. Nothing had any effect on the Arabs' refusal to negotiate.

What the Israelis offered was not much; but there was not much they felt able to give up. Their willingness to make concessions diminished as they saw that they could survive despite Arab hostility. The doubling of the population, the extension of border settlements and the country's stability and military superiority seemed to preclude the need for concessions: political sacrifices were 'not only unnecessary but dangerous'.[1] The Arabs, it was believed, would treat proffered concessions as a sign of weakness and raise their prices accordingly.

This argument was supported by the general tenor of Arab propaganda. Year in and year out the Israelis listened to the Arabs vie with each other in calling for their destruction. No matter how much they might have told themselves that the propaganda was exaggerated, its effect on their state of mind, particularly over such a long period of time, must have been considerable. The Israelis considered that 'the idea of wiping out Israel is not just a catchword intended for Arab local consumption, but an obsession to be tried out in practice by some Arab Government or other. The slogan has been in use for too long not to have wrought a deep impression on the Arab mind'.[2]

The Israelis hoped to integrate eventually into the Middle East. But how could they integrate into a world in a state of violent flux and revolution, especially when it was to some extent directed against them? It was not enough to want to come to terms with the Arabs, one had to decide which Arabs one was going to come to terms with. Was it to be Egypt or Jordan or Syria? Was it to be the reactionary effendis or the social reformers? Was it to be the government of this man, or the government of that and 'turning rapid somersaults every time

---

[1] 'No Israel Government can afford to cede as much as ten square miles without falling, unless it received a reasonable *quid pro quo*. And a peace settlement in itself would not be regarded as a reasonable *quid pro quo*'—*Israel Economist*, September 1954, p. 166.

[2] Colonel Ya'acov Harakkabi, Chief of Army Intelligence, *Jerusalem Post*, 9th October 1955.

16

one of them falls . . .'?[1] The Israelis faced the problem in 1950 in the abortive negotiations with King Abdullah over the draft peace treaty. They were not the first to face this difficulty, but for them it was insurmountable.

Another development worth noting was the progressive decline of Western influence over Middle Eastern affairs. Because of their conflicting interests the Western countries made no sustained, cooperative effort to establish a peace settlement. In so far as there was any kind of Western policy it was usually initiated by the Americans, with the British and the French lagging behind. The emphasis was on peace through economic development, typified by the McGhee Plan and later, in 1950, the UN Reintegration Fund. Neither of these was successful, so another attempt was made on a more limited scale in 1953 on the basis of a Jordan Valley water development scheme. The diminishing scope of these plans reflected increasing lack of control over Middle Eastern affairs generally. The Arabs and the Israelis each believed that the West could if it wanted exercise control over the other. In fact, the progressive consolidation of the forces within the various countries gave the West less and less opportunity to exercise influence in the traditional manner.

By the latter half of 1955 Arab–Israeli relations were out of control. This was illustrated by the changing status of the Tripartite Declaration. In May 1950, worried about the rapidly deteriorating situation and the possibility of another Arab–Israel war, the Americans, British and French issued a Declaration[2] stating that they were opposed to an Arab–Israel arms race, and that they would sell arms only on the basis of internal security and legitimate self-defence requirements: in other words, an arms balance. The Powers declared their 'unalterable opposition' to the use of force or the threat of force. If any of the disputants were found to be preparing to violate borders the signatories would, consistently with their obligations as UN members, 'immediately take action, both within and outside the United Nations, to prevent such violation'.

[1] See *Israel Economist*, June 1950, pp. 143–5 evidently written with the crisis over the draft peace treaty still fresh in the editor's mind.

[2] For text see J. C. Hurewitz, *Diplomacy in the Near and Middle East*, vol. 2, pp. 308–11.

Comments on the Armistice and Arab–Israeli Relations

The Arabs and the Israelis were suitably impressed and the immediate danger of war receded. Apparently the situation was under control. In 1954 Prime Minister Eden told the House of Commons that he knew of 'very few international agreements, if any, which carry as strong a commitment' as the Declaration. He thought it improbable, he said, that it could be strengthened in any way.[1] This simply was not true. The injunctions regarding the use of force and the threat of force were unenforceable. Armies or sanctions were not going to be used to stop infiltration or the *fedayeen* (Egyptian-controlled raiders operating in Israel) or reprisal raids or propaganda attacks. The arms balance could be maintained only if the West controlled the sale of arms to all Middle Eastern countries. Once the Russians decided to ship Egypt and Syria large quantities of arms, the whole system of control broke down. The Americans, who had been the prime movers behind the Declaration, were more interested in withdrawing from the Declaration than in improving on it. The Powers wrangled; instead of cooperation it was *sauve qui peut*. And in 1956 Britain and France supported Israel's invasion of Egypt.

The weakness of the West was reflected in the growing ineffectiveness of the United Nations. The impotence of the Security Council was not surprising, considering its make-up and the interests of its delegates. Ordinarily, however, when the Council fails the General Assembly is there to carry on the work. But in this case the General Assembly abdicated from its position of responsibility. The Assembly had called for partition in 1947, had appointed a mediator and then a conciliation commission in 1948, and set up the Reintegration Fund in 1950. Over the next few years there was not a lot it could do. But in 1952 the Free Officers came to power in Egypt and established contacts with the Israelis, which augured well for the future. It looked as if an Arab–Israeli *rapprochement* was in the making.

That autumn an eight-power draft resolution[2] was brought

[1] *House of Commons Debates*, 2nd November 1954, vol. 532, cols. 326–7.

[2] Canada, Cuba, Denmark, Ecuador, The Netherlands, Norway, Panama and Uruguay. *GAOR*, A/AC. 61/L.23/Rev. 4, and *First Committee* meetings from 25th November to 11th December 1952. The Arabs' reaction had its humorous side since they had been responsible for bringing the matter to the Assembly's attention, in the form of a complaint against Israel (A/2184).

before the General Assembly, urging the Arabs and the Israelis, 'without prejudice to their respective rights and claims', to enter into 'direct negotiations' for a settlement, bearing in mind 'the principal objectives of the United Nations on the Palestine question, including the religious interests of third parties'. The Arabs opposed the draft resolution because it called for direct negotiations and included no specific reference to re-patriation or to the 1947 Partition Plan. The draft resolution passed safely through the First Committee, but by the time it reached the Assembly floor the Arabs had succeeded in lining up a formidable opposition. The Asian bloc supported them. The Vatican supported them because it refused to countenance continued Israeli control of Jewish Jerusalem, although it would accept Arab control of all Jerusalem. A last-minute attempt to find a compromise failed and the Latin American states either gave in to Vatican pressure or else abstained from voting. The Russians, who had abstained in the First Committee, came out against the resolution. The resolution still got a majority of votes, but not the necessary two-thirds and so it was lost: 24–21–15.

The Israelis were treated to the spectacle of twenty-one states voting against peace, and fifteen abstaining. So far as the Assembly's effectiveness, and the Israelis' faith in it, were concerned this was the final blow. There was now no disinterested authority to look to for guidance, or to protect Arab–Israeli relations from the deadly morass of Power politics. As the international situation worsened, Arab–Israeli relations were dragged down with it. Each year that passed there was that much less control over events. By the end of 1955 the situation resembled a juggernaut, irresistible, unmanageable.

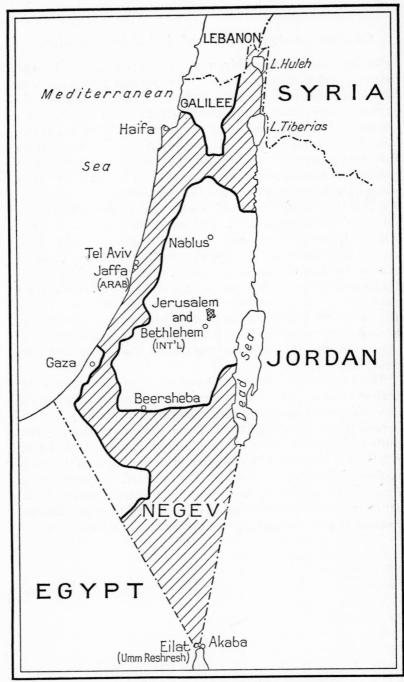

Palestine According to the UN Partition Plan.
Shaded Areas: Jewish.   White Areas: Arab.

Chapter Three

ARMISTICE NEGOTIATIONS
(January–July 1949)

ON 28th November 1947, the United Nations General Assembly adopted a resolution calling for the partition of Palestine into Jewish and Arab states bound together by economic union.[1] The Jewish State was to include Eastern Galilee, most of the coastal plain, and the Negev. Jerusalem, Bethlehem and their environs were to be internationalized. The Arab State was to comprise the remainder of Palestine

The announcement of the Partition Plan was followed by the outbreak of violence and eventually civil war. The Arab States announced that they would oppose, by force if necessary, any attempt to implement the Plan, and the hastily-formed volunteer Army of Liberation moved in from Syria. The British refused to support the Plan and began withdrawing in such a way as to leave much of the advantage with the Arabs. The Russians, continuing their efforts to frustrate the British, began to give active support to the Zionists. The Americans, worried about the possible repercussions of partition, undertook a policy designed, in all futility, to fulfil their promises to the Zionists and to placate the Arabs. The French confined themselves to embarrassing the British and trying to restore their own influence in Syria. Faced with the need for action the Arabs found themselves even more divided and jealousy-ridden than

[1] *GAOR*, (11) 181.

previously. The Zionists alone were adequately unified and disciplined.

On 14th May 1948 the State of Israel was proclaimed and its Provisional Government was immediately recognized by the United States and then Russia. On 15th May, the Arab States announced that their armies would enter Palestine. The first Arab–Israeli war had begun.[1]

On 11th June, when the Security Council's first truce came into effect, a military stalemate had been reached. The Israelis still held most of the coastal plain, but both they and the Arabs were exhausted. During the four-week truce both sides rearmed and reorganized. The Arabs refused to extend the truce period and fighting broke out again on 9th July. During the ten days of fighting the Israelis extended their holdings, and by the time the second truce came into effect on 18th July they had clearly established their military supremacy. But their continued existence depended upon gaining more territory, particularly in the north and in the south, in order to make their state viable and defensible. By this time the UN's mediation and conciliation machinery had begun to take hold and both sides came under increasing pressure to make peace. The Israelis refused to agree to any discussions which left the Arabs in possession of Eastern Galilee and the Negev. The Arabs refused to enter into any kind of discussions at all. The next few months were marked by a constant manœuvring at the conference-table and on the battlefield as everyone jockeyed to place themselves in the best possible position before the UN.

In September, the UN Mediator in Palestine, Count Folke Bernadotte, reported the failure of his mission and made several suggestions for a UN-imposed settlement. The 'Bernadotte Plan' was intended to be a sensible compromise between the promises of the Partition Plan and the existing military situation.[2] There would still be two states. All of Galilee was to go Israel. All of the Negev, including Ramle and Lydda, was to go to the Arab State. There would be no economic union.

---

[1] For accounts of the fighting see John and David Kimche, *Both Sides of the Hill*; E. O'Ballance, *The Arab–Israeli War*; N. Lorch, *The Edge of the Sword*; G. Kirk, *The Middle East: 1945–50*.

[2] *GAOR*, A/648, 17th September 1948; see also Folke Bernadotte, *To Jerusalem* (London 1951).

Instead the Arab State would be united with Transjordan. Under the Partition Plan Israel would have had an area of about 5,579 square miles; under the Bernadotte Plan, 2,124. The day after signing his Report Bernadotte was assassinated by Israeli terrorists and his Plan, originally intended as a set of tentative proposals, became the inviolable testament of a man who had died in the cause of peace. UN revulsion over the assassination and Britain's speedy support for the Plan foreshadowed its wholesale endorsement by the Assembly; something which neither Israel nor most of the Arab States were willing to accept.

Before the Plan came up for debate in the General Assembly trouble broke out first in the Negev, and then in Galilee. In both instances the Israelis were looking for opportunities to exploit and the Arabs provided them by refusing to adhere to provisions of the cease-fire. The Israelis occupied the northern Negev, including Beersheba, the important road junction, surrounded Egyptian troops at El Faluja, and reduced their positions at Gaza. Later, in October, Israeli troops moved against the Army of Liberation in the north, driving it out of Upper Galilee and following after it into Lebanon north to the Litani River. On 4th November, the Security Council ordered both sides to return to the positions held before 14th October when the fighting first broke out in the south.[1] The Israelis refused, claiming that the Arabs had instigated the fighting and must bear the consequences. Finally the Council began to take firm action. On 16th November, the withdrawal order was repeated. More important, the parties were ordered to negotiate an armistice with a view to facilitating the transition to permanent peace: refusal to comply would be treated as a breach of the peace under Articles 39 and 40 of the UN Charter and action taken accordingly.[2]

The meaning of the 16th November resolution was clear:

[1] *ibid*, S/1070, 4th November 1948.

[2] *SCOR*, S/1079, 16th November 1948.

Articles 39 and 40 provide the Security Council with the authority to determine the existence of a threat to or breach of the peace; and to order the disputants to comply with such provisional measures as are necessary to prevent an aggravation of the situation, it being understood that 'such provisional measures shall be without prejudice to the rights, claims, or position of the parties concerned'.

armistice negotiations would take place after the Israelis had withdrawn back to the lines of 14th October. The fine hand of British diplomacy was obvious. They had been trying right from the beginning to manœuvre the Israelis into an area smaller than that allotted under the Partition Plan. They had held off Security Council intervention throughout May and June when the Arabs looked like winning, and, in July when the Israelis were advancing rapidly, had tried to get a cease-fire implemented as soon as possible. Generally speaking, they were anxious to obtain the best settlement possible for the Arabs, in the belief that this would in one way or another work to their own benefit. The Bernadotte Plan suited them well: the Arabs were unlikely to get anything better, and it would increase Abdullah's, and hence their, influence considerably. It was, therefore, important to have the Israelis withdraw, particularly from the Negev, before the armistice negotiations began—on the basis of the Bernadotte Plan. To this end, the British persuaded the Council to pass the two withdrawal orders and a third on 29th December.

The Israelis were adamant. They wanted negotiations but they refused to withdraw. In order to avert Council action they arranged a compromise with Acting UN Mediator Ralph Bunche. The Egyptians would remain where they were; the Israelis would withdraw back to their 14th October lines; and the disputed area would be demilitarized—except for those Israeli mobile forces which had been there before 14th October.[1] This did not satisfy the Egyptians or the British, but it alleviated the Council's pressure on the Israelis.

In the meantime, the Assembly was debating a British resolution to adopt the Bernadotte Plan. The Russians were opposed. So were Egypt and Syria, because it gave everything to Jordan. The Americans, on whom the British counted heavily for support, were divided: the State Department favoured the resolution, the White House opposed it. Anglo-American efforts to settle their differences with each other were eventually successful and a compromise resolution was drafted. But there were other people to consider, and the resolution was defeated

[1] *Times*, UN Correspondent, 12th November 1948; *NYT*, Hamilton, 14th November 1948; *NYHT*, 15th November 1948; *Times*, 24th November 1948.

by a unique combination of Israel, Egypt, Russia and their supporters.

The Bernadotte Plan was dead. Now the problem was to get the armistice negotiations under way. The key to the impasse lay in Cairo. The Egyptians had been largely responsible for the continuation of the fighting and no Arab State would move until they did. But, backed up by the British, they refused to negotiate until the Israelis withdrew from the Negev.

There were important issues at stake. The Negev provided Egypt with her only land route to the other Arab States, and Israel with her only port on the eastern seas and the only territory suitable for large-scale exploitation and colonization. Egyptian troops had been sent across the Negev in May, establishing a line running through Beersheba and Hebron to Jerusalem. That line had been broken in October, and now the main Egyptian force was lying south and west of Beersheba. The Israelis made one last attempt to induce the Egyptians to negotiate by offering to lift the siege of Faluja. Egypt still refused. On 23rd December Israel attacked, and on the 28th her troops were across the international frontier at El Auja. The complete collapse of the Egyptian Army was imminent.

At this point Britain intervened. The Anglo-Egyptian Treaty of 1936, to which Egypt objected so much, was invoked and Britain ordered Israel to leave Egyptian territory. Consequently Israeli troops swung north back across the frontier and began to seal off the main body of Egyptian forces around Gaza. The Egyptians, caught between Britain's unwanted help and Israel's unwanted army, agreed on 6th January to enter into armistice negotiations. The one condition was that Israeli troops withdraw from Rafah heights, just inside Egyptian territory. Tension ran high. Five British reconnaissance planes were shot down over Israel. British troops were arriving in Akaba. Israel gave up one of her strongest bargaining points and withdrew. Armistice negotiations began at Rhodes on 12th January.

The Israelis were optimistic about the outcome. For the first time in thirty years an Arab State had agreed to negotiate a formal agreement with the *Yishuv*. That the Arab State was Egypt seemed to mean that the Arab–Zionist deadlock was at long last over, and that a general settlement was now in sight. The Israelis believed that there were no real grounds for conflict with Egypt, and that a settlement agreeable to both sides could be reached quickly. They were particularly anxious to finish before their first national election, on 25th January 1949. During the first week, despite some early awkwardness, the talks went well. A cease-fire agreement was signed, arrangements were made for the evacuation of the Faluja garrison with full military

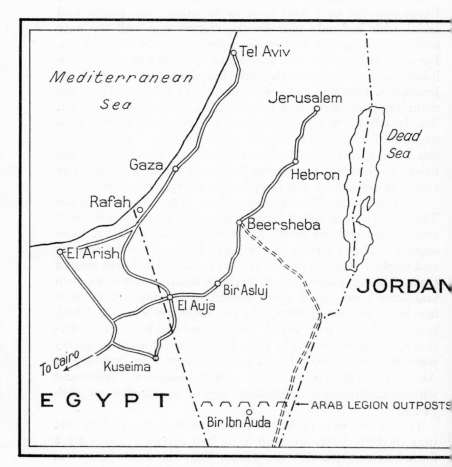

Egyptian Negotiations

26

honours, and an agreement was reached in principle regarding the establishment of an armistice commission. But progress ended as soon as the discussions moved on to the question of armistice demarcation lines (ADL). On the 25th, the delegates went home for further instructions. The Israelis postponed the withdrawal of the Faluja garrison for 'technical reasons'. The deadlock persisted. Finally, in mid-February Bunche formulated a set of proposals which set the talks moving again.

The crux of the issue was, as it had been from the begininng, who was to have what in the Negev. The Egyptians insisted that the Israelis withdraw behind the lines of 14th October. The Israelis insisted that the Egyptians withdraw from Gaza. Bunche suggested that the Israelis withdraw, but that the Egyptians retain their existing positions, and that the area in dispute be internationalized. This was rejected by Israel. Finally both sides agreed to accept the existing military lines as the ADL. It was agreed that Egypt would have a civilian administration in Gaza.

The Egyptians asked to have a governor of sorts in Beersheba, the crossroads of all east–west, north–south routes in the Negev. It was not necessary that he have any power, they said, only that he be there to save face. The Israelis rejected the request as 'absurd', incompatible with national sovereignty, and a possible basis for future claims by Egypt. A similar request was then made for a governor in Bir Asluj, a mud village on the main road just west of Beersheba. The Israelis refused again. Then Egypt asked Israel to withdraw from El Auja, a small village on the border: the strategic road junction in the area. At one end lies Beersheba and the Israeli hinterland; at the other, two roads branch off into Egypt, one north to El Arish on the coast, and the other west to Ismailia, the Suez Canal and Cairo. It is possible that the Egyptian delegates were thinking of their countrymen's feelings when they asked for concessions in Beersheba and Bir Asluj. But El Auja was a military matter.[1]

The Egyptians claimed that it was the eastern gateway to the Sinai and could not remain in the hands of a powerful and potentially hostile neighbour. The Israelis replied that it was

---

[1] According to a senior Israel army officer who took part in the negotiations. Walter Eytan disagrees: see his *The First Ten Years*, pp. 33–4.

also the only entrance from Egypt into the Negev, and that any army controlling it was in a position to reach Beersheba and so seal off the south: their security requirements precluded any concession to Egypt in that sector. The negotiations deadlocked. Bunche attempted to find a basis for compromise by proposing that the sector be internationalized. Egypt agreed, but the Israelis refused, claiming that this would detract from their national sovereignty and would, in any case, provide them with no protection against an Egyptian attack. Finally, Bunche proposed that the area be demilitarized, thereby satisfying the Israelis' claim to sovereignty, and the Egyptians' desire for security. The Israelis hesitated. They did not like demilitarization. At the same time they accepted that the Egyptians did have a point. Furthermore, they wanted to finish these negotiations so that others could begin with Jordan and Lebanon. In the event this last consideration seems to have been decisive. The Israelis accepted demilitarization on condition that a similar zone be set up on the Egyptian side of the line. On this basis agreement was finally reached.

Before the Agreement could be signed one more point had to be settled. According to the stipulations laid down in the 16th November resolution both parties had to undertake a withdrawal and reduction of armed forces in the vicinity of the ADL. The Israelis were unwilling to reduce their forces in the Negev while there was no armistice with Transjordan. Eventually it was agreed that for the purposes of the armistice the Negev would be divided into an Eastern and a Western Front, and that the armistice agreement with Egypt would apply only to the Western Front. In the Eastern Front the Israelis could do as they pleased without impinging on their arrangements with Egypt. This apparently innocuous arrangement was of considerable political importance. In effect, the Egyptians had agreed to let the Israelis move south from their existing positions in the Eastern Front: in other words to control all of the Negev —the southern end of which was still unoccupied—right down to Eilat on the Gulf of Akaba. The Egyptians made only one condition. This was that Beersheba be included in the Western Front, probably because this might have afforded them some control over Israeli troop movements and concentrations.

There was even a suggestion that the town be demilitarized and placed under the supervision of the Mixed Armistice Commission. The Israelis refused absolutely to accept any control over Beersheba, even if this meant the breakdown of the conference. Bunche accepted their position and the Egyptians finally agreed to leave all mention of Beersheba out of the agreement.[1] With all the other issues resolved, the details concerning the evacuation of the Faluja garrison were quickly settled. A General Armistice Agreement (GAA) was signed on 24th February.[2]

The basis of the GAA was the restoration of the former Palestine frontier, except that Egypt kept control of the Gaza Strip. From the territory taken after 14th October the Israelis had to withdraw all their troops except for the light defensive forces defined in the GAA. This in effect was a repudiation of the Council's resolutions of 4th and 16th November, and an indirect reference to this is included in Article IV, paragraph 2, of the GAA.

Negotiations with Lebanon were straightforward. Contact had been made before October 1948 when Elias Sasson from the Israel Foreign Ministry met with the Lebanese Prime Minister, Riad el Solh, in Paris. But Lebanon, the weakest of the Arab States, striving to maintain her delicate equilibrium between Christian and Muslim, could not afford to be the first to negotiate with Israel. Consequently, official talks did not begin until after the Egyptian negotiations were under way.

The only question of any importance concerned the sixteen Lebanese villages occupied by the Israelis as they followed the retreating Army of Liberation. On 14th January, two days after the Egyptian negotiations began, Israel agreed to withdraw from four villages immediately, and from the rest as soon as an armistice was signed. In turn, the Lebanese withdrew from a small sector of Palestine north of Ras en Naqura.[3] On this basis a draft agreement was drawn up and sent off to Tel Aviv and Beirut for approval on 19th January.

Final agreement, however, was held up until late March

---

[1] *NYHT*, Bilby, 22nd February 1949; *MG*, 23rd February 1949.

[2] *SCOR*, 4th year. Special Supplement 3.

[3] *NYHT*, 12th and 17th January 1949; *NYT* and *Times*, 16th and 17th January, 1949.

because of difficulty with Syria. There were Syrian troops in Lebanon, and it was not certain that they would feel bound by any armistice agreement signed by Lebanon. This was settled when the Syrian troops withdrew. Also Syria occupied the north-eastern corner of Palestine, where the borders of the three countries meet. The Israelis pointed out that an armistice agreement with Lebanon would necessitate withdrawing and reducing their troops in this area. They could not do this while Syrian troops occupied this part of Palestine. The Syrians refused to withdraw, stating that this was a matter outside the purview of the Lebanese negotiations, and concerned Israel and Syria only. In almost the same breath they rejected Bunche's invitation to enter into armistice negotiations with Israel. The matter was somewhat embarrassing for the Lebanese who had a treaty of diplomatic cooperation with the Syrians. Possibly the Syrians refused to withdraw because they felt that it would compromise their hold on the parts of Palestine they occupied near Lake Tiberias. In any case nothing could be done until 19th March when Syria finally accepted Bunche's invitation to negotiate, and evacuated the north-eastern area.

The Lebanese GAA (signed on 23rd March 1949)[1] was straightforward. The former Palestine boundary was taken as the ADL; there was almost complete demilitarization on both sides; and there were mutual undertakings of good behaviour. It should be emphasized that the Israelis' readiness to withdraw from Lebanese territory and to have the old boundary act as the ADL indicates the political importance which they attached to this GAA. If they had felt, and there is no reason to believe that they did, that the Lebanese did not also consider the negotiations as the penultimate step towards peace they would never have withdrawn. Instead they would have remained in Lebanon as Egypt remained in the Gaza Strip, or Jordan in eastern Palestine. As it is, there seems to have been full confidence on both sides.

In the early stages, negotiations with Jordan followed the Lebanese pattern. Informal secret talks began in the fall of 1948. A cease-fire for Jerusalem and an exchange of prisoners

[1] *NYHT*, 7th, 9th, 21st and 24th March 1949; *SCOR*, 4th year, Special Supplement 4.

were arranged in late November. Talks continued into the new year, but still secretly for fear of outside interference. There were powerful considerations pushing Jordan to a settlement with Israel. She was a very poor country, largely dependent upon the Palestine Jews as a market for her crops and surplus labour, and most of her trade went through Haifa. The split between the two countries was rapidly leading her toward bankruptcy. The military situation was not much better. The Arab Legion had fought well, but its manpower and material resources were gravely depleted and now it could fight in only the most limited battles. The feud with Egypt was steadily approaching crisis proportions. As we now know the Arabs, despite their declarations, had not planned on actually intervening in force in Palestine. What had brought them to it was King Abdullah's decision, with Britain's consent, to occupy those parts of Palestine allotted to the Arab State under the Partition plan.[1] However reluctant they were to commit their armies in Palestine, they were even more reluctant to see Abdullah carry away all the prizes, particularly Jerusalem. Once it was clear that he was determined to move in, they had no choice but to invade Israel also. In the event, Abdullah succeeded in capturing most of central Palestine and the holiest parts of Jerusalem. Egypt was determined to see that he did not retain them. Throughout the fall and winter of 1948–9 his position in the Arab world grew increasingly isolated and precarious, and his need for a settlement with Israel more pressing.

These pressures suited the Israelis. Unlike the Lebanese negotiations, those with Jordan had to deal with a list of military, political and economic problems too formidable to allow for any hopes of an easy settlement. Furthermore, these problems involved more than one would normally associate with armistice negotiations. In fact, it would not be incorrect to describe

---

[1] Except for Gaza and Galilee which would be divided up amongst the other Arab countries; see Glubb, *Soldier with the Arabs*, pp. 62–6; Kedourie, *Pan Arabism and British Policy*, in Laqueur, *The Middle East in Transition*, and Frye (ed.) *The Near East and the Great Powers*. More details can be found in *MEA*, April 1950 and March 1955; *MEJ*, Autumn 1951; and *Foreign Policy Reports*, 1st March 1950.

In August 1948 the Iraqis claimed that during the Portsmouth talks the British had agreed to work for an 'Arab solution' in Palestine. The British denied that there had been any formal agreements or commitment; *JP*, 19th August 1948.

Situation on the Eve of the Jordan Negotiations

these armistice negotiations as being in the nature of exploratory peace talks. Abdullah even suggested skipping the preliminaries and moving right into peace negotiations. There were, however, too many complications and the armistice talks began as planned at Rhodes on 2nd March.

There were three main areas in dispute: the Jerusalem–Latrun area, the Negev, and the Triangle.[1]

The Jerusalem–Latrun area was potentially the most dangerous of the three. The fighting in both places had been especially severe. Latrun straddled the main Tel Aviv–Jerusalem road, and Jerusalem was of great strategic, political and, of course, spiritual importance to both sides. The November cease-fire left Jordan holding the walled Old City, and Israel the sprawling New City. Neither side was willing to cede what it had to the other. Both were equally determined that no third party should take away what they held. When the General Assembly passed its resolution of 11th December calling for a permanent international régime in Jerusalem[2] they closed ranks, and began working for a settlement which would leave the UN no scope to intervene. During the armistice negotiations they agreed to disagree; set up the ADL along the military lines; and made arrangements for the future settlement of the following claims.

The Israelis wanted a passage through the Arab-held Sheikh Jarrah quarter to the Hebrew University on Mount Scopus; access to the Wailing Wall in the Old City; and the Latrun salient, so that the road to Tel Aviv could be opened. Jordan wanted the Jerusalem–Bethlehem road opened, and the part of it running through the Israeli-held Baka'a quarter neutralized. For various reasons it was decided not to put the settlement of these issues into the General Armistice Agreement. Accordingly, a Special Committee was to be set up (Article VIII) to deal with these and other matters. At the time this was considered to be a formality since, as was expressly stated in the Article, agreement in principle already existed. The Committee was empowered

[1] Jordan wanted to discuss refugee repatriation. Israel refused, but offered funds for resettlement in Jordan and Iraq. Jordan also asked for Lydda and Ramle, and for a sea outlet at Gaza. Israel refused to cede the towns and suggested that a sea outlet at Gaza was the concern of Egypt.

[2] *GAOR*, (111), 194, 11th December 1948.

to deal with any other matters which the signatories might bring before it. There is little doubt that it was conceived as the operative basis for a peace settlement.

The situation in the Negev, before the negotiations began, was roughly as follows. In the north, the Israelis occupied the road system centring on Beersheba. In the west, i.e. the Western Front, they held territory as far south as El Auja. In the east, they had troops in various places between Ein Gedi and Beersheba. Except for these troops, the southern and central parts of the Negev were empty. After the military collapse of Egypt in January, Jordan sent about a hundred Arab Legionnaires into the southern sector where they drew up a picket line running east and west through Bir Ibn Auda, approximately fifty-five miles north of the Gulf of Akaba. These troops provided Jordan with the basis for her claim to the southern Negev. Israel based her claim on the Partition Plan. According to the terms of the Egyptian GAA, Israeli movements in the Western Front were restricted. In the Eastern Front they were not. On 7th March Israeli troops crossed the Arab lines at Bir Ibn Auda and on the 10th occupied Umm Reshresh (Eilat) on the Gulf of Akaba. Israeli possession of the Negev was now complete and the question of its ownership was dropped from the negotiations.

This move south had its dangers. British troops had been arriving in Akaba since early January. For a while, particularly during the Israeli advance, it appeared that given a plausible excuse they would move against the Israeli troops. But the Israelis took care to stay away from the border, and in the end matters passed off peaceably with an exchange of Anglo–Israeli assurances regarding frontier crossings. Israel now had consolidated her position in the Negev. She had a port, Eilat, on the eastern seas and land for development and settlement. Jordan could have no direct access to the Mediterranean except with Israel's permission. Egypt had no land connexion with any of the Arab States. In the next years Israel found herself squarely in the path of Egyptian expansionism. The struggle for the Negev had by no means ended.

To the east of the Israeli-held coastal plain lay a great bulge of former Palestine held by Iraq and Jordan. Labelled the

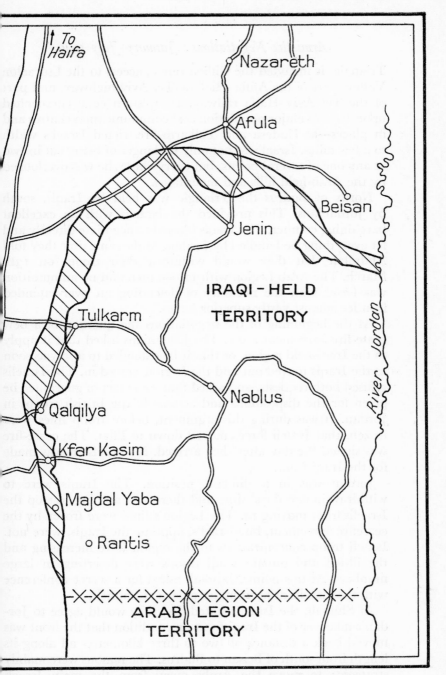

To
Haifa

Nazareth

Afula

Beisan

Jenin

IRAQI - HELD

TERRITORY

Tulkarm

River Jordan

Nablus

Qalqilya

Kfar Kasim

Majdal Yaba

Rantis

—X—X—X—X—X—X—X—X—X—X—X—X—X—X—X—

ARAB LEGION
TERRITORY

Area Ceded to Israel in the Triangle During the Jordan
Negotiations

Triangle, it included the Gilboa range, access to the Esdraelon Valley, part of the Afula–Hadera–Tel Aviv highway, and part of the Tel Aviv–Haifa railway. Its western edge encroached upon Israel's major population and communication centres and in places—at Hadera and Tulkarm—restricted Israel's width to a few miles. Israel was not only in danger of being cut in two at any one of several points, but everywhere she was overlooked by the Arab-held hills and mountains.

North of Budrus the Triangle was held by Iraqis, south by Jordanians. This provided the Israelis with an excellent bargaining counter. The Iraqis refused to negotiate directly and let everything be handled by Jordan. At the same time they told Abdullah that they would withdraw their troops on 13th March. The Arab Legion with 11,000 men and no ammunition was faced with the necessity of defending an over-extended frontier against vastly superior forces.

At the beginning of the negotiations the question of a new cease-fire agreement arose. The Jordanians asked that it apply to the Iraqi-held region, or that it be extended to apply as soon as the Iraqis moved out and the Legion moved in. The Israelis refused both requests, and asked that some sort of guarantee be given for the dispositions and actions of the British troops in Jordan. It was during this argument, before troop lines were frozen, that Israeli forces moved down to Eilat. The cease-fire was signed the day after they arrived. No provision was made for the Iraqi front.

Jordan was in a difficult position. The Iraqis were to withdraw in two days' time and there was nothing to stop the Israelis from moving in. The Legion's lines were frozen by the ceasefire agreement, but Israel's, opposite the Iraqis, were not. Israeli troop concentrations in the region were increasing and the ill-fed and unpaid Iraqi troops were deserting in large numbers. At this point Abdullah asked for a secret conference with the Israelis at his summer palace at Shuneh.

At Shuneh, the Israelis stated that they would agree to Jordan's takeover of the Iraqi front on condition that the front was moved back a distance of two to three kilometres all along its length from south of Beisan to Budrus. The reasons were mainly strategic: to move the Arabs away from the main Israeli

36

centres, and to put Israelis in the foothills to provide some defence against Arab positions in the mountains. The Israelis were insistent: if Abdullah did not agree, their troops would move into the Iraqi sector and right on to the Jordan River. Probably this was bluff—the risks were very great—but Abdullah believed them. He turned to the United States and Britain for help. In the meantime he authorized the initialling of a preliminary agreement providing for the withdrawal, with the proviso that it would not be valid until countersigned by the Prime Minister, Tewfiq Pasha, who was then in Beirut. It was hoped that this would stall the Israelis until the two Powers came to his aid. The Americans, however, replied that since a preliminary agreement had already been initialled they thought it best not to interfere. Abdullah had no choice but to agree to withdraw and the General Armistice Agreement was signed on 3rd April 1949.[1]

Everything about this GAA indicated that the main concern was with impending peace talks, and not with the details of an armistice settlement. The ADL was drawn on the map with a 'thick blue pencil'. No one was concerned that it divided villages in two, or that farmers were cut off from their wells or from their fields. No one expected the armistice to last long enough to make a difference: otherwise neither delegation would have agreed to it. Peace talks were just around the corner; the machinery had already been set up; a final settlement was imminent—so it was believed.

Negotiations with Syria did not begin until 5th April and an agreement was not signed until 20th July. Once again the major obstacle was the dispute over the ADL. Syria held three small areas near Lake Tiberias which, according to the Partition Plan, were to go to Israel. Their strategic and economic importance was considerable, putting Syria in a position to cut off the Israeli settlements east of Tiberias and all of the northern Galilee, and to control a large proportion of Israel's water supply. The Israelis demanded an unconditional withdrawal. They claimed the areas by virtue of the Partition

---

[1] *SCOR*, 4th year, Special Supplement 1. To compensate her for her withdrawal, involving some of the most fertile land in Palestine, Jordan received an equivalent area of land near Hebron.

Plan. In any case, they said, Syria had no business west of the Palestine border; in similar circumstances they had withdrawn from Lebanon. The Syrians replied that what Israel had done in Lebanon was not their concern; moreover, if Jordan could remain on the West Bank pending a peace settlement why could Syria not do the same at Tiberias? Finally, if Israel was using the Partition Plan as her criterion, then she could not keep western Galilee, and would she give it up? The Syrians had strong arguments, but as the months passed Arab–Israeli relations deteriorated, and the Israelis grew increasingly reluctant to assume that peace, and not hostility, was likely in the future. Bunche's deputy, Henri Vigier, suggested that the areas be demilitarized but remain in Syria's possession. The Israelis rejected this as well as a Syrian proposal for an exchange of territory.[1] After months of fruitless negotiations Bunche suggested, and it was agreed, that the Syrians withdraw, and that the Israeli troops remain where they were. In this way the areas evacuated would be demilitarized.

The obscurity of the provisions made for the civilians in the Demilitarized Zone points up the difficulties inherent not just in this but in all the armistice negotiations. No formula explicitly involving any kind of political settlement would have been acceptable to the Syrians. Yet something had to be done about the civilians in the DZ. So we find a delicate compromise (Article V),[2] sufficiently vague to satisfy everyone, but clear enough to work with. Provision is made for 'the restoration of normal civilian life', and an explanatory letter from Bunche stipulates that this process will be carried out by local administrations, Arab and Jewish, under the supervision of the Chairman of the Mixed Armistice Commission. The obscurities of this formula admirably suited the immediate situation, but it could work only until the time when the needs of normal civilian life and national development outstripped the capacities of local administration.

The successful completion of the final set of negotiations was greeted with general relief by the Security Council which

[1] *MG*, 29th April 1949; *NYHT*, Bilby, 18th May 1949; *NYT*, 24th May 1949.
[2] *SCOR*, 4th year, Special Supplement 2.

characterized the four General Armistice Agreements as 'a milestone on the road to a settlement of the Palestine question'. Dr. Bunche described the GAAs as equivalent to 'non-aggression pacts', and stressed that there was absolutely no reason to doubt the good faith or the future intentions of the signatories. The Israeli delegate, Abba Eban, enthused at great length that it was 'a matter of considerable satisfaction to my government to find its essential relations with its four contiguous neighbours resting . . . upon foundations of mutual consent. On every inch of ground where the authority of the Government of Israel is effective, we have at this moment the agreement of the Arab State concerned . . .'[1] He was, perhaps, overly optimistic. The Egyptian delegate spoke briefly, pointing out that the GAAs were purely military not political arrangements, and that Egypt had not yet given up the struggle.[2]

Numerous factors brought about the success of the negotiations. A few worth noting were Israel's military superiority, her willingness to fight to defend her interest, and her need to begin the monumental tasks of internal construction; increasing unrest in the Arab countries and an unwillingness to continue fighting; and the great pressure exerted by the Powers. These were essential ingredients but not necessarily enough to overcome deadlock. That the negotiations were completely successful is due to the efforts of Ralph Bunche, Acting UN Mediator after Count Bernadotte's assassination.

He succeeded where no one else has, either before or afterwards, and the reasons why are worth examining. He was an extremely able person, and devoted to his job. He worked hard. He controlled the negotiations, and prevented them from getting out of hand, alternately bullying and cajoling the delegates to keep them talking. He told the Powers not to interfere. And he told the delegates that they would have to bear the responsibility for any breakdown in the talks. He insisted on meeting the Council's stipulations regarding ADLs and the withdrawal and reduction of armed forces, but apart from this he was flexible. When the success of the Egyptian negotiations

---

[1] *SCOR*, 433rd mtg., 4th August 1949, p. 12.
[2] See statements: *ibid*, 413th mtg., 3rd March 1949, and 434th mtg., 4th August 1949; also S/1357, 26th July 1949.

was at stake he agreed to disregard the Council's resolutions regarding withdrawal to the lines of 14th October. His integrity was such that no responsible accusation of bias has ever been made against him, a considerable achievement in the Middle East. He insisted upon direct negotiations between the two delegations actually concerned and refused to allow any other delegations to participate. This is the ordinary way of conducting negotiations but it was rarely used in Arab–Jewish relations. It was only in these circumstances that the tools of compromise and concession could be used to good effect, and positive results achieved.

An impetus toward peace had been created and utilized. The negotiations with Egypt, Lebanon and Jordan augured well for the future.[1] But after the GAAs were signed, the pressures were relaxed. The dangers of further fighting diminished, and the UN's attention was diverted elsewhere. The Arabs grew increasingly reluctant to expand the area of settlement with Israel. It remained to be seen if the Conciliation Commission for Palestine would be able to overcome the growing inertia.

[1] The Syrian negotiations were still on when the CCP began its activities.

Chapter Four

THE CONCILIATION EFFORT
(February–October 1949)

THE Conciliation Commission for Palestine (CCP) was set up according to the terms of the General Assembly's resolution of 11th December 1948. It was given three major tasks. The first and most important was to bring about a peace settlement.[1] The others were to facilitate the repatriation and resettlement of the refugees, as well as their economic and social rehabilitation and the payment of compensation; and to draw up a scheme for a permanent international régime in Jerusalem.

Not only did the CCP fail to achieve any of its goals, but by its ineptitude it hastened the destruction of whatever chances for peace still existed. Superficially, the CCP's failure was the result of Arab–Israeli antagonism and intransigence. A closer look shows that even more important was the CCP's own weakness and incompetence. But as one probes deeper it becomes clear that in the final analysis the responsibility must be laid at the door of the countries represented on the CCP. The conciliation effort provides an excellent example of how power-politicking complicated, distorted and aggravated Arab–Israeli relations. It is a tale of selfishness and incompetence; of how a short-sighted pursuit of 'national interest' could result in

[1] In order to allay Arab opposition to the resolution, this term is not used; nonetheless, the resolution's meaning is unmistakable.

41

irreparable harm to those interests, to the United Nations—and to the countries needing conciliation.

To examine the conciliation effort properly we have to approach it at three different levels: power politicking, the incompetence of the CCP itself, and the course of the actual conciliation negotiations. This means covering the same period—February to October 1949—three times with unavoidable repetition. To lessen confusion, the reader should keep in mind that we are concerned with the events surrounding the Beirut Conference in March 1949 and the Lausanne Conference which followed at the end of April.

According to the General Assembly's resolution, the CCP was to consist of three UN member-states to be picked by the five permanent members of the Security Council. The states chosen were France, Turkey and the United States. Representatives from these three countries were to form the CCP itself. Here we have the fundamental reason for the failure of the conciliation effort. The CCP was composed of men chosen by and responsible to their respective Governments, not the UN. Each acted as an agent of his government while he was carrying out his duties as a member of a United Nations commission. The CCP became a medium for the expression of the national policies of its member-states rather than of the United Nations. These states had wide and conflicting interests in the Middle East. They were agreed on one thing only: that an Arab–Israeli settlement must not harm these interests. What this involved can be realized by considering it within the context of the four great struggles taking place in the Middle East: the anti-imperialist struggle, the East-West struggle, the conflict amongst the Western Powers, and that amongst the Arabs themselves. The CCP members had important interests involved in all these areas of conflict, interests which would be affected seriously by the actions they took in the conciliation effort, and by the results of that effort. Even assuming that all the CCP members were anxious for a settlement—something that is by no means certain—they could not devise a policy agreeable to themselves which would meet the needs of the Arabs and the Israelis. In the circumstances it was preferable that the conciliation effort fail.

42

For example, in the spring of 1949 French Middle Eastern policy had, among others, two aspects. One was the restoration of friendship with Syria. The other was to weaken the power and prestige of the British. Thus, during the early stages of the Lausanne Conference the French member of the CCP, Claude de Boisanger, openly sided with the Syrian delegation. He also encouraged the Arabs to negotiate with Israel *en bloc* rather than separately and thereby diminished the likelihood of a peace agreement. Similarly, by playing upon the Israelis' dislike of Abdullah's occupation of eastern Palestine and their fear of his defence treaty with the British, he persuaded them to concentrate their peace efforts in the CCP, instead of trying to reach a separate agreement with Abdullah.[1] The purpose of these efforts was to limit the influence of Abdullah and the British both at the conference and in the Fertile Crescent, but they also handicapped the conciliation effort.

The activities of Hussein Calhit Yalcin, the Turkish member, were equally dubious. The Turks, fearing an attack by Russia, were anxious to establish some sort of alliance with the Arab States. One would have thought that this alone would have been sufficient to disqualify them from being represented on the CCP. Yalcin, however, made matters worse by going about giving public expressions of Turkey's friendship for the Arabs and of her desire to establish a military alliance with them.[2] If Turkey's desire for the Arabs' friendship was such that Yalcin was authorized to compromise himself so heavily in public, one can only wonder how much farther he was authorized to go in the privacy of committee meetings.

But it is to the United States that we must look for a real understanding of the failure of the CCP. It was only the United States which had the influence and power necessary to weld the CCP into an effective organ of conciliation. But, like the French and the Turks, the Americans appear to have rated peace as secondary to the protection of their own interests. To complicate matters further they were never able to formulate a clear-cut

[1] *JP*, Kimche, 12th July 1949; see also 8th and 9th June 1949; *NYT*, Sulzberger, 5th May 1949.

[2] *NYT*, 4th January, *LaB Egypt.*, 5th January, *Times*, 7th January and *NYT* Ross, 16th February 1949.

and consistent approach to the problem. This was due not only to the usual conflict between the pro-Israeli and the pro-Arab factions in the U.S. government, but to a real uncertainty about what to do. None the less the State Department took the initiative in the conciliation effort. Its plan was to impose a settlement, through the offices of the CCP, based on Arab demands. Any other basis was thought to be detrimental to American interests in the Middle East. Not only did this approach weaken the influence and effectiveness of the CCP, but it opened the way for a host of complicating factors which should not have been allowed to intrude. Power politics came first and successful conciliation second.

This brings us to an interesting point relevant to the question of imposing an 'Arab peace' on Israel. If such a peace was to be imposed, which one was it to be? We have already seen how there were sharp divisions amongst the Arab States regarding Palestine. If the Americans were going to support the Arab side, they had also to decide which Arabs they were going to support. Was it to be Amman, Damascus, Cairo, or Riyadh? If Israel was to lose the Negev, who was to get it? If she was to obtain territory in return, where was it to come from? Did the Americans expect, for example, that there could be an arrangement whereby Farouk took the Negev, while Abdullah lost Arab Palestine? Would Syria be satisfied with nothing? Would Abdullah agree to let Syria hold land on both sides of the Jordan if he lost the West Bank? Would Ibn Saud agree to let Abdullah hold all of Jerusalem? Which Arabs wanted an 'Arab peace'? What about those who would accept less? Would this 'Arab peace' have been a stable peace? Would the partition, complete or incomplete, of Israel have led to further strife and wrangling? These were questions to which the State Department did not seem to have given much thought.

The State Department pressed on. It gave strong support to official Arab League policy, and openly attempted to persuade the Israelis to make unilateral concessions. Complaints by the U.S. Ambassador in Tel Aviv, James McDonald, that this was an unreasonable approach met with the curious reply that the Israelis had to be coerced, otherwise they would be able to overawe the Arab States and apply unfair duress (*sic*).[1]

Whatever the justification for this policy, it had several undesirable results. It weakened the position of the more moderate Arabs who were inclined to accept some of the Israeli offers. If the Americans thought these offers insufficient, it was pointless and dangerous of these men to disagree. Thus it fortified a tenuous unity, and destroyed any incentive to make a separate peace with Israel. These moderate, separatist sentiments did exist. They had played an important role during the armistice negotiations and could have done so again.

Instead the State Department took the official pronouncements of the Arab League at face value and declined to act on any other basis. On the face of it these pronouncements were clear-cut and uncompromising. There would be no separate or direct negotiations with Israel. The Arab States would negotiate collectively and indirectly through the medium of the CCP. There could be no peace negotiations until the Israelis had agreed 'in principle' to repatriate all the refugees, and had promised to allow a specific, large number of them actually to return. Only after this had been settled could there be negotiations on the boundaries. Here the basis for discussion would be the boundaries described in the UN Partition Plan in 1947, and not those set out in the Armistice Agreements. This was the official Arab policy.

Within the first week of the Lausanne Conference Egyptian and Jordanian delegates had met secretly with the Israelis, and before the Conference was over members from the other delegations had done so, without the knowledge of the CCP. As the conference wore on some Arab delegates began, unofficially, to express a desire for direct negotiations and regrets that Bunche was not in charge. There was no unity on the questions of refugees or borders. During the early stages of the Conference both Jordan and Lebanon indicated a willingness to negotiate directly with Israel on the frontier question without first settling the refugee problem. In September 1950, President Shishakli of Syria quietly broke with the League's official policy and agreed to settle 82,000 refugees in Syria with the aid of UNRWA—

[1] James McDonald, *My Mission in Israel* pp. 170–1.

before the refugee question was settled with Israel.[1] In the private negotiations with Abdullah the refugee question does not appear to have arisen at all (see below, Chapter Six). And finally, both Jordan and Lebanon indicated their willingness to negotiate a frontier settlement, not only before the refugee question was settled, but on the basis of the armistice lines, not the Partition Plan. These were the realities behind the Arab unity which the State Department was supporting.

The Americans began by trying to persuade the Israelis to make some unilateral concessions to pacify the Arabs who were about to meet at the CCP's first conference in Beirut. The Israelis finally agreed to implement a 'reunion of families' scheme whereby certain categories of refugees would be allowed to return to their families.[2] The Arabs gave no official sign of relenting, and the State Department continued its well-publicized efforts to extract concessions from the Israelis. Just before the Lausanne Conference began in April the American member of the CCP, Mark Etheridge, publicly declared that he agreed with official Arab policy on the refugee question, and that its settlement was a test of Israel's good faith. At the same time the State Department declared that Israel would have to accept a boundary settlement based upon the Partition Plan, and repeated its demands for unilateral concessions.[3]

The Israelis replied that the United States was being unrealistic. They said that, in the first place, the U.S. was cutting the ground out from under the Arab moderates and strengthening the extremists. Second, they said, it was impossible for them to make large concessions on the refugee and border questions until after the Arabs entered peace negotiations; then there could be discussion and concession. But until the Arabs agreed to enter into peace negotiations—and at that time none of the Arab delegates had any authority to negotiate peace—nothing

[1] The agreement was never implemented: Peretz, *Israel and the Palestine Arabs*, p. 25.

UNRWA (PRNE) UN Relief and Works Agency (for Palestine Refugees in the Near East).

[2] About 6,000 came in under this scheme. All told about 25–30,000 refugees were repatriated in one way or another.

[3] *NYT*, Hoffman, 26th April and *MG*, 20th May 1949.

The State Department also insisted upon the internationalization of Jerusalem despite both Jordan's and Israel's protests.

could be done. Furthermore, the Israelis said, because of the hostility implicit in the Arab League's policy and in the threat of war by some Arab leaders, no concessions could be offered without the Arabs giving some effective guarantee of peace in return. The Americans treated these arguments as a 'pedantic quibble'. The Israelis, however, refused to relent.

Then, on 29th May, a very strong Note was sent in President Truman's name to Ben Gurion. The Israelis were told that their attitude was dangerous to the peace, that the Partition Plan must be used as the basis for boundary negotiations, and that they must make large concessions for refugee repatriation before peace negotiations began. The Israelis refused to accept these terms. Ben Gurion told Ambassador McDonald that the note was unrealistic and unjust, and that there could be no substantial repatriation until there was peace. 'How can we permit potential enemies to come back so long as Arab States openly threaten a new war of destruction? To whom should we turn if Israel were again attacked? Would the U.S. send arms or troops?' Ben Gurion asked. President Truman showed no enthusiasm for pressing a matter of which he seems to have been only vaguely cognizant. After hemming and hawing, the State Department had to back down. The deadlock continued.

The Note seems to have been part of the 'McGhee Plan', named after the new Assistant Secretary of State for Near and Middle Eastern Affairs, which the Americans continued to push. The specific proposals were not new, but the whole idea had an original twist. In essence it involved having the Israelis make sufficient concessions so that the Arabs would be mollified to the point where they would allow the Americans to bribe them into negotiating a peace based on more concessions from Israel. The Americans believed that the key to peace was the refugee problem. Total repatriation was obviously out of the question. Therefore there had to be large-scale resettlement and this would have to take place 'within the economic and social rehabilitation of all the countries in the Near East'. The United States would foot most of the bill for this vast development plan, of which refugee resettlement would form only a part. Al the Arabs had to do was agree to take the money. According to the

Americans, they were on the verge of doing so but would require unilateral concessions from Israel in order to overcome the political drawbacks. She was to agree to repatriate 100,000 refugees immediately, and to take in more as part of the actual peace settlement. Secondly, she was to give up both Galilee and the Negev in return for the Gaza strip.[1] Attached to these demands was the threat that if the Israelis did not agree the whole matter might be placed before the General Assembly with disagreeable results for Israel.

The Israelis turned down the Plan for the same reasons that they had turned down the Note. They agreed that resettlement and economic development were important—they had been saying so for some time—but they could not agree even to consider such far-reaching concessions until the Arabs first agreed to enter peace negotiations, especially now that the Arabs were engaged on extensive rearmament programmes. The people to talk to were the Arabs, since it was they, not the Israelis, who were refusing to negotiate.

The Americans continued to press for unilateral concessions. Finally, in August, Ben Gurion, despite considerable domestic opposition, offered to repatriate 100,000 refugees as part of an overall peace settlement. The State Department and the CCP expressed their dissatisfaction with the offer. The Arabs then rejected it. The Israelis withdrew the offer and there the matter rested. By this time they had succeeded in establishing a short-lived *rapprochement* with the British who were anxious to promote an Israel–Jordan settlement on the basis of Jordan's occupation of Arab Palestine, and to prevent a partitioned, weak and discontented Israel from becoming another source of friction and strife in the Middle East.[2]

---

[1] Peretz, *loc. cit.*, p. 64; cf. *NYT*, Sulzberger, 12th June 1949.

[2] British support at this time was invaluable to Israel. The British thought that a durable settlement might be based on these premises: to prevent trouble in the future Israel and Iraq should exchange their Arab and Jewish populations; Israel should not repatriate more than 100,000 refugees; the rest would be compensated and resettled in Jordan, Iraq, Syria, and perhaps Cyrenaica; if Israel was to be viable for a population of two million there could be no territorial concessions, although some frontier adjustments were necessary; and the future status of Jerusalem should be settled by Israel and Jordan.—*Observer*, Special Correspondent 11th September 1949; *MG*, 1st September 1949; *JP*, 12th September and 14th December 1949.

The State Department was at a loss. The Israelis refused to be dictated to. The Arabs saw no reason to consider concessions or even negotiations so long as the State Department was doing all the work. The CCP itself had ceased to be the focus of conciliation and was now without power or prestige. Nothing had been gained, and a great deal had been lost. At this point the State Department decided to leave the disputants to find their own settlement, and to work through the UN and the CCP which despite their obvious lack of success were 'useful for the long pull'.[1] In this manner a certain vestige of dignity was maintained as the State Department daintily stepped clear of the sordid details of peace-making. It is interesting but fruitless to speculate on what might have happened had the State Department given the conciliation effort the same support that it gave to Bunche; had it chosen to support the organization rather than a particular policy; and had it concentrated on encouraging the parties to negotiate with each other, rather than to negotiate only on one particular basis.

The ineffectuality and the incompetence of the CCP itself is highlighted by even the most cursory comparison with what was done by Bunche. He never allowed this kind of Great Power intervention. There was never any serious suggestion that he represented anyone other than the UN and the best interests of the parties directly concerned. The armistice effort was run by one man, appointed by and responsible to the UN. The conciliation effort was a tripartite affair, with a rotating chairman, and outside interference. Bunche moved forward steadily, never letting up the pressure to negotiate, quick to see the obstacle and to devise the necessary formula. The CCP moved at an incredibly slow rate. It began its talks in February 1949. Its first conference (Beirut) was held in March in order to clarify issues. The next conference, still to clarify issues, began at Lausanne at the end of April and lasted until mid-September. The CCP then adjourned to consider the positions of the parties. By January 1950 two more conferences had been held, and absolutely nothing had been accomplished. All the CCP could say was that it would be very difficult 'or even impossible to

---

[1] *George McGhee to US ambassadors in the Middle East*, McDonald, *loc. cit.*, p. 182.

carry on constructive negotiations . . . with any chance of success'.[1]

Time was of the essence in the conciliation effort. A situation conducive to peace existed for a few months, a year at the most. It was up to the CCP to push ahead firmly and surely, to exploit every opportunity, to deal decisively and intelligently with every obstacle. The armistice was meant to be a period of transition: there could be either war or peace in Palestine. Yet the CCP dithered along, while every favourable opportunity was destroyed.

The CCP had no outstanding men on it; certainly no one who gave any indication of having the personality and ability necessary to deal with the situation. Lacking effective leadership, it is not surprising that it retained little respect, or that the Arabs and Israelis steadily lowered the level of their delegations. The Commission members themselves do not appear to have taken their tasks seriously, it being reported that, even in the early days, they were frequently absent on other business, and that when present approached their duties in an off-hand manner.[2] The CCP did not even ensure that the various delegates had the necessary authority to negotiate. None of the Arab delegates had authority to negotiate a peace settlement, and some were empowered to discuss only the refugee question. Bunche had been particularly careful to ensure that all delegates had the necessary authority, and this was stated in each armistice agreement. The CCP never saw fit to mention the matter.

Little interest was shown in what Bunche had learned. Despite the fact that he had been the only man ever to succeed in getting the Jews and Arabs to make and carry out an agreement, no attempt was made to set up an effective liaison with him. In general the CCP showed considerable independence from outside help or advice. An excellent example was the Beirut Conference: a meeting of the Arab delegates only, to discover their point of view prior to meeting with the Israelis. Almost every expert, Bunche and the British included, opposed holding such

[1] CCP, *6th Progress Report, GAOR,* A/1255, 29th May 1950, p. 6.

[2] *Times,* Special Correspondent, 18th May 1949; *Zionist Review,* 20th and 27th May 1949.

a conference on the grounds that treating the Arab delegations as a bloc beforehand would only weaken the position of the moderates, and strengthen that of the more intransigent. The CCP pressed ahead with the conference regardless, with the expected results.

The Arab League announced, as was predicted, that all delegations would act as a bloc and speak collectively, and that there would be no direct negotiations with Israel. Everything would have to go through the CCP. Bunche had refused to countenance similar demands. He had insisted upon and gotten separate and direct negotiations. He had overcome—with only slight difficulty—the same problems of Arab reluctance that the CCP faced. But there is no evidence that the CCP ever really tackled these problems. When the Israelis complained, it replied that it could do nothing; that the decision on whether or not to negotiate directly lay with each Arab delegation. Later when its incompetence had forced the UN Secretary-General to institute an investigation and it had been severely criticized for its failure in this respect, it spoke rather weakly of promoting 'the greatest possible flexibility in the exchange of views', and went so far as to say that it had 'not thought fit to relinquish the possibility of holding meetings with one or more Arab delegations separately'.[1] Such courage was unlikely to impress anyone. Fawzi el Mulki, the Jordanian delegate, once described the CCP as a 'post office' transmitting letters from one side to another, usually after a long delay.

Bunche had held his negotiations in secret. He had issued few statements to the Press, made no comments on the various problems or on the attitude of the delegations, and his reports to the Security Council were brief, uninformative, and infrequent. Only in this kind of atmosphere did the delegates feel free to enter into the give-and-take so essential to the successful conclusion of negotiations. The CCP chose to give itself and its activities full sterilizing publicity. There were detailed and frequent reports to the General Assembly. Statements were made to the Press. There was free comment on the various problems and the attitudes of the respective parties, and the Americans particularly had no hesitation in declaring their preference for

[1] CCP, *3rd Progress Report*, A/927, 21st June 1949, p. 2.

one delegation as against another. The delegates were stripped of all protective secrecy. They could hardly make a move without everyone knowing about it. The CCP could not have done more to strengthen the intransigents without holding mass demonstrations. How, in these circumstances, could concessions be offered—or accepted?

In his report in May to the UN Secretary-General on the reasons for the CCP's failure, Andrew Cordier[1] charged that the CCP members were interested primarily in carrying out the policies of their respective governments, and not in furthering the conciliation effort. He criticized the CCP for failing to institute direct negotiations. He also pointed out that there was a general regret that Bunche was not in charge. None of this, however, had any effect upon the CCP, and things went on much as before.

The CCP began work in the spring of 1949 and is, in a very minor way, still in operation. But the crucial period, the time when effective possibilities of a peace settlement did exist, was February–October 1949: the period covering the Beirut and the Lausanne Conferences. To review briefly: the Commission began with a tour of the various capitals in February. The armistice negotiations had barely hit their stride and it was too early for the parties to be precise about what they wanted. Official Arab policy was that there could be no negotiations until Israel had accepted in principle the refugees' right to repatriation. The Israelis refused to discuss any question—particularly this one—until the Arabs stopped threatening war and entered general peace negotiations. But, on the whole, the CCP found the parties favourably inclined to peace. It was decided to hold a conference of just the Arab States in Beirut to see if their position on the refugee question might be moderated. Despite the barrage of expert advice to the contrary the CCP went on with the conference[2] with the expected results. The

[1] Executive Assistant to the Secretary General. *NYT*, Hamilton, 13th June 1949. Later Cordier told Hamilton that at the time he had felt that there was no chance of an agreement being reached: letter from T. J. Hamilton, 1st May 1959.

[2] Just before it began, Mark Etheridge, the US CCP delegate, tried to extract a concession from the Israelis to placate the Arabs. Foreign Minister Sharett refused to act on the spur of the moment but promised to consider the idea. From this grew the 'reunion of families' scheme.

only CCP proposals to which the Arabs agreed were the internationalization of Jerusalem, and a general conference in a
neutral city. In the meantime the Israelis tried to submit a
memorandum, which has never been published, on the refugee
question. The CCP rejected it as contrary to the provisions of
the General Assembly's resolution, and refused to pass it on.

The Commission's acknowledged attitude was one of general
agreement with the Arab position regarding the pressing nature
of the refugee problem and the need to gain from the Israelis an
agreement in principle on repatriation. At the same time it
recognized the need for Arab agreement to resettle those
refugees who did not wish to be repatriated. One of the most
difficult problems of all, it foresaw, would be to distinguish
correctly between those refugees who did and those who did not
wish to return to their homes.[1]

Subsequently the Lausanne Conference was held, attended
by Israel, Egypt, Jordan, Syria and the Lebanon (Iraq refused
to attend until the refugee question had been settled). The
official Arab policy has already been outlined: this was not a
peace conference, but merely an extension of the previous discussions at Beirut to examine the problems of refugees and
Jerusalem. There would be no direct negotiations with Israel,
and the Arab States would discuss all matters collectively.[2]

The CCP agreed. It stipulated that there was no intention of
assembling the delegates at one table or even under the same
roof. It also stated that ' . . . the fact that the scope of these new
conversations may eventually be broadened does not imply that
they should be considered as peace negotiations . . .': a general
conference was being held to save the CCP the trouble of having
to travel from city to city. Committees were set up to discuss
only the refugee problem and Jerusalem. The territorial question was ignored even though the CCP itself had admitted that
it was inseparable from the refugee problem. The dispute over
Jerusalem was never very serious despite the publicity which it

[1] CCP, *2nd Progress Report, GAOR*, A/838, 19th April, 1949.
[2] *Egyptian Gazette* 5th May 1949.
Evidently, at least partially through the influence of the British and the French,
the Egyptian delegation had control of the Arab delegations: see Kimche, 12th
July 1949; *Observer*, Special Correspondent, 1st and 22nd May 1949, and *MG*,
18th May 1949.

received. Israel and Jordan refused to accept internationalization. The other Arab States agreed to it. But by all accounts it seems to have been agreed tacitly that if the other questions were settled that of Jerusalem could be resolved with little difficulty.

The Israelis were taking the Lausanne Conference very seriously. Not only did they hope for a peace settlement, but also for a breach in the boycott and blockade and a series of bilateral trade agreements with their neighbours. They found themselves unexpectedly handicapped by having to counter the demands of the CCP as well as those of the Arabs.

At best the Israeli's position on the refugee problem was evasive. They would not accept the principle of repatriation, but they did not reject it. Instead they took refuge behind the clause in the Assembly's resolution in which it was stated that those refugees wishing to return must be prepared to 'live at peace with their neighbours'. The Israelis said that the refugees' promises could not be relied upon unless repatriation took place as part of a general peace settlement; the real answer lay in resettlement. Clearly the Israelis did not want the refugees back except in the comparatively small numbers of a 'reunion of families' scheme. The population as a whole was in no mood to take into its bosom large numbers of people who, rightly or wrongly, were considered to have attempted to destroy Israel. Those responsible for national security and defence felt that the danger was too great even to consider the possibility of substantial repatriation. The government and the people were extending themselves to the utmost to cope with the problems of post-independence and post-war development, and to absorb vast numbers of immigrants flooding into the country. To accept in addition the difficulties of taking back and settling large numbers of probably hostile Arabs was to them unthinkable—certainly unless there were definite guarantees of cooperation from the Arab States.

The Israelis submitted a list of proposals to the CCP in the form of a draft protocol to be signed by all parties before negotiations began. In the preamble, the signatories expressed their desire to reach a settlement consistent with the UN

Charter. In the following paragraphs the parties resolved to deal with any disagreement 'entirely by peaceful, direct negotiations'. In the case of continuing disagreement they agreed to submit to third-party arbitration. There was to be mutual recognition of the frontiers agreed upon at the projected negotiations. Until borders were agreed upon regular contact between the various frontier posts was to be established so as to eliminate incidents'.[1] The CCP was asked in the memorandum to arrange direct negotiations between the Israelis and the separate Arab delegations, to whom the Israelis were willing to submit proposals for frontiers. The Israelis indicated that they would prefer to negotiate first with the Lebanese, with whom a tentative arrangement had already been worked out. After the Lebanese would come the Egyptians, and then Jordan; there could be no negotiations with Syria until an armistice had been signed. Once the frontier question was out of the way the Israelis wanted to discuss Jerusalem, and then the refugee question.

The CCP rejected the draft protocol and refused to inaugurate direct and separate negotiations, claiming that this had to be decided by the Arab delegates themselves. It then drew up a draft protocol of its own in which the parties agreed that the Partition Plan boundaries would serve as 'a basis' for negotiations.[2] When the protocol was signed (two separate copies to preclude direct contact between the Arabs and the Israelis) the Israeli delegate reserved his right to reject parts of the partition boundaries and to suggest others. Later on he pointed out that the partition boundaries were to provide 'a basis', not 'the basis' for negotiations. The CCP then announced that it was ready to transmit proposals from one side to the other. It was now mid-May, two and a half months since work was begun.

The Israelis immediately submitted a list of proposals for a settlement with Egypt, Lebanon and Jordan (the armistice negotiations with Syria had still not ended). With regard to boundaries they proposed that those with Egypt and Lebanon remain as they had been prior to 1948—in effect that Egypt

[1] *MG*, 30th April 1949; *Observer*, Special Correspondent, 1st May 1949; *NYT*, 9th May 1949.

[2] CCP, 3rd *Progress Report, loc. cit.*, Annexes A and B.

withdraw from the Gaza Strip. The Jordan border would also remain as it had been, but the Jordanian-controlled Triangle would remain under Jordan control, except in so far as minor frontier modifications were necessary to rectify certain anomalies. The Israelis stated that they did not want to discuss the future status of the Triangle at that time nor did they have any ambitions there. Its future disposition was a matter to be agreed upon by the Arab States, the inhabitants of the area, and the refugees—in other words by a plebiscite. Until such agreement was reached, Israel would continue to recognize Jordan as the *de facto* occupying power. The question of Jerusalem was a separate problem which did not enter into the proposals. If the Arab States accepted these proposals then Israel would be willing to repatriate the refugees living in the Gaza Strip : about 250,000. This would bring Israel's total Arab population to just over 400,000 compared to a Jewish population of about 800,000. This was considered to be the maximum the country could absorb. If the Gaza Strip were not ceded, the Israeli delegate stated, he would not be in a position to submit proposals concerning the number of refugees who might be repatriated.[1]

The CCP was not pleased with the 'Gaza Plan' and said so. It contained no references to Israeli-occupied territory allotted to the Arabs by the Partition Plan, and it dismissed somewhat summarily the position of the Arab States in Palestine. Israel's suggestion of a plebiscite seems to have been completely disregarded by the CCP. Then the Arabs denounced the Plan as calling for 'annexations rather than territorial adjustments envisaged by the Protocol'. In turn they submitted their own proposals.

The Arab Plan was not as detailed as the 'Gaza Plan', and it concentrated more on the refugee question. It was proposed that all the Arabs originating from Israeli-occupied territory allotted to the Arab State by the Partition Plan should be allowed to return home : an estimated 350,000 people were involved. These areas were '. . . in principle to be recognized as Arab areas.' Further, it was expected that the Israelis would repatriate

[1] *CCP*, pp. 4, 7–8; *Observer*, Special Correspondent, 15th May 1949; *NYT*, Currivan, 21st June 1949.

another 100,000 into the area which they still held. No indication was given of who was to control these Arab areas or of what was to happen to the Triangle. Apparently the Arabs wished to contain Israel within the 1947 Partition Plan boundaries without according her the compensation of economic union.[1] The Israelis rejected the Arab Plan because it was based so nearly on the Partition Plan, and they would not accept a certain proportionate distribution of population and land agreed upon in 1947 as a criterion for a settlement under existing circumstances.

The first attempt at a settlement had failed. The CCP did nothing. The talks dragged on for another month and were then recessed. Just before they were, the Israelis made another attempt to break the deadlock. They submitted a set of proposals which called for the establishment of five sub-committees to deal with the major problems: the Arab delegations would be empowered by their governments to negotiate a peace settlement; the negotiations would be direct; and finally, the armistice provisions would provide the basis for discussion. The CCP dismissed all these proposals as 'procedural' and did nothing about them.[2] The reason for this seems to be that the State Department had sent Israel its Note a few days earlier, on 29th May. The Americans had taken over from the CCP, and it in turn had little to do except watch while the Americans tried to pressure the Israelis into accepting the 'McGhee Plan'. The Israelis resisted American pressure, and the Lausanne Conference recessed on 1st July.

The position of the CCP was now serious. Four months had gone by and nothing had been accomplished. Andrew Cordier, the Executive Assistant to the UN Secretary-General, had come and gone, leaving behind him charges of incompetence and self-seeking. The Arab delegates themselves, or at least the more moderate among them, were becoming increasingly outspoken in their criticism of what was happening. Prospects brightened considerably when the Conference reconvened on 19th July.

---

[1] CCP, *3rd Progress Report, loc. cit.*, p. 8; *MG*, 25th May 1949.

[2] *NYT*, Gruson, 12th and 14th June 1949. Strangely, the CCP *Reports* make no mention of these proposals.

Both sides compromised. The refugee problem would be discussed first, but within the framework of comprehensive peace negotiations. On 28th July, Israel agreed to submit concrete proposals regarding the number of refugees it would be willing to repatriate. The only conditions were that repatriation would have to form part of an overall settlement of the refugee question, and that it would be implemented only as an integral part of a comprehensive and final peace settlement. On 2nd August, the Arabs accepted these two conditions, but rejected another request for direct negotiations.[1]

On 3rd August Israel formally offered to repatriate 100,000 refugees. This was the long-awaited offer. According to the first reports out of Lausanne the Arabs were inclined, with some misgivings, to accept it as a basis for discussion.[2] Ordinarily this would have been sufficient. But before a formal Arab reply could be given, both the CCP and the State Department denounced the offer as inadequate, and the CCP refused to transmit it to the Arabs as a formal offer. Not surprisingly, on 15th August the Arabs rejected it as a basis for discussion.

At this point the CCP divided its activities. On the one hand it, or more properly the United States, began to emphasize the economic side of the refugee question, and a Survey Mission was set up to study the problems involved in resettlement, repatriation and rehabilitation. On the other hand the parties were asked to set forth detailed proposals for a boundary settlement.

The Israelis replied briefly: all the territory controlled by them according to the terms of the four General Armistice Agreements should be acknowledged as Israeli territory. In their reply the Arabs claimed all the territory allotted to the Arab State according to the Partition Plan, plus a great deal more.

---

[1] CCP, *4th Progress Report*, A/992, 22nd September 1949, pp. 1 *et seq.*

Other conditions, which the Arabs accepted, were: no member of the Husseini faction or any known anti-Zionist would be included among the repatriated; the repatriated would be settled according to national development schemes the same as Jewish immigrants; and for security reasons and to prevent smuggling none of the repatriated would be settled along the border.

[2] *MG*, 4th and 5th August 1949; *Observer*, 7th August 1949; *Zionist Review*, 5th August 1949.

The Arabs wanted a time limit imposed, and no deductions made for refugees already repatriated.

Lebanon claimed Western Galilee which she intended to use to maintain her existing population balance between Christians and Muslims. Syria claimed Eastern Galilee. Jordan claimed all of Jerusalem, central Palestine, and a corridor to the sea. Egypt claimed the Gaza Strip and the Negev. This last is interesting. The Egyptians stated that Israel's development plans in the area, that is for ports, railway and roads, endangered their vital interests and necessitated control of the area.[1] Of the 17,000 sq. km. controlled by Israel, the Arabs claimed 12,000.

After waiting a few weeks to think things over the CCP concluded that all the proposals were unreasonable, exceeding the limits of what might be called 'adjustments' to the Partition Plan. It asked the parties to reconsider their respective positions.

The Lausanne Conference had ended. For all practical purposes the conciliation effort had failed and was over. A conference was held in Geneva from January to July 1950, and another in Paris in the latter part of 1951. It was here that the CCP submitted its own proposals for a peace settlement. They were rejected not because they were unworthy—they were not —but because in September 1951 there was not an Arab politician in the Middle East who could have accepted any kind of reasonable settlement with Israel and expected to remain in power—or alive. In November 1951, the CCP announced that it could not carry out its mandate. The General Assembly instructed it to carry on, but in the following years it confined itself to things like cadastral surveys.

[1] CCP, *General Progress Report*, A/1367 and Add. 1, 23rd October 1950, pp. 36–49.

Chapter Five

THE ARMISTICE RÉGIME

THE failure of the conciliation effort meant that Arab–Israeli relations remained within the legal-political framework of the régime established by the four General Armistice Agreements. To understand the deterioration of Arab-Israeli relations within its proper context we must understand what this armistice régime involved: what kind of armistice the Security Council had asked for, and what kind of armistice the Arabs and the Israelis had drawn up and agreed upon.

The armistice régime had come about as a result of the Security Council's intervention in its resolution of 16th November 1948. Its description of the kind of armistice it wanted had been brief: the armistice was to 'facilitate the transition from the present truce to permanent peace . . .'; there were to be permanent armistice demarcation lines; and the armed forces on both sides of the armistice demarcation lines (ADL) were to be withdrawn and reduced. In fact, each of the four GAAs includes much more than this, going far beyond what the Council had asked for.

In the Preamble[1] the armistice's purpose of facilitating the transition to permanent peace is stated. In Article One the signatories agreed:

[1] The four GAAs differ because of varying local circumstances; however, in so far as the armistice itself is concerned, each GAA is considered to mean the same as the other three. Unless noted to the contrary all references will be to the Lebanese GAA, *SCOR*, S/1296/Rev. 1, Special Supplement No. 4, 1949.

1. not to resort to force in the settlement of the Palestine question;
2. not to undertake, plan or threaten aggressive action by armed forces against the armed forces or people of the other side;
3. to respect fully 'the right of each Party to its security and freedom from fear of attack'; and
4. that the establishment of the armistice is an indispensable step toward the restoration of peace in Palestine.

The terms of the armistice itself were set forth in Article Three:

1. a general armistice was declared;
2. each party agreed to forbid hostile or warlike action by its military, para-military or non-regular forces against the military or para-military forces of othe other, or against its civilians;
3. each party agreed that no warlike act or act of hostility would be conducted from territory under its control against the other.

Articles Four and Five provided for the delineation of ADLs and the withdrawal and reduction of armed forces. Neither military nor civilian personnel were to be allowed to cross the ADL. Article Two provided that the terms of the GAA would not prejudice 'the rights, claims and position of either Party hereto in the ultimate peaceful settlement of the Palestine question . . .' In Article Eight it was stated that the armistice was permanent, and would remain in force even after the final peace settlement. The signatories were free to revise or suspend any provision of the GAAs, excepting Articles One and Three. These, the actual armistice provisions, could not be altered or revoked.

This was the armistice.[1] It went beyond anything the Council had asked for. Presumably the signatories knew what the words meant and what responsibilities they were undertaking when they signed. According to traditional jurisprudence an armistice involved little more than a temporary cessation of military hostilities. But this armistice was 'permanent'. All the signatories agreed that Article One constituted continuing 'non-aggression pacts'. Paragraph three of the Article contained an

---

[1] For a detailed legal analysis of the GAA's, see S. Rosenne, *Israel's Armistice Agreements with the Arab States.*

explicit provision for the right of each Party to its security—not just a limited 'military security'—and freedom from fear of attack. Without going into the complicated legal questions regarding the definition of 'preliminary peace' it is obvious that the purpose of this Article was to maintain peaceful relations and involved the acceptance by each party of the other's right to exist and develop as did other nations. No allowance was made for backsliding. Each GAA was studded with phrases stating that the armistice was part of the transition to a final peace settlement.

This was fundamental. Neither the UN officials nor the Israelis thought that it would take more than six months to work out peace agreements, a year at the most.[1] The GAAs were not designed to last longer than that. Unexpected stresses and strains would emerge. There could be no standing still. Either the movement toward peace would be sustained, or the armistice régime would crumble.

Because movement was not sustained, the rot set in almost immediately. The responsibility lay with the Arabs. The trouble stemmed from their refusal to implement the spirit or the letter of the General Armistice Agreements.

There is no moral judgement involved here. I am not suggesting that the Israelis were 'right' and the Arabs 'wrong', or that one side was 'good' and the other 'bad'. Four agreements were signed, agreements based upon certain assumptions about the present and the future, agreements involving certain obligations, explicit and implicit. To put it briefly: the Arabs agreed to the existence of Israel and to live in peace with her. Then they decided that it was not in their interest to carry this out; that it was more important to continue the struggle. Whether or not this was right or wrong, good or bad, is irrelevant. What does count are the consequences; it is with these that we are concerned.

---

[1] In December 1950 General Riley said, 'neither Bunche nor myself visualized any of the Armistice Agreements continuing this long ... we talked of six months as the maximum time necessary ... to reach an agreement that might lead to the basis on which final peace could be signed. Then we added another six months and said the the parties themselves are bound to reach an agreement in that period': *HKJ–IMAC,* 43rd mtg., 6th December 1950, p. 2; also *E–IMAC,* 11th mtg., 31st May 1949, p. 5.

While the Security Council was celebrating the successful conclusion of the armistice negotiations the Egyptian delegate stated pointedly that his Government would continue the struggle against Israel. This attitude was already reflected in the CCP, in the tightening up of the blockade and boycott, in the whittling away of the MACs' authority, and in the increasing ferocity of anti-Israel propaganda. The Israelis were forced to alter fundamentally their concept of the armistice. They believed that if Arab propaganda proclaimed the coming of a 'second round' then this was the trend of Arab policy, against which no Arab leader would dare move. The Israelis also believed that the Arabs were using the armistice to injure and defeat them. Consequently they had to think of it in terms of security and survival, and not of facilitating the transition to peace. As they trusted the Arabs less, so the Israelis relied on their army more. So long as they believed that the Arab must be taken at his word—that the destruction of Israel was his prerequisite for peace—they had no choice.

The breakdown of the armistice régime was not solely the result of Arab–Israeli differences. External pressures, the inter-Arab, Great Power, and Arab–West conflicts constituted powerful disruptive forces. Against these the armistice machinery was ineffectual. Local issues were caught up in extraneous international disputes and used for ends which bore no connexion with their origin or with local needs. The time factor was inexorable. Even if, in the first few years, the Arabs did not want another war, by choosing not to make peace they laid the situation open to pressures which they could not control. As time passed these pressures took hold and it became easier to move away from than on towards peace. The armistice régime as an instrument of action lost its importance.

Three interlocking sets of machinery constituted the armistice régime.

The first was the Mixed Armistice Commission (MAC)[1] set up under the terms of each GAA to provide for the implementation and supervision of the armistice provisions. The MACs

---

[1] Legally and politically each MAC is separate from the other three. But they faced similar problems and were subjected to similar pressures and hence tended to behave alike. The Lebanese MAC was the exception.

were bipartite military commissions to which each side sent an agreed-upon number of military delegates. Often civilians were present at the meetings, but only as advisers to their respective delegations. The Chairman of each MAC was the Chief of Staff, UNTSO, who usually sent one of his senior officers to act in his stead. The functions of the MAC were mainly administrative. But it also had the authority to interpret armistice provisions where this was necessary for supervision. Its decisions were final. It could make recommendations for alterations to the GAAs, excepting Articles One and Three, but these were not binding. Decisions if possible were to be unanimous, but a simple majority was sufficient. This meant that the MAC could still function even if one party boycotted it. It also meant that on contentious issues the decision lay with the Chairman. Complaints relating to the application of the GAA were to be referred immediately to the MAC through the Chairman. Appropriate action would then be taken 'with a view to the equitable and mutually satisfactory settlement' of the complaint. Each MAC had at its disposal for purposes of observation and investigation a number of Observers from the UNTSO.

The MACs were the only place where the Israelis met with their neighbours continually to discuss the questions outstanding between them. They were very important in the early years. Once the set tasks of arranging for the delineation of demarcation lines and the withdrawal and reduction of armed forces had been completed, they had to deal with other problems outside their formal authority: for example, carrying out the 'reunion of families' scheme, arranging land transfers, and above all dealing with the numerous cases of theft, murder, reprisal and *fedayeen* raids along the border. The problems involved here were of a civilian and political nature. Everything depended upon the various governments' willingness to let the MACs deal with these questions, and to abide by their recommendations. As time passed this occurred less and less frequently.

A dispute of fundamental importance underlay this lack of co-operation. The Israelis expected that the MACs would play an active, effective role in the settlement of questions outstanding and in bringing about final peace. This was especially so after the other media of conciliation had failed. Thus they were anxious that the MACs operate on as broad a basis as possible. The Arabs took exactly the opposite view. They regarded the armistice as a purely military arrangement, concerned only with the cease-fire. They tried to ignore and pass over every provision concerned with non-military matters. Thus, they refused to discuss the implementation of Article One, or anything else which had political implications. This meant, in effect, that there was no adequate machinery for resolving those problems disrupting the armistice régime.

It soon became clear that something had to be done. Late in 1950 General Riley, Chief of Staff, UNTSO, told the Security Council that the MACs had outlived their usefulness. He said that to cope with post-armistice developments it was necessary to broaden the MACs' authority.[1] The Council, however, had no authority to order such a move, and the Arabs refused to countenance the idea.

They went even farther, and tried to utilize the MACs as a weapon against Israel. The Arab delegates to the four MACs began to meet, and in 1952 a common policy was agreed upon. The Israelis claim, and the evidence available supports them, that there were four major points: the scope of the GAAs was to be limited; no new arrangements would be made for border control; local incidents were to be exploited so as to nullify existing agreements; and the activities of the MACs were to be reduced to a minimum. The Israeli reaction was calculable.[2]

Steadily deprived of their opportunities to ameliorate border violence, the MACs become little more than courts *cum* scoreboards. Complaints were so numerous that it became impossible to deal with them all. It was decided that the Chairman would call emergency meetings within twenty-four hours to handle complaints dealing with loss of life. Other complaints were put on the agenda of the regular meetings, and came up for discussion months after the event. Delegates presented the longest list possible of complaints for propaganda purposes. By October

---

[1] *SCOR*, 517th mtg., 30th October 1950, pp. 16–17.
[2] *Times*, Beirut Correspondent, 15th July 1951, Amman Correspondent, 18th November 1951, Cairo Correspondent, 20th April 1953; *MG*, 20th April 1953; *Times* and *LaB Egypt.*, 22nd August 1955; *JAD*, 5th December 1952, p. 216, 20th February 1953, p. 497; *JOMER*, 24th April 1953; *JP*, Achimogel, 10th July 1952.

1952, the Egyptian MAC had 429 complaints on its agenda, the Jordan MAC 506. In such circumstances discussions were futile and time-wasting. Often complaints would be cleared from the agenda *en bloc*. Later they would appear as statistics in the regular UNTSO reports to the Council, grist for the propaganda mill. Unanimity became the exception rather than the rule. Walkouts and boycotts were not uncommon. The Israelis argued against turning the MACs into courts or score boards and insisted upon more constructive action.[1]

The Arabs, however, refused to agree to enlarge upon the MACs' role, and so nothing was done. The position of the Chairman with his deciding vote was invidious. He had to act as judge while the various delegations brought in bits of evidence, trackers' reports, blood samples, cartridge cases, and other debris, but he had no authority to formulate the verdict. Resolutions were drafted by each delegation to provide the maximum of propaganda value and he had to vote for one and often both. Several attempts were made by the Chief of Staff, UNTSO, to alter the procedure so as to give the Chairman more authority to formulate decisions and to regulate the work in general, but without Arab–Israeli agreement nothing could be done.

The MACs broke down. The Syrian MAC stopped meeting in 1951, did not meet again until 1954, and after that only sporadically. The Egyptian MAC broke off meeting in October 1951 for seven months, and when it reconvened was useless. The Jordan MAC met regularly and serious efforts were made to hold the situation in check. But the pressures were so strong that sustained government action was necessary. This was not forthcoming until it was too late. In all cases arrangements were made for informal cooperation—including sub-committees and local commanders' agreements—which were often very useful, particularly when relations were so bad that formal MAC meetings would have been politically compromising. But these informal arrangements could not replace a vigorous MAC supported by governments in active cooperation.

The second piece of machinery was the UNTSO. Created

---

[1] For example, vd. *HKJ–IMAC*, 65th mtg., 28th August 1951; *E–IMAC*, 30th emergency mtg., 2nd October 1954, pp. 17–24.

by the Security Council in 1948 to supervise the truce, it remained on after the armistice was established to carry on this same function. It also had another task: to provide, not only Chairmen, but Observers for the MAC investigation machinery. For reasons which have never been adequately explained, the UNTSO usually ignored its broader duties and confined itself almost solely to writing reports of investigations of complaints to the MACs. Even here it acted in a very cautious and circumspect manner. This was its gravest weakness. The UNTSO saw itself as neutral, and neutrality seems to have been equated with inoffensiveness. This was quite different from the forthright objectivity which the situation demanded. The UNTSO made few attempts to discuss the factors undermining the armistice and the cease-fire, or to discuss the difficulties surrounding the implementation of Article One, or even mention that Article One was not being implemented. Most UNTSO reports read as though the real issues were military, not political. The emphasis was upon day-to-day events: who crossed the line? who fired first? how many were killed?

Two instances are revealing. In his report to the Council on the Qibya Raid, UNTSO Chief of Staff General Bennike—who seems to typify the most serious weaknesses of the UNTSO—stated that he had 'deliberately refrained' from mentioning anything other than the 'immediate problems connected with their [UNTSO] daily work'.[1] Later, in 1954, when Israel–Jordan relations were chaotic and bloody incidents frequent, the Israelis made a major effort to improve the situation by calling the special conference, provided for in the GAA, to review the whole armistice régime with Jordan. Attendance at the conference was obligatory. Two months of effort went into persuading Jordan to attend. On 17th March, eleven Israelis were killed near the border. A few days later Jordan stated definitively that she would not attend the conference. Shortly afterwards Israeli troops raided Nahalin. Reporting on the raid Bennike concentrated almost exclusively on previous border incidents. About the attempts to convene the conference, their failure, and the implications, he found nothing to say except that it had 'not contributed to create a better atmosphere

[1] *SCOR*, 630 mtg., 27th October 1953, p. 15.

between the two countries'.[1] To discuss border incidents solely within the context of other border incidents was like thinking the symptoms more important than the disease—and just as disastrous.

As time passed the UNTSO took on a new role. The armistice régime had broken down, all corrective measures had failed. The Security Council and the Western Powers, unwilling or unable to rectify matters, tended to use the UNTSO as a poor substitute for effective action. The Council began to give it the attributes of a third, sovereign party in the dispute. By its very nature this development was detrimental to Israel.

The UNTSO operated mainly within the former boundaries of Palestine. Any expansion in its powers—for example, by the creation of UNTSO-controlled buffer zones, or freedom of access, flying rights, and authority on the ground—meant placing limitations on Israel. With the exception of Jordan, the other Arab States were not much affected. There was also a growing tendency of the Security Council and the Arabs to treat the GAAs themselves as arrangements between UNTSO and the various parties, rather than as between Israel and the separate Arab States. In 1955–6, the Israelis considered that the UNTSO stood between them and the *fedayeen*; that while they were arguing with the UNTSO about what could be done, the Egyptian raiders were free to carry on as they pleased.

Attributing powers to the UNTSO could not disguise its inability to stop or alleviate the Arabs' war of attrition against Israel. Armed marauders, propaganda and incitement, boycott and blockade were used with impunity. The UNTSO did not condone these actions, and there were few measures it could take against them. But the Israelis saw it as standing between themselves and adequate defence, as an involuntary shield protecting the Arabs from having to implement the letter or spirit of the GAAs. Trying to delegate authority to it only served to aggravate its weaknesses in the eyes of the Israelis. Again and again the situation went from bad to worse because the Israelis did not trust the UNTSO, or were reluctant to

[1] *Report of the Chief of Staff, UNTSO . . . ibid*, S/318 and Corr. 1, 1st March 1954, p. 26.

cooperate with it because they believed that cooperation would not secure them protection.[1]

Most of the important UNTSO officials had serious accusations of bias and dishonesty levelled against them by one side or the other. This was an important issue, but unfortunately not much reliable evidence is available. In fairness it should be pointed out that the UNTSO was understaffed, overworked, and usually lacked support from either side or from the UN. The very nature of its task was bound to generate antagonism. The job itself was backbreaking, thankless and dangerous, and most officers carried it out to the best of their ability. Also, the UNTSO Observers came from different countries with different military traditions, and these inevitably shaped their attitudes towards their duties along the ADLs, creating not only difficulties with the parties but amongst themselves as well. UNTSO was an institution with its own bureaucracy and its own rules for behaviour and personal advancement. The nature of an institution is to develop its own interests, which it seeks to protect, possibly to the detriment—although it would not be considered as such by the UNTSO—of the cause of peace. Now, this is not meant to imply that UNTSO was some sort of evil growth or that it deliberately sought to perpetuate itself, or that its officers deliberately evaded their duty in order to secure their advancement or to ensure that their contracts were renewed, as some Arabs and Israelis claim. But, even with the best of intentions, UNTSO was subject to all the faults of an organization and as such it could not be expected to remain truly impartial and disinterested.

The Arabs considered UNTSO Chiefs of Staff, General William Riley (1949–53) and General E. L. M. Burns (1954–6) to be pro-Israeli. Riley was a continual embarrassment because he had first-hand knowledge of the disparity between what the

---

[1] Also the UNTSO was in Israel—everywhere in Israel. The vast majority of Arabs never saw a UNTSO official or car from one year to the next. The Israelis saw them every day. Their conspicuous vehicles travelled the countryside from one incident to the next. To a young, sensitive, chauvinistic nation they were a foreign, impeding presence, a constant reminder of other foreign 'troops'. Furthermore, the UNTSO officials were highly paid by Israeli standards, able to afford the best of everything. The story is an old one. There was a fertile breeding ground for discontent and dislike on both sides.

Arabs had promised during the armistice negotiations, and how they acted afterwards. Burns was criticized for discussing the Gaza Raid within the wider context of Egyptian provocation.[1] Both men tried hard to extend the area of cooperation and to get the whole of the GAAs enforced. The Israelis thought them to be impartial and capable, and in turn, claimed that UNTSO Chief of Staff General Vagn Bennike (1953–4), Jordan MAC Chairman B. L. de Ridder (who was Acting Chief of Staff for a time), and his successor Commander E. H. Hutchison, were pro-Arab.

There is considerable doubt about the competence of Bennike and de Ridder. Bennike's UNTSO reports and a speech he made after retiring indicate that he had no clear understanding of the armistice régime. De Ridder's reports on the fighting at Tel el Mutilla in Israel in May 1951 indicate that he had little idea of how to go about his job. Bennike and Hutchison convict themselves of bias by their own words: the former in his speech after retirement, and the latter in his book. Both believed Arab charges that Israel was bent on the domination of the Arab world; both accepted as valid the Arabs' conception of the restricted scope of the armistice; and neither seems to have been aware of the dynamics of the forces at work in the area.[2] This, however, does not mean that these men acted in a deliberately dishonest manner or consciously broke the trust placed in them during the performance of their duties. De Ridder may belong to a different category. If he spoke and acted as the Israelis claim[3] he did then he is open to serious charges. All three men were decorated by the Arabs on their retirement from the UNTSO.

The third piece of machinery was the Security Council. The GAAs provided for three stages in the enforcement and alteration of the armistice provisions. The first was negotiations carried on through the MAC perhaps, where the parties had the power to revise or suspend by mutual consent any provision of the GAA, with the exceptions of Articles One and Three which

[1] For example *MEM*, 29th November 1952, p. 11; *LaB. Egypt.*, 2nd July 1955 *NYT*, Gilroy, 4th and 10th July 1955.

[2] *JP*, 13th December 1954; vd. also Hutchison's *Violent Truce*.

[3] *JAD*, 1st August 1952, pp. 1,459–60; *JOMER*, 1st August 1952, p. 7, and 8th August 1952, p. 5.

were immutable and permanent. Failing agreement, either signatory was entitled, after the GAA was one year old, to ask the UN Secretary-General to call a conference of the signatories to review and revise it. Attendance was obligatory. If there was no agreement at the second stage, then either side could bring the matter before the Security Council 'for relief sought, on the grounds that this Agreement has been concluded in pursuance of Security Council action toward the end of achieving peace in Palestine' (Article Eight of the Lebanese GAA). At this point the Council could review and revise the GAA as it saw fit (except for Articles One and Three). Presumably its authority would derive from the GAA itself rather than from the UN Charter, with all its limitations, and thus the scope for action would be much greater. If, however, complaints were brought before the Council without going through the proper stages then it would have to act solely within the framework of the Charter. This meant that the Council would not have the authority to take any steps or order any measures prejudicial to the rights, claims or position of the disputants.

The three stages were implemented only once. In 1954, when relations with Jordan were particularly bad and the MAC ineffective, Israel asked the Secretary-General to convoke a conference. Jordan refused to attend. Subsequently Israel took the matter to the Council for redress of grievance. The Council adjourned to consider a technicality and that was that. There was no discussion at all of the question of review and revision. The only chance the Council ever had to grasp firmly and shape Arab–Israeli relations into something better was simply relinquished. Unwillingness to come to grips with the fundamentals of Arab–Israeli relations was implicit in almost all the Council's deliberations. One found it in the platitudes about mutual cooperation and agreement when obviously it was their absence which was the real problem. One found it in the tendency to give all the responsibility to the UNTSO. One found it in the Council's reluctance to deal with anything except breaches of the cease-fire.

The Council's scope of action was never adequately delineated. The Charter referred to breaches of the peace and threats to the peace. Both phrases were open to various interpretations. Obviously a broken cease-fire agreement was a breach of or threat to the peace. But were there others: threats of war? incitement to violence? There was no indication that the Council ever gave its serious attention to this question. Eventually this emphasis on just the cease-fire destroyed whatever lingering belief existed in the integrity of the GAAs. By 1956, UN Secretary-General Dag Hammarskjold was arguing, and the Council agreeing, that there was a clear distinction between the cease-fire provisions in the GAAs (Article Three) and all the other provisions including Article One.[1]

The Israelis objected strongly to Hammarskjold's interpretation of the GAA, maintaining that according to the terms of each GAA the two Articles were inseparable and unchangeable. They argued that it was impossible to divide one from the other without destroying the whole armistice régime. Article One, they said, with its provisions for security and freedom from fear of attack was the touchstone of the armistice. The Secretary-General replied that the cease-fire provisions were based upon Charter commitments binding on all UN members, and upon the Council's cease-fire resolution of 15th July 1948. Therefore it took priority over the other provisions; anyway, there was no machinery for enforcing the other provisions including Article One. The Israelis took the view, in vain, that since the situation came under the restrictions of the Charter and the July 1948 cease-fire resolution there was no reason to bring in the GAAs as support at this level. It would have been sufficient to say that raids must cease because of the Charter and the resolution. The parties could then have been asked or ordered to reinstate the GAAs, or at least Articles One and Three, as a whole.

The effect of the Secretary-General's interpretation was to validate the Arabs' concept of a limited, static armistice, with the result that for all practical purposes the Council considered the GAAs to be dead and the situation back to what it had been in July 1948. There is no doubt that in adopting this restricted interpretation the Council, and probably the Secretary-General, were influenced largely by the exigencies of the international situation, and by the interests and involvements of the

[1] *Report of the Secretary-General . . . SCOR*, S/3596, 9th May 1956.

individual Council members. This, the crucial weakness of the
Council in all important matters, is too well known to need explanation. Clearly no one (at least until after the Suez Canal
Company was nationalized) was going to risk trying to force
Egypt or Israel to do things they did not want to do. Thus, the
Council, which was to be the bedrock of the armistice régime,
turned out to be muskeg. In politics, like road-making, it is
notoriously difficult to build on or over muskeg. One simply
sinks.

The only attempt made to find out what the armistice really
meant was during the Council debate in 1951 on the Suez
Blockade.[1] Very briefly, the situation was this. Egypt was preventing Israeli ships and goods, for or from Israel, from passing
through the Canal, an international waterway through which
free passage was guaranteed by treaty. Egypt's arguments were
as follows:

1. Israel was a threat to Egypt and the blockade was an act of
   self-defence justified by the Convention of Constantinople
   (1888) and the UN Charter.

2. A state of war existed between the two countries. The GAA put
   an end only to the fighting but the state of war was still in
   effect.

3. Consequently Egypt had the right of visit, search and seizure
   as guaranteed by international law.

4. According to traditional usage an armistice is a purely military
   arrangement and can have no effect on the political *status quo*.

5. No interpretation could be put upon the GAA which would
   affect Egypt's rights, claims or position in the Palestine dispute.
   (This same argument was used to justify the Arabs' refusal to
   discuss political matters in the MACs, and Egypt's and Jordan's
   reluctance to mark the ADLs properly on the ground.)

Egypt's emphasis on a 'technical *status belli*' raised some fine
legal points. At the time of their intervention in Palestine the

[1] For comprehensive statements of the various positions vd. *SCOR*, 549th mtg.,
26th July 1951 and subsequent meetings. A bibliography for the legal arguments
can be found in L. M. Bloomfield, *Egypt, Israel and the Gulf of Aqaba in International
Law*.

Arab States had taken great pains to show that no state of war existed, because if it did then they were liable to formal charges of aggression under the Charter, with the possibility of sanctions being applied against them. Also, it would have implied recognition of Israel: a state can declare war only on another state, not on groups of terrorists and bandits. The Arabs did not 'declare war' on Israel until a year *after* the GAAs had been signed.[1] There was no formal declaration, only a rather casual comment as to the war's existence by an Egyptian delegate during a MAC discussion on the Blockade.

The Egyptians argued that all this was unimportant. They pointed out that according to traditional usage no formal declaration to the enemy was needed in order to legalize hostilities. Furthermore, there could be a unilateral declaration of war, the dissent of the other side notwithstanding: the *status belli* and the whole paraphernalia of belligerent rights could come into effect merely on Egypt's statement to that effect.

The Israelis maintained that all these arguments were based on traditional international jurisprudence and that no account was taken of contemporary jurisprudence, the Charter régime, and, most important of all, the actual wording of the General Armistice Agreements. First of all, they said, contemporary practice was for armistice agreements to contain provisions of a political nature. Second, since 1947 the Palestine question had been dealt with under the UN Charter, hostilities in 1948–9 had been handled according to the provisions of the Charter, and, finally, some of the armistice provisions had been lifted bodily from the Charter. Clearly the armistice had to be viewed within the context of the Charter. The Charter made no provision for a *status belli* or for the continuing exercise of belligerent rights. The purpose of the Charter régime was to maintain the peace, not to protect the rights of war. No distinction was made in the Charter between an armistice and peace. Once the hostilities ended so did all those rights and privileges which arose solely out of the existence of hostilities. Also, the Israelis went on, it was now accepted that if an armistice was permanent, as this one was, then it fell into the traditional category of 'pre-

[1] In August 1949 the Arabs were still claiming that there had been no formal state of war: *SCOR*, 549th mtg., 26th July 1951, p. 11.

liminary peace', which meant the abolition of belligerent rights. Third, it was incorrect to try to fit this particular armistice into a traditional form which might or might not be relevant. What was important was the wording of the GAAs themselves, the obligations, responsibilities and commitments which they set out, and which the signatories had agreed to accept.

The Israelis pointed out:

1. that they and the Arabs were agreed that Article One constituted a permanent non-aggression pact;

2. that the provisions of this Article were not of a purely military nature, and involved restrictions of a political kind;

3. that each was bound to respect the right of the other to his 'security' and 'freedom from fear of attack';

4. that the word 'security' stood unqualified, there was no reference to just military security; and

5. the very fact that the Arabs insisted upon a *status belli* and the exercise of belligerent rights was a violation of the GAAs because it threatened Israel's security and freedom from fear of of attack.

So far as the Israelis were concerned, there was no *status belli*, and they were bound together with the Arabs in a state of peace, even though the final arrangements had still to be worked out.

These, in brief, were the arguments brought before the Council. The issues were complicated and obscure. The Council's authority extended to some aspects and not to others. Even so, the dispute was handled in an unsatisfactory manner. All legal issues were avoided.[1] Most delegates disregarded the provisions of the Charter and of the GAAs except for general references. Instead the approach was 'commonsensical'.[2] The British delegate summed it up when he said that whether or not a *status belli* existed was unimportant: what mattered was

[1] According to one source the Security Council even refused to take legal advice: 'The Security Council and the Suez Canal,' in *International and Comparative Law Quarterly*, January 1952.
[2] For delegates' opinions see *op. cit*, 552 and 553rd mtgs., 16th August 1951.

whether the actual exercise of belligerent rights was 'reasonable, just and equitable', particularly after the armistice had been in effect for over two years. Only the French delegate asserted that Egypt's arguments had no legal validity, but he did not say why. The Chinese and Indian delegates said that by depriving Egypt of belligerent rights the Council members were disregarding her legal position under international law.

The Council's decision that the blockade must be lifted was formulated in such a way as to render it ineffective regardless of whether or not it was the proper decision to make. Egypt was ordered to desist because it was unreasonable to exercise belligerent rights two and half years after an armistice had been signed; she had no need to claim self-defence; and the blockade interfered with the right of other (i.e. European) nations to their freedom of navigation and economic reconstruction.

The resolution was futile. Nobody was going to force Egypt to implement it. It was prejudicial to her substantive rights and therefore *ultra vires*. The resolution was not placed within the context of those Charter provisions which gave the Council binding authority, and therefore it was a 'recommendation' rather than an 'order'. These criticisms, however, were of secondary importance to the main issue which was the Council's role in the maintenance of the Armistice. Now, obviously the Council did have some authority in this dispute. It could not decide upon the substantive issue, which in effect was what it tried to do. But it could, for example, have dealt with the question of the right of self-defence within the context of Article Fifty-one of the Charter where that right was defined. Also it could have determined that the blockade was a violation of Article One of the GAA. Under the terms of Chapter Seven of the Charter it would have been justified in ordering the parties to take the dispute to the International Court of Justice. In this way it would have been acting strictly within the limits of its own authority and, at the same time, ensuring that the dispute was settled once and for all. At the same time it must be admitted that these were not actions which the Powers, enmeshed in their struggles with each other, would undertake lightly.

And so the matter was passed off. No proper decision has ever been handed down, and the dispute still goes on. Now, perhaps, it is not too important, but in 1951 the proper handling of the dispute and an authoritative statement by the Council on the nature of the GAAs might have accomplished a great deal.

Chapter Six

ISRAEL AND JORDAN (1949-56)

R ELATIONS between these two countries started off well. It was taken for granted that peace negotiations would follow immediately after the armistice conference. The terms had been adumbrated in Article Eight of the GAA; a Special Committee was provided to do the necessary work; the armistice was to be only a minor, brief interlude between war and peace.

Yet nothing was done for seven long months, while one by one the opportunities for successful peace-making were lost. When serious talks did begin, in October 1949, it was already too late. The difficulties of the questions still outstanding compounded with the external complications had created a hopeless situation.

If it had been left to King Abdullah peace talks would have begun immediately. His claims to the West Bank of the Jordan, to Jerusalem, and ultimately to leadership of the Fertile Crescent drew growing opposition from Egypt, Saudi Arabia and the republican and nationalist circles in Syria. If he was to succeed he had to settle his differences with Israel. It was the Israelis who held back. They were reluctant to enter into negotiations on the basis of Jordan's occupation of the West Bank. Despite the Arab Legion's withdrawal, the Israelis were still at a considerable military disadvantage. Jewish Jerusalem was surrounded on three sides. The corridor to the sea was narrow, and threatened by the Latrun salient. The coastal plain was still only ten miles wide in places and dominated by the Legion's hill positions. The Israelis, encouraged by the French CCP delegate de Boisanger, hoped to eject Jordan by working together with the other Arab countries at the CCP conference in Lausanne.[1] The Israelis believed that they and the Egyptians had common interests *vis-à-vis* Jordan and that a joint policy could be formulated in which Syria and Lebanon would join. The hope was not without foundation. During the armistice negotiations the Egyptian delegates gave Israel the impression that their government was not averse to a peace settlement or to cooperating to limit Abdullah's—and Britain's—influence.

Egypt was the most powerful of the Arab countries. Jordan depended almost entirely on British support, and Abdullah himself was suspect as an anglophile. Many Israelis argued that the road to peace lay through Cairo. If there were negotiations with Abdullah on the basis of his occupation of the West Bank Egypt would be antagonized. She would turn against Israel. The chance of a settlement between the two countries would be lost. Also there could be little hope of peace with Syria or Lebanon unless Egypt went first. Even if Abdullah did sign a peace treaty it was a dead end, others would not follow. If, these people argued, Israel wanted to make peace with all her neighbours then she had to do it through Egypt. Abdullah would have to wait.

As the spring wore on into the summer even the most optimistic Israeli realized that there was no chance for peace negotiations with Egypt. None the less, the same problem remained. Egypt's consent to an Israel–Jordan settlement was essential if that settlement were to be implemented. But what could be offered Egypt as an inducement? Abdullah could not give Egypt the West Bank. Anything (apart from the Negev) Israel could concede—free ports, corridors to the sea—would benefit Abdullah, not Egypt. By October it was impossible to procrastinate any longer. The CCP was obviously a failure. Both Israel and Jordan were undergoing economic crises of extremely severe proportions. In both countries the situation was critical to the point of unreality. Peace could not be delayed. The Israelis decided to risk Egypt's displeasure.

[1] According to Sharett the Israelis wanted to see Arab Palestine turned into a separate, independent buffer state: Bilby, *loc. cit.*, p. 97.

Secret negotiations began, on Abdullah's initiative,[1] but with little success. There was no agreement on the disposition of the West Bank, the Negev or Jerusalem, and the talks hung fire. News of the negotiations had leaked out, however, and in retaliation the Egyptians began, in December 1949, to organize support in the UN for another resolution calling for the internationalization of Jerusalem. The idea had originally been adopted by the General Assembly for its Partition Plan. At that time, in 1947, all the Arab States were opposed to internationalization. The Zionists accepted it because it seemed the only way to get a Jewish State. Then, the Arabs' siege of Jerusalem, and the UN's lack of concern for the fate of the Jews there, persuaded the Israelis that Jewish Jerusalem could not be left under UN administration. They made the New City their capital, and declared internationalization unacceptable. Jordan followed suit.

Egypt then persuaded the Arab–Asian bloc, the Russian bloc and the Vatican to support a new resolution reaffirming internationalization. The Vatican which had previously supported internationalization, and then accepted Bernadotte's proposal that Jerusalem become an Arab city, now refused to consider any suggestion that the Israelis govern half of it. Despite the efforts of the United States the Latin-American countries were herded into line and the resolution was adopted.[2] (A few months later the Russians announced that they were withdrawing their support for internationalization.)

Faced with the prospect of UN intervention, Israel and Jordan agreed to lay aside their efforts for a comprehensive agreement and to concentrate on settling their differences over Jerusalem before the UN moved in on them. Abdullah seems to have wanted the Israelis to cede some Arab sections of the city

[1] See McDonald, *loc. cit.*, p. 192 for a summary of the negotiations. Dearden and Kirk have different accounts. For background see *Scotsman* and *MG*, 18th August 1949; *NYT*, 19th August 1949; and *MG*, 2nd September 1949.

In August, after it was obvious that the CCP was a failure, Abdullah went to London and evidently received British support for his plans to annex Arab Palestine, to establish a union with Syria, and to oppose Egyptian aspirations in Palestine and Syria.

[2] *GAOR*, 303 (iv), 9th December 1949. For detailed studies see G. Pollak, *Jerusalem and the Protection of the Holy Places* .. Unpubl. Thesis (University of London 1957) also E. B. Glick, in *International Organization*, Spring 1957.

but offered them nothing in return. Once again no agreement could be reached.

Despite his several failures Abdullah could not afford to let matters rest. In February 1950, he proposed a set of interim measures designed to provide the benefits of a peace settlement without, it was hoped, its drawbacks. The measures were a five-year non-aggression pact based upon existing boundaries. These would remain unchanged pending a final settlement. Borders would be open to ordinary trade and traffic, and Jordan would regain her free port of Haifa. Both countries would guarantee the freedom of, access to, and protection of the Holy Places. The supply of electricity from the New City to the Old would be resumed. Committees would be set up to work on the other questions still outstanding. Presumably, this included the refugee problem.[1]

The Israelis were most hesitant. There were Russia and Great Britain to consider. Relations with Russia were causing considerable concern. Russia's diplomatic support and trade were badly needed: so was access to her three million Jews. But, according to the Russians, Zionism and Communism were incompatible doctrines. Also Israel's policy of non-identification was seriously compromised by her dependence upon American aid and charity. Anti-Israel and anti-Jewish campaigns were gaining momentum in the Soviet *bloc*. The Russians told the Israelis that they regarded Abdullah as a puppet of British Imperialism and his annexation of the West Bank as an un-friendly act, and that Israel's agreement to it would be viewed with disfavour.[2]

The British supported Abdullah's proposals—which fell in

---

[1] McDonald, *loc. cit.*, pp. 193–4; *NYT*, 1st March, Currivan 2nd March 1950; *Observer*, Special Correspondent, 5th February 1950.

[2] *Zionist Review*, 30 December 1949, p. 11; *JP*, 13th December 1949. Laqueur, *The Soviet Union . . .*, pp. 148–9. In the autumn of 1949 an exchange of Notes took place between Sharett and Vishinsky. The latter noted Israel's dependence upon US economic aid for her existence, and expressed his understanding of the situation. This assurance was preceded and followed by heavy Soviet propaganda attacks on Israel for being a tool of American Imperialism. Laqueur postulates that one of the main reasons for Russia's violent campaign against Israel was Russian Jewry's immediate and powerful emotional response to Israel's creation. The Soviet government suddenly found that it had not been as successful with its Jewish Problem as it had thought and regarded Israel as a centrifugal and disruptive force.

with their previous arrangements with him for Palestine—
and told the Israelis that the other Arab States would in time
also accept them as the basis for a general settlement. The
Israelis, despite the recent *rapprochement*, were still suspicious of
Britain. In particular they were worried about the implications
of the Anglo–Jordan military alliance. They did not want the
treaty provisions extended to include the West Bank; they did
not want British troops on their borders; and they did not want
the British to be involved in any future argument over Arab
Palestine.

In Israel the argument swung back and forth. Opponents of
Abdullah's plan insisted that it meant giving up all effective
claims to Arab Palestine. The Communists and left-wing
Mapam opposed the extension of British influence and the
alienation of Russia. The right-wing parties, *Herut* and the
General Zionists, argued that all of Palestine belonged to Israel
by virtue of her religious and historic destiny, and that the plan
was a fatal compromise. Prime Minister Ben Gurion and Army
Chief of Staff Yigal Yadin suggested that the plan placed
Israel at a strategic disadvantage. Furthermore, agreement to
it would be taken by the other Arabs as a sign of weakness, and
they would be encouraged to demand even more concessions as
the price of peace. Only the Foreign Ministry, which had done
the negotiating, considered the plan acceptable. Eventually
it was decided to accept the offer. A draft treaty was drawn
up and initialled[1] by both parties toward the end of February.
Now the Israelis had to wait to see if Abdullah could weather
the storm which followed.

He stood alone, shrewd, stubborn, ambitious; a gambler, a
bedu contemptuous of city people, corrupt yet with honour,
brave with hints of greatness. An old man, an anachronism,
he fought the new Arabs with their modern ideas, their Western
education, and he lost. The issue was never in doubt; defeat
followed inexorably upon defeat. And there was nothing the
Israelis could do but wait and watch. His Prime Minister and
Cabinet refused to approve the draft treaty, which had been

---

[1] Eytan, *loc. cit.*, p. 41, who acted for Israel, is explicit about the initialled draft
treaty, but Glubb, *loc. cit.*, p. 258, and Dearden, *loc. cit.*, pp. 81–3 deny that
negotiations ever went this far.

negotiated without their knowledge, and resigned. Several
hours later they were back in office; another government could
not be formed. On the West Bank there were riots. Egypt,
determined to break Abdullah's influence once and for all,
decided to expel Jordan from the Arab League. Abdullah pre-
tended to ignore the move, but his representative went to the
League meeting on 25th March and, aided by Iraq and the
Yemen, defeated expulsion. The price was signature to a resolution that League membership would be forfeited by any
country signing a separate agreement with Israel. Probably
Abdullah intended to break his word once the national elections on 11th April had demonstrated that his people were
behind him.

The election were a personal disaster. Everyone voted, including the refugees. The mood of the Palestinians was unmistakable: annexation to Jordan was acceptable, peace with
Israel was not. Prominent opponents of Abdullah were elected
to the Assembly and almost half of the new cabinet were
Palestinians. Abdullah turned to the British for help. He was
their man, they had put him where he was, they had supported
and encouraged his plans for Arab Palestine and the Fertile
Crescent, and for peace with Israel. Now he wanted them to
persuade Egypt to moderate her position. But the British had
to think of their own difficulties with Egypt over the Suez Canal,
a matter of greater importance than Abdullah's career. Strong
representations on their part would have only angered the
Egyptians and accomplished little. Instead a cautiously worded
Note was sent to Abdullah expressing disapproval of the
League's resolution and forecasting that sooner or later the
Arabs would have to make peace with Israel.[1] This was less
than Abdullah needed. The back of the peace attempt was
broken, and the draft treaty laid quietly to one side. Talks with
the Israelis continued fitfully up until his assassination, but both
sides knew that nothing could be done.

The Palestinians with their greater numbers and better

[1] *JOMER*, 25th April 1952, pp. 9–10.
In April 1950, Arab Palestine was formally incorporated into Jordan. The
British awarded *de facto* not *de jure* recognition to the addition, and announced that
British troops would not be stationed on the West Bank.
The Israelis noted the incorporation, but declared that they were not bound by it.

education soon became the most influential single group in the Jordan government. Whatever loyalty they might have felt for their new king had been undermined by the Legion's withdrawals after the armistice negotiations, and destroyed by Abdullah's attempts to make peace. Their allegiance lay with Cairo. Their aim was to restore their homeland. The interests of Jordan were not their main concern.

The Israelis continued to press for a settlement. They reckoned that if Jordan would not come to terms voluntarily then she could be compelled to by insisting that she fulfil her obligations under the GAA. The Special Committee, set up under Article Eight, even if it were not used for peace negotiations, had duties to fulfil which would bring peace closer. Originally, the Israelis had expected that the Committee would settle the questions on its agenda within a few weeks or months of the armistice. But Jordan had refused to cooperate and meetings had been suspended. After the collapse of the draft treaty negotiations, the Israelis insisted that the Committee meet and carry out its tasks. Jordan declined, and the dispute was carried to the Security Council. Jordan then agreed to recommence meetings. But at the meetings Jordan refused to implement the arrangements set forth in the article on the grounds of national security. The Israelis rejected this as hypocritical: Jordan talked of a 'second round', yet at the same time she maintained that her security was threatened.[1] Jordan, however, was adamant, and after Abdullah's assassination in July 1951 attempts to resuscitate the Committee ended. Later, in 1956, the Israelis made another fruitless attempt to reactivate it in one of their last peaceable efforts to crack the Arab ring closing in around them.

The Special Committee was designed to carry out vital functions, and its collapse, serious enough in itself, further weakened the already declining authority of the armistice régime. Yet the UNTSO and the Council gave its demise only passing comment. What might have been—famous last words—the most effective provision of the GAA was effectively neutralized.

---

[1] *SCOR*, 517th mtg., 30th October 1950, statement by Eban, p. 13; *JAD*, 13th October 1950, p. 106, 17th November 1950, p. 312, 29th December 1950, pp. 568–9.

Along the winding furrow on the ground which marked the border between the two countries was enacted day in and day out the tragedy of Palestine; a story of misery, bloodshed and waste. The human suffering has been so great, the national interests so pressing, that one is swamped; to retain an equitable sense of proportion taxes us to our very limit. It is easy to say that the refugees should not have infiltrated into Israel to rob and sabotage and murder; that the Jordan government should have stopped them. But this ignores the dynamics of the problem. It is easy to say that the Israelis should have treated the infiltrators leniently; that understanding and cooperation held the answer, not shooting and reprisal raids. But was effective cooperation possible? If not, what was? How does one juxtapose misery, hatred and injustice to the will to national self-preservation, legal rights and obligations, and to fear? To state these questions is to bare the heart of the Israel–Jordan armistice régime.

The refugee problem dominated the scene. But the problem was not, from the point of view of maintaining the armistice régime, intractable. In the past few years we have seen that illegal border crossings can be stopped, that order can be maintained. What brought the armistice régime crashing down in ruins before 1956 was the Jordan's government's refusal to take the measures necessary to control the refugees.

Admittedly this statement is open to dispute. The contention here is that Jordan did not fulfil her obligations under the GAA, at least she did not fulfil them until it was too late to arrest the deterioration. The Israelis were not angels; they did most of the killing. But the records of the Mixed Armistice Commission indicate that in the early days, when border crossings both ways were numerous and often tragic, both MAC delegations considered the situation to be an unhappy but unavoidable result of the war's aftermath. There were no accusations of evil intent, and much evidence of good faith and sincere cooperation. The trouble began after unorganized infiltration began to diminish and infiltration organized for robbery and violence began to rise. Then the Israelis came to the conclusion that the Jordan government was not doing all that was necessary and possible to control the situation. They retaliated in force. From that time forward the turn of relations depended, in the last analysis, upon Israel's success in intimidating the peoples and government of Jordan. The road to success was a bloody one.

About 700,000 people were jammed into Arab Palestine; about one-third of these were refugees. The effect upon the West Bank's feeble economy was disastrous. Large numbers of people infiltrated into Israel: to steal food, to rejoin their families, to cultivate land, or simply because they did not know where the ADL was or what it meant. A smaller number of Israelis fround themselves in Jordan for similar reasons. This was usually described as 'innocent' infiltration. On both sides the situation was complicated by inexperience, disorganization, inadequate means, and pressing problems elsewhere.

The attitude of the Jordanian authorities varied. The MAC delegation and the Arab Legion realized the dangers involved and wanted strong measures taken to stop infiltration. The Legion's effectiveness was limited because strategic and internal security considerations required that most of its forces be stationed away from the border. In July 1950, it suggested to its government that all refugees be moved at least twenty kilometres from the frontier, and that local authorities be held responsible for infiltration from their districts. The government rejected the proposal. Border supervision was left to the local police and to the National Guard, a volunteer organization made up of local villagers under the command of Legion officers.

Officially the government opposed infiltration but it did not view the situation with any sense of urgency until 1952. Some controls were implemented but these were inadequate, and the government was reluctant to give the MAC delegation or the local authorities sufficient power to act effectively. Furthermore, the whole weight of evidence available indicates that there was within the government itself an influential group of former Palestinians who opposed any measures which would have lessened the pressure on Israel.

The Israeli government wanted infiltration stopped. Apart from the number of lives lost, innocent infiltration was causing incalculable damage to agricultural development and adding considerably to the already acute shortage of food. It was thought that the economy could not sustain the continuation of these losses. On the frontier itself the situation was similar to that in Jordan. The people on the spot acted very much as they pleased. The soldiers were mainly immigrants, newly recruited, raw and ill disciplined. The chain of command was weak, and junior officers were accustomed to act on their own initiative, orders notwithstanding. The settlers, however, were the most active group. They bore the brunt of the infiltration, had their crops, livestock, and equipment stolen, and lived in a not un-reasonable fear for their lives. To these men the differences between an 'innocent' and a 'violent' infiltrator were not always immediately apparent, and the results of both were often the same. Most settlers were war veterans. The traditional principle of *Havlagah* (self-restraint) was a dead letter. They believed that the local authorities on both sides of the border were ineffective and that the only way to protect themselves and their property was to apply the brutal 'law of the land': an eye for an eye, or in their case, two for one, this being the only law which they felt the Arabs understood.

Considering the difficulties it faced, the MAC did well for the first few years. The delegations trusted and cooperated with each other. Even when the border situation was unusually tense and blood flowed freely, the MAC meetings were marked by an atmosphere of dispassion and mutual interest.

Gradually innocent infiltration came under control, but the number of acts of violence began to increase. In February 1951, the Army Chiefs of Staff from Israel and Jordan met to discuss what was turning into an explosive situation. A new system of Local Commanders' Agreements (LCA) was devised which provided for frequent meetings between opposite local commanders to settle minor disputes on the spot. The situation improved and a year later a new, comprehensive LCA was set up providing for daily meetings between local commanders at ten points between Eilat and Beisan: no complaints would be submitted to the MAC if they could be handled on the spot; stolen property would be returned; infiltrators would be tried and Israel informed of the sentences. This LCA worked so well that Israel claimed that infiltration fell off by seventy-five per cent.[1]

Most of the decline still related, however, to innocent infiltration. Violent infiltration continued to increase steadily. In the seven weeks following the signing of this LCA, eight Israelis were killed. Israel passed on various warnings through the MAC but there was no improvement. Relations in the MAC were still good, but it was obvious that the Jordan delegation was not getting the necessary support from its government. Meetings were broken off in the summer. They were resumed in September but the situation continued to deteriorate. It reached 'alarming proportions' in Israeli Jerusalem, and the Israelis claimed to have captured 1,800 infiltrators in 1952 alone.[2] A new LCA was signed on 29th December but it made little difference to the trend of events. It was no longer possible to ignore or gloss over the important areas of disagreement between the two governments. It was these, rather than the day-to-day events on the border, which persuaded the Israelis of Jordan's bad faith.

The first and most important was so obvious that outsiders seldom took it into consideration. But for the Israelis, at all times, in all circumstances, it was the keystone of their persuasion, the gravamen of their accusations. Jordan would not make peace with them; Jordan had associated herself with the policy of a 'second round'. Consequently, Jordan was trying to limit the sphere of the GAA, to restrict the activities of the MAC, to reduce it to a court sitting in judgement on complaints regarding only military and para-military activities, to exclude completely from discussion everything not of a military nature.[3]

Another influential consideration was the Jordan government's lack of support for its MAC delegation. Time and again agreement was reached in the MAC for the implementation of some measure or other. Almost invariably the Jordan delega-

[1] *NYT*, 15th February 1951; *JAD*, 22nd February 1952, p. 691, 29th February 1952, p. 725.

[2] *Israel Economist*, December 1952, pp. 259–60; *HKJ–IMAC*, 104th mtg., 30th January 1953, p. 35. On 30th November Israelis killed several people at Silwan near Jerusalem. After that infiltration in the area fell off sharply.

[3] For example see *HKJ–IMAC*, 65th mtg., 28th August 1951, esp. pp. 14–16.

tion had to come back to say that its government would not act. It was agreed in the MAC on numerous occasions that the frontier must be clearly demarcated on the ground. Numerous incidents resulted from an inaccurate knowledge of where the frontier was; army patrols crossed accidentally, or were attacked because it was thought that they had crossed, or shot at civilians because it was thought that they were crossing the line, and so on. There were instances of Arabs cultivating land illegally in Israel (at one time about 20,000 dunams were involved). Stipulations regarding demarcation on the ground were included in the terms of the LCA. Yet the Jordan government refused to implement them.[1] It was only after years of trouble and bloodshed that most of the dangerous areas were marked more or less adequately.

There was a major dispute over who was responsible for controlling infiltration, and for the acts of infiltrators. In 1949 and 1950, the MAC had agreed unanimously that according to Article Four, paragraph three, of the GAA each government was responsible for preventing its civilians as well as its armed forces from crossing the line. Similarly, each government was responsible for the actions of its people once they had crossed the line, even if they acted without the consent or knowledge of their government (the exception being an unarmed individual). The MAC was considered the competent authority to deal with complaints arising out of civilian infiltration.

Then, late in 1952, when the border situation was deteriorating rapidly, the Jordan government announced that it could not be held responsible for acts committed by its civilians without its knowledge or consent, regardless of the crime committed, and that from now on it would refuse to discuss such activities in the MAC.[2] The Jordan delegation agreed that this contradicted what had been agreed upon three years earlier. The Israeli delegate asked why Jordan was reversing her policy at a time when the border situation was so bad: was the Jordan government embarking on a tougher anti-Israel policy?

[1] *HKJ–IMAC*, 70th mtg., 25th October 1951, p. 8.

[2] *ibid*, 98th mtg., 13th November 1952, pp. 6–8; vd, also 34th mtg., 18th April 1950; emergency mtgs, of 27th and 28th November 1950; and Rosenne, *loc. cit.*, pp. 45–6.

During the spring of that year it had rejected an anti-infiltration bill which had been drawn up under the guidance of the senior Jordan Delegate to the MAC. Captured infiltrators were being sent to jail, but since the longest sentence was only sixty days—the draft bill would have meant a substantial increase—neither the infiltrators nor the Israelis were much impressed. The Jordan Government had also turned down an Israeli request that the refugees from at least the most troublesome areas be moved back from the border. Obviously this was a matter in which the Israelis could not intervene but Jordan's refusal to implement such an obvious corrective was discouraging.

The Israelis were unimpressed with Jordan's argument that the proper instrument for handling civilian infiltration was the LCA, since they did not believe that the LCA was working. In May they had been most reluctant to renew it because that implied approval of what they considered to be an unsatisfactory state of affairs. Jordan's local commanders and police authorities were denied sufficient powers to carry out their duties properly.[1] Jordan refused to carry out the agreement embodied in the LCA to demarcate the frontier on the ground. Essentially, however, the Israelis distrusted the people administering the LCA. Most of the police and civilian authorities were former Palestinians. The National Guardsmen were all former Palestinians. Many considered it in their interest to see Israel harassed. Evidence obtained by the MAC and other sources showed that much of the violent infiltration was encouraged, and in some cases organized, by local Jordan authorities. Stolen Israeli goods were being sold openly in Hebron, Nablus and even in Alexandria. Bands of armed marauders often included National Guardsmen. In many instances National Guardsmen provided fire cover for farmers illegally cultivating land in Israel. There was also good reason to believe that some officials in the central government were active in protecting and organizing infiltration.[2]

---

[1] Hutchison, *loc. cit.*, p. 102.

[2] For example see *HKJ–IMAC*, 68th mtg., 4th October 1951, p. 3, and 93rd mtg., 24th September 1952, p. 15; *JAD*, 4th May 1951, p. 1,293; *Times*, TA Correspondent, 11th February 1952.

Israel and Jordan: 1949–56

The Israelis made a number of attempts to remove the economic causes of infiltration by offering to restore the lands of certain Arab villages. The proposals[1] were negotiated with and approved by the Jordan MAC delegation. In each case the Jordan government rejected them. In January 1951 the Israelis proposed an exchange of land in the Qalqilya area. At one time Qalqilya had been a large, prosperous town. During the armistice negotiations Jordan had insisted on keeping it even though its fertile fields went to Israel. It was now packed with refugees and impoverished, a major centre of infiltration. The proposed exchange involved about a dozen Arab villages, 4,000–5,000 people, and over 45,000 dunams. Half the people would regain their land by entering Israel under guarantee: the other half would have their land ceded to Jordan. Part of the Latrun enclave would be ceded to Israel to enable her to reopen the old Jerusalem–Tel Aviv highway. Also Israel would restore some wells to other Arab villages in return for access to water supplies near Sdom (Sodom) on the Dead Sea. All in all, Jordan would have gained 25,320 dunams, and Israel 20,210. The Jordan delegations accepted the offer in January. The government turned it down in May. It also rejected another Israeli proposal to restore just Qalqilya's land. Later the MAC delegations agreed upon an exchange of land in the Zeita area but this too was rejected in November 1952. Evidently opposition to all these proposals came from Palestinians in the government who were afraid that any alterations in the frontier implied an acceptance of the *status quo*. Later the Israelis offered to allow refugees to cross from Jordan to Gaza to rejoin their families. The offer was declined on the grounds that Jordan could not sanction any legal arrangements with the Israel government.

As 1952 drew to a close the Israelis were reaching the end of

---

[1] Details can be found in Eban's statement, *SCOR*, 637th mtg., 12th November 1953, pp. 23–6; *Times*, TA Correspondent, 3rd and 5th June 1952, Amman Correspondent, 2nd June 1952; *NYT*, Schmidt, 5th June 1952; *MG*, 9th June 1952; *LaB. Egypt*, 30th May 1952; *JOMER*, 23rd and 30th May and 6th June 1952; *MEM*, 31st May 1952.

In 1955 the Israelis suggested dividing up the uninhabited no-man's land around Latrun with seventy per cent going to Jordan. This also was rejected: Dearden, *loc. cit.*, p. 136.

their tether. Infiltration generally had fallen off, but organized marauding was becoming increasingly frequent. The MAC Chairman stated unequivocally that the Armistice Agreement was obsolete; the situation was such that 'the Armistice is hardly not breached any more'.[1] The Israelis described the situation as 'semi-warfare'. Militant Israelis were exerting pressure on the government to take stronger counter-measures. None of the Powers had shown any inclination to support Israel's case in the Security Council. The economic position was critical; national morale was very low. Israelis began to feel that they could not withstand the strain of Arab hostility. The Arabs had just succeeded in preventing the General Assembly from passing the eight-power peace resolution. There was growing talk in Israel of deliberately precipitating a crisis to force the Powers to take action to end the 'war.'[2]

Israel sent out surveyors at mutually agreed times to mark the frontier unilaterally. Each time they were attacked by the National Guard.[3] Three Israeli soldiers who had crossed the line at another time were not returned despite a prior agreement that all such people would be. On 7th January 1953, Israel withdrew from the LCA, explaining that Jordan had undertaken 'a systematically organized' campaign of theft and violence in the central sector, and that she was not cooperating in the implementation of the LCA or the GAA.[4] The LCA expired on 22nd January.

On the 23rd Israeli troops attacked Falama (the surveyors had been fired on from here). In the next few weeks other centres of infiltration were attacked. The Israelis claimed that there was no alternative to taking up 'an active defence all along the border'. Arabs blew up a train at Nir Eliahu opposite Qalqilya. Jordan invoked the Anglo–Jordan Treaty of Alliance. The Israeli government, under strong public pressure for military action, appealed to the United States, Britain and France to use their influence to persuade Jordan to stop infiltra-

[1] *HKJ–IMAC*, 97th mtg., 30th October 1952, p. 7.
[2] *Israel Economist*, August 1952, p. 169 and February 1953, pp. 27–8.
[3] *HKJ–IMAC*, 93rd mtg., 24th September 1952 and 102nd mtg., 6th January 1953.
[4] *ibid*, and 103 mtg., 7th to 8th January 1953, Appendix; see also 105th mtg., 3rd session, 4th February 1953; and 114th mtg., 16th to 17th March 1953, esp. p. 9.

tion. In the MAC Jordan reiterated her refusal to discuss complaints arising out of the actions of civilians. The situation continued to deteriorate. On 7th and 19th April Israel delivered more *démarches* to the Tripartite Powers and to Turkey. The Israelis claimed that because the Powers were indifferent Jordan was not taking the matter seriously. Infiltration could no longer be attributed to the refugees' economic circumstances, it was now well organized, and local authorities were involved. The Israelis wanted the MAC, which was 'of no practical value', replaced by new, more effective machinery.[1]

On 22nd April, in Jerusalem, the tension became unbearable: someone fired a shot that started off a bloody shooting fray. Ten Arabs were killed and twelve wounded; six Israelis were wounded. The Arab Legion refused a joint investigation on the grounds that only Jordanian civilians were involved. The MAC found it impossible to decide who had fired the first shot.

In his report to the Security Council, General Riley described the situation as potentially the most dangerous yet. The MAC was 'inadequate': the time had come for the two governments to review the whole situation. He announced that he had called for high-level talks and that Israel had accepted.[2] Jordan made no reply. In the following weeks infiltration into Israel purely for the sake of murder increased. In one night alone there were three attacks on Israeli settlements, leaving two dead and five wounded. Once again Jordan refused to allow a joint investigation on the grounds that only civilians were involved. At the same time fighting broke out in the Hebron area over illegal cultivation. The armistice line was close to being 'uncontrolled'.[3]

On 29th May, Riley held a special meeting of the MAC. Israel agreed to renew the LCA (and to go ahead with the demarcation of the armistice line). After some hesitation Jordan accepted. On 8th June a new three-month LCA came into effect. On the following three nights Israeli villages were attacked with the consent, if not the active support, of some local

---

[1] *HKJ–IMAC*, Special Meeting, 23rd April 1953, pp. 6–9, 20.
[2] *SCOR*, S/3007 and Corr. 1, 8th May 1953. Shortly afterwards Riley resigned.
[3] Chairman de Ridder, *op. cit.*, 118th mtg., 26th May 1953, pp. 2–3.

Jordan authorities.[1] Once again the situation was critical; and Jordan still had not agreed to high-level talks. Amongst themselves the Israelis talked seriously of a wholesale invasion or the occupation of strategic hills in the Jerusalem corridor. Jordan began to move. The Anglo–Jordan treaty was invoked again. Extra police were put on the border.

Talks between high-ranking military officials finally took place on 29th June and general principles were laid down for the cooperative handling of infiltration. Other considerations aside, the Israelis were pleased that Jordan had once again acknowledged her responsibility to stop border crossings. For their part the Israelis consented to rely less on the military and to set up a Border Police force. It was agreed that high-ranking police officers would meet in the near future to work out these principles in detail. An uneasy quiet reigned along the border. After some Israeli soldiers were killed in July the Israel MAC delegate warned of the cumulative effect which even isolated incidents were having on Israeli public opinion.

Early in August violence broke out again. In one week eleven armed engagements took place inside Israel. Subsequently the Israelis retaliated by attacking three villages. On 31st August the LCA was extended for another three months and it was agreed to regard all complaints outstanding as settled. However, by this time the Israelis were angry, frustrated and disillusioned. Jordan was still not cooperating. National Guardsmen continued to attack soldiers trying to stop illegal cultivation. Jordan, supported by a meeting of the Arab MAC delegates, reneged on her promise to demarcate the border. The meeting between senior police officials from Israel and Jordan had been fruitless and no detailed programme of cooperation was worked out. The Army officers from both sides were supposed to meet again, but Jordan refused to attend. The border situation continued to deteriorate in a vicious cycle of attack and retaliation. Some local Jordan authorities were still cooperating with the infiltrators. During September there was an increased number of murders and attacks on railways and buses in Israel. Then on 12th October 1953, a mother and child were

[1] *HKJ–IMAC*, 123rd mtg., 8th June 1953, esp. Observers' reports; also 119th–128th mtgs., 26th May–11th June 1953.

killed at Yahud in the heart of Israel. The tracks of the attackers led back to a Jordan police station. At the subsequent MAC meeting the Israel delegate rejected Jordan's denial that Jordanian officials were implicated. He described the murders as a 'provocation, a challenge', part of a 'systematically organized small-scale war'. The Jordanian delegate asked Israel not to retaliate and provided all assistance possible in the investigation.[1]

On 14th October, Israeli troops attacked the village of Qibya, destroying it and killing over fifty men, women and children.

What prompted this calculated act of horror was not just the border situation, bad though it was. The Israelis had been under an exceptionally severe strain going back to the early 30's and they were no longer reasonable men. The writings and speeches of the period reveal a deep-seated, powerful sense of frustration and the shrill, rising tone of growing hysteria.

The year 1953 was a very bad year in Israel. There had been no peace. Statehood had brought grinding austerity and crippling taxes. There was not enough food. Morale was dangerously low, discontent ran high. Aid and charity from overseas was falling off drastically. The boycott and blockade were increasingly effective. The New Economic Policy was a last-ditch stand to ward off bankruptcy. The new Republican government in the United States seemed unfriendly. The British were negotiating their withdrawal from Suez. The UN had done nothing. Egypt had ignored the Security Council's resolution on the Blockade. Tel el Mutilla had been disregarded and now the Syrians were blocking the new B'nat Ya'acov water project, and UNTSO Chief of Staff General Vagn Bennike was supporting them. Jordan MAC Chairman Bennett de Ridder was considered to be an Israelophobe. Abba Eban told the Council, 'We are besieged, we are blockaded, abused, threatened, encircled, ambushed, harried, and subjected to murderous onslaught at every turn . . . there is no parallel for this situation in the life of any other nation.'

What this meant in plain terms was that circumstances over a long period of time had so weighed down on the Israelis, had so

[1] *HKJ–IMAC*, 150th mtg., 14th October 1953.

increased their desperation at the cost of reason, that they were ready to use a blood-bath in an attempt to create more favourable political and diplomatic conditions. The Israelis hoped that the Qibya Raid would convince the Jordanians that infiltration had to be stopped; and that it would precipitate a general crisis which would force the Powers to step in and insist that Arab–Israeli relations be based on arrangements more comprehensive and substantial than the GAAs. The Israelis apparently did not realize that, moral considerations apart, the raid was bound to increase the Arab peoples' demands for revenge, against which any Arab government whatever its inclinations would find it difficult to stand. The Israelis knew that the Jordan government, despite the actions of many of its officials, was not condoning armed infiltration, and that the murder and sabotage were being carried out by small groups of men organized and financed mostly by people outside of Jordan. These people were unlikely to be deterred by indiscriminate slaughter. Also the Israelis did not remember that because the Western Powers were assiduously courting Arab friendship the raid would make them that much more unwilling to try to impose an unacceptable settlement on the Arabs; rather, by necessity and temperament they would be inclined to act against the perpetrators of such a crime.

Once the Israelis had launched one massive raid they were forced to launch others whenever there was provocation. Failure to do so would be interpreted, the Israelis thought, by the Arabs as a loss of nerve, and Arab pressure would be increased accordingly. In effect the Israelis had placed themselves in a position where they had to terrorize all likely infiltrators, and the Jordan government, into good behaviour. Ultimately they succeeded, but the process was long and bloody, both sides suffered heavily and the long-term costs were beyond counting.

Criticism of one policy implies a practical alternative. The Israelis were convinced that the Jordan government was unwilling to take the extraordinary measures necessary to stamp out violent infiltration. They knew that any of their own defence measures would be inadequate; that most of the work had to be done by Jordan. So far nothing they had done—

representations in the MAC, through the UNTSO and the Powers, petitions to the Security Council, an 'active border defence policy', land exchange proposals—had persuaded Jordan to do the work. The Israelis claimed that the situation was intolerable, and that they were desperate. Judging from their circumstances and actions at the time there is no reason to doubt that this was so. What then was the alternative? To state the matter so bluntly is not to condone what was done but to describe it as the Israelis saw it.

The Israelis' plans for using the raid to goad the Powers into positive action[1] were ill-conceived. Britain stated flatly that there had been 'no possible justification' for the raid. (Anglo–Egyptian relations being what they were this was no time for the British to show anything but the utmost concern for the Arabs' welfare.) The Americans, despite British urging, refused to join in outright condemnation. They wanted to restrict the effects of the raid as much as possible, in order not to jeopardize Eric Johnston's chances of success.[2] Eventually they agreed to a joint draft resolution in the Security Council condemning Israel.

At the UN during the Security Council debate[3] the Israeli delegate, Abba Eban, argued that the Council must examine the raid within the total context of Arab–Israeli relations. He hoped the Council would undertake 'a broad and fundamental discussion on peace and security in the Middle East'. After a detailed listing of Israel's complaints against Jordan and the other Arab States he described the raid as 'a most unfortunate explosion of pent-up feeling and a tragic breakdown of restraint'. But, he argued, many governments regarded with 'nonchalance' the Arabs' war against Israel and the news of Israelis being killed, and become alarmed only when the Israelis failed to react with perfect restraint. He asked the Council for a resolution embodying six points. Tension would

---

[1] The Israeli Foreign Ministry described the Council's debate as a 'heaven-sent opportunity' to put an end to the conditions which led to Qibya, and to bring about a general settlement.

[2] Eric Johnston had just arrived in the Middle East as Special Ambassador from President Eisenhower with a water development plan for the Jordan River: vd. below, Chapter Nine.

[3] See *SCOR*, 630th mtg., 27th October 1953, *et seq.*

be diagnosed as a threat to security arising out of the absence of peace. Attention would be drawn to the need to fulfil the main object of the GAA, the transition to peace. The Council would note that its own resolutions on peace and security and Article Eight of the Jordan GAA had not been implemented. The Council would recognize that Israel and Jordan agreed that the most specific source of current tension was infiltration, and urge that special attention be paid to the armistice provision requiring the restraint of illegal border crossings. The Council would direct the UNTSO to devote special attention to those provisions of the Council's resolutions and of the GAA which had not been implemented, especially those calling for the transition to permanent peace. And finally, the parties should be ordered to enter into direct negotiations for a peace settlement to replace the transitional armistice régime. Eban argued that it was unreasonable to refuse to make peace with Israel, and at the same time claim to be acting in conformity with the terms of the GAA.

The Lebanese delegate, Charles Malik, dismissed all this as a red herring designed to draw attention away from the Qibya Raid. There had not, he said, been 'any really hostile acts or designs' against Israel by the Arabs. He asked for only 'the mildest action'. The Council should call upon Israel to bring the men who carried out the raid to trial, to pay compensation, and to refrain from such acts in future. Also the Council should ensure that Israel received no military or economic assistance until these terms were met, and should warn her that in future similar acts would lead to the invocation of Article Seven of the Charter.

The American and French delegates said very little. But the British delegate, discussing only the raid and the 'alleged provocation' of Israel, stated flatly that he did not accept Eban's account of the situation.

An Anglo–American–French resolution was submitted[1] emphasizing the need to maintain and strengthen the armistice régime. In addition it included the 'strongest censure' of Israel for violating the cease-fire of 15th July 1948. Note was taken of the substantial evidence of unauthorized border

[1] *SCOR*, S/3189, 20th November 1953.

crossings, and Jordan was asked to continue and to reinforce her anti-infiltration measures. Both governments were called upon to ensure effective cooperation of local security forces, and the implementation of the armistice provisions and Council resolutions. The importance of cooperation with the Chief of Staff UNTSO was emphasized and he, in turn, was asked to consider ways of strengthening the UNTSO.

Eban objected strongly saying that the resolution revealed a stringent attitude towards Israel's defence policy, and a marked indulgence to the Arab siege. Furthermore it contained, for the first time, no reference to peace negotiations or to concrete, substantive proposals for alleviating the situation—apart from those which had already been tried and found wanting. Eban asked the Council to drop its 'timid and conservative' approach and embrace 'a bold leap into the future'. He then invoked Article Twelve of the GAA.[1]

This, it will be recalled, provided for the calling of a conference for the purpose of reviewing and revising the armistice provisions: attendance at the conference was obligatory. In his first statement to the Council Eban had proposed that senior political and military representatives from the two countries should meet immediately at UN Headquarters to discuss armistice problems. Subsequently, Notes were sent to Britain, France and the US asking for support for this move. The response was unenthusiastic. Then the Israelis decided to invoke Article Twelve.

The Council took little notice. A phrase was tacked on to the draft resolution asking the Chief of Staff, UNTSO, to take into account any agreement arising out of Israel's request. The French delegate remarked that the conference 'may lead to satisfactory results . . . Thus we have found it impossible to avoid mentioning [it] . . .' This was not what the Israelis had expected, and their comments on the final resolution—adopted with Russia and Lebanon abstaining—were bitter and disillusioned.

Then began a long-drawn-out attempt to persuade Jordan to attend the conference when the UN Secretary-General called it. She, evidently, was strongly tempted but after much argument

[1] Article Eight in the Lebanese GAA.

the other Arab states persuaded her not to go.[1] UN Secretary General Dag Hammarskjold did not make the refusal public, and, strongly supported by the British and the Americans, pressed her to change her mind. Jordan protested that if she went she might be forced into a peace treaty. Hammarskjold then had the Israelis promise not to bring up the question of peace. Jordan replied that in this case there was nothing to be discussed which could not be dealt with by the MAC. Hammarskjold then asked the Israelis to withdraw the request for a conference. They, however, insisted that they were entirely within their rights, and that this was exactly the situation for which Article Twelve had been designed.

On 19th February 1954, Hammarskjold formally convoked a conference. On 24th March, Jordan replied with a definitive refusal. He then told the Israelis that he did not intend to pursue the matter further.[2] A few days before Jordan's refusal the Syrians had shelled Israeli fishing boats. And just before that, on 19th March, eleven Israelis had been killed and two wounded when a bus was attacked at Scorpion Pass near the Jordan border. At the time the coincidence—it does not seem to have been more than that—appeared most ominous.

In the meantime in the weeks following the Qibya Raid the border situation had improved somewhat. A new LCA had been signed on 16th November 1953; the Israelis had strengthened their Border Police; and the Jordanians had improved their anti-infiltration measures. But having committed themselves to massive reprisal the Israelis were forced to stick to it, and when, in mid-December, infiltration began to rise again they struck back hard. For example, when two soldiers were killed well inside Israel they responded with three raids in which four Jordanians were killed and two wounded. Their mood was not improved by Jordan's continued refusal to attend the conference, nor by Bennike's comment that Israel's request for a

[1] *MEM*, 9th January 1954, p. 3; *Le Monde*, Clairmont, 16th January 1954.

[2] *Exchange of Correspondence . . .*, SCOR, S/3180, 19th February 1954. S/3180 Add. 1, 24th March 1954, and Add. 2, 31st March 1954; *NYT*, 6th January 1954; *Times*, 8th January 1954 and NY Correspondent, 23rd January 1954; *NYT*, Rosenthal, 9th February 1954; *NYT*, 20th February and 26th March 1954.

conference had 'not contributed to create a better understanding between the two countries'. Considering that every
other attempt to come to terms with Jordan had proved fruitless, and that the armistice was in the last stages of disintegration, the Israelis felt that, to put it mildly, Bennike was not
doing his job, and that he was out of sympathy with the spirit in
which the armistice had been devised. Then in March 1954
came Scorpion Pass, the shelling of the fishing boats, and
Jordan's final refusal to attend the conference.

Jordan denied any knowledge of the attack on the bus and did
everything possible to assist the investigators. (One Jordan
official made the ill-timed suggestion that Israelis had been
responsible.) But the Israelis were in no mood to listen, and
submitted a resolution to the MAC condemning Jordan. The
Chairman of the MAC, Commander E. H. Hutchison, after an
exhausting and fruitless investigation, asked them to postpone
their resolution until he had made more inquiries. They refused.
He abstained from voting. They walked out of the MAC and
cut off all contact and cooperation along the border with Jordan. Hutchison they submitted to a prolonged and vicious
propaganda campaign.[1]

Moshe Sharett was now Prime Minister (Ben Gurion had
retired in December) and the public's strong reaction against
the excesses of Qibya had given him and the other moderates
considerable influence over border policy. But now, after
Scorpion Pass, he found his authority seriously threatened by
the activists led by the Minister of Defence, Pinhas Lavon,
and the new Army Chief of Staff, Moshe Dayan, who had
helped initiate and plan the Qibya Raid. Behind them lay Ben
Gurion's enormous influence. The activists began to act on their
own initiative without Sharett's consent. Scorpion Pass was too
important a challenge for them to overlook, and on 28th March
Israeli troops attacked, unsuccessfully, the village of Nahalin,
north of Hebron. The split between the moderates and the
activists was now extremely serious. The government no longer

[1] *HKJ–IMAC*, 177th mtg., 22nd to 23rd March 1954; also Hutchison, *loc. cit.*;
and *SCOR*, S/3252, 25th June 1954.
In 1956, in Gaza the Israelis found evidence substantiating Hutchison's theory
that the attackers had come from Egypt.

had control over the vital question of border policy or, if it came to that, war and peace.[1]

The Nahalin Raid did have the effect of bringing Jordan back to the Security Council with another complaint against Israel. The Israelis countered with complaints, *inter alia*, of Jordan's refusal to implement Article Twelve. Now, for the first time, all the procedures laid down in the GAA for the peaceful settlement of disputes had been exhausted. For the first time the Security Council had the authority, according to the provisions of the GAA, to review, suspend and interpret such terms of the GAA as it saw fit. It could, if it wished, resolve many of the ambiguities of the armistice régime, and place Israel–Jordan relations on a much firmer and more effective contractual basis. The Western Powers seem to have been willing to move in this direction. But the Council discussed neither of the two complaints nor the general situation.[2]

For a month the Tripartite Powers argued with Lebanon and Russia over whether the complaints should be discussed together or separately. Lebanon wanted separate discussions, with Jordan's complaint coming up first. Evidently they hoped for a resolution censuring Israel for Nahalin, and a Russian veto against any subsequent resolution. Eventually it was decided to discuss the complaints together. The Israelis, determined to press home their advantage, pointed out that since Jordan was not a member of the UN she could bring a complaint before the Council only if she accepted in advance, for the purposes of the dispute, Article Thirty-five of the UN Charter relating to the obligation to settle all complaints by peaceful means. Lebanon tried to pass off this reference to Article Thirty-five as unimportant, but the Israelis made a formal submission regarding Jordan's compliance with the Article. They were determined that Jordan should declare openly whether or not she intended to settle the Palestine question by peaceful means. The French delegate asked for an adjournment in order to seek instructions from his government. Subsequently, Jordan announced that she

[1] Also the 'Darling' spy ring was set up in Cairo, this time without even Lavon's knowledge. While he was busy trying to weaken Sharett's influence others were busy trying to oust him from office: vd. below Chapter Twelve.

[2] See *SCOR*, 665th mtg., 8th April 1954, *et seq.*

would withdraw her representative and refrain from participating in the Council debate rather than submit to the obligations of peaceful settlement. The Council did not meet again to
discuss the matter.

All three channels set forth in the GAA for the redress of
grievances were now useless. The MAC did not function
properly. The Special Committee was a dead letter. Article
Twelve had been ignored. And now the Security Council, the
last remaining source of authority, had chosen to opt out. At
this point we can leave the Israel–Jordan armistice régime. For
all practical purposes it had ceased to function. From now on
there was a straightforward struggle between Israel and recal-
citrant groups in Jordan. Eventually the border situation improved, not because the armistice machinery was reactivated,
but because Israeli military superiority persuaded the government and people of Jordan to stop the infiltration. When infiltration began to increase again on this border in 1956 it was
carried out by Egyptian-controlled *fedayeen*. At this point raids
against Jordan did nothing except weaken the already shaky
government. Egypt was the target.

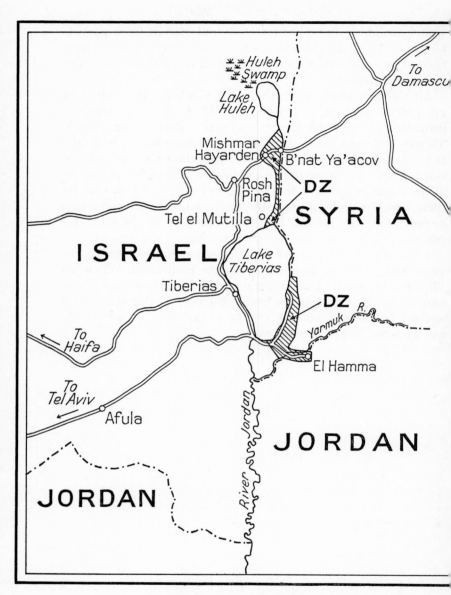

The Northern Demilitarized Zones

Chapter Seven

ISRAEL AND SYRIA (1949–56)

ISRAEL–SYRIAN relations were concerned almost solely with the struggle for control over the Demilitarized Zone, and the question of who was to have how much of the precious waters of the Jordan River.

The DZ, it will be recalled, is that part of Palestine which was occupied by Syria during the war. The Israelis had insisted that the Syrians withdraw, and they had agreed to do so on condition that the area was demilitarized. The DZ comprised two seperate sectors, not connected with each other. The central sector ran from the south-eastern half of Lake Huleh along the Jordan River to the mouth of Lake Tiberias. For most of its length it was about a kilometre wide, but at one point it widened to form a triangle with its apex about four kilometres inside Israel at Mishmar Ha'yarden. The southern, or Ein Gev, sector lay along the south-eastern shore of Lake Tiberias, with a tail projecting directly eastward for about four or five kilometres, like a wriggly thin wedge between Syria and Jordan. It is important to remember that both sectors lay entirely within Palestine. So also did Lake Tiberias, Lake Huleh, and the Jordan River. At no point did the Syrian border touch either of the Lakes or the River.

In many places the strip separating Syria from the water was only ten metres wide, not very wide but none the less there, and to Israel of great importance. Ordinarily their separation from the water would mean little to the Syrians. The few people living on the border had a traditional right to draw water for their domestic and agricultural needs and to fish, although this was a somewhat more complicated matter, and the topography was such that Syria could not use the waters of Lake Tiberias for extensive irrigation schemes.

But in the abnormal circumstances typical of Arab–Israeli relations even limited control over the DZ would improve Syria's ability, in the event of fighting, to cut off northern Galilee and to strike for the coast and Haifa. It would enable her to prevent or limit Israeli development projects both inside and outside the DZ. It was only within the DZ that Israel could carry out the work necessary to drain the Huleh swamps, to build hydro-electric power stations, and to bring water to the Negev. Of all her neighbours, Syria was the best placed to handicap or even cripple Israel's economic development. Rightly or wrongly, the Israelis always assumed that this was what the Syrians had in mind.

According to Article Five of the Syrian GAA,[1] the civilian status of the DZ was defined 'with a view towards providing for the gradual restoration of normal civilian life', without prejudice to a final settlement. The MAC Chairman was responsible for the supervision of this process. He was to set up local administrations throughout the DZ—Jewish administration and police for Jewish settlements, and local Arab for the local Arab villages. All complaints of a civilian nature were to be handled by him, not the MAC. While supervising the restoration of normal civilian life he had also to protect the rights of the parties concerned, the Israelis and the local Arabs. The obscurities of this arrangement plainly concealed a delicate compromise, the implications of which the armistice delegations obviously had chosen not to examine closely for fear of the effects upon their tenuous agreement to agree. But as normal civilian life was restored it became increasingly difficult to avoid the important questions.

Disagreement was apparent as soon as the Chairman went to the MAC for assistance in determining what was meant by the

---

[1] See also Bunche's Note of 26th June 1949, in *SCOR*, S/2157, 18th May, 1951.

phrase, 'restoration of normal civilian life'.[1] Eventually it was agreed that the Syrians had no authority in the DZ nor any rights there, and that so long as the Israelis were working on their own lands and the work was of a non-military kind the Chairman had no authority to intervene.[2] During this period relations between the two countries, at least on this level, were good. Continual and, evidently, promising negotiations took place regarding a final settlement of the status of the DZ. There was some trouble in the DZ itself: Israeli police were active outside their settlements and often interfered with the local Arabs; and the Syrians sent in agents and in general exercised substantial control over the local Arabs. But although at one point General Riley felt it necessary to admonish the two sides for their behaviour,[3] neither country seems to have regarded this muted struggle for power as one of immediate importance.

The Huleh project was straightforward. The Huleh swamps lay entirely outside the DZ. Draining them would release about 45,000 acres for cultivation. The drainage canal to the Jordan River would run through the DZ only on Israeli-owned land. Preparatory work began in October 1950 and the project itself in January 1951. It was then discovered that a road would have to be built affecting about a hundred acres of Arab-owned land in the DZ, seven of them permanently.

The Israelis entered into negotiations with the landowners and at one point tentative agreement was reached on the terms of compensation. The Arabs were then called to Syria and on their return rejected these terms.[4] The Israelis offered 'practically any price' for the use of the land but the Arabs refused.

---

[1] *I–SMAC*, 5th September 1949. The Syrians argued that restoration meant the same number of settlements, buildings and people as had been there prior to 14th May 1948.

[2] *ibid*, 60th mtg., 19th March 1951, p. 6; see also 8th mtg., 26th September 1949, p. 4; 55th mtg., 25th January 1951, p. 5; 58th mtg., 21st February 1951, p. 9; 59th mtg., 7th March 1951, p. 16.

[3] *ibid*, 45th mtg., 31st August 1950, pp. 2–3.

[4] *ibid*, 59th mtg., 7th March 1951, p. 28. Unless noted otherwise references to the Huleh dispute are drawn from *Reports of the Chief of Staff, UNTSO. . . .* beginning *SCOR*, S/2049, 12th March 1951.

Finally the Palestine Land Development Company, the Israeli concessionaire, expropriated the land under the authority given it by the Palestine Government Ordinance of 17th March 1938. On 14th February Syria lodged a complaint with the MAC on two counts: drainage of the swamps would remove a natural military obstacle in violation of the GAA;[1] and the work would prevent the restoration of normal civilian life. The Israelis agreed to discuss the complaint in the MAC and eventually it was decided to ask General Riley for his opinion just on the question of military advantage.

In his memo on 7th March Riley dealt with three questions: military advantage, private rights, and sovereignty. On the first two he decided in Israel's favour. He pointed out that the DZ had not been created to compensate for the absence of natural obstacles to military action. In any case, the question of military advantage was irrelevant both inside and outside the DZ: 'Neither side could dictate to the other side what it did in territory under its control.' The same held true for private rights. So long as the work affected only Israeli-owned land, Syria had no more grounds for complaint than Israel would have had if similar work had been carried out in Syria. Since, however, some Arab land was affected, against the wishes of the owners, the restoration of normal civilian life was affected, and the work constituted a violation of the armistice provisions. Riley then came on to the question of whether or not the Company could expropriate land on the basis of a Palestine Government ordinance. He explained that the GAA included no provisions relating to sovereignty in the DZ. The Chairman was responsible for supervising the restoration of normal civilian life which would be undertaken by the local administrations in the Arab and Israeli areas. Consequently no party was sovereign in the DZ. All 'laws, regulations or ordinances' in force prior to demilitarization were now 'held in abeyance'. The right of compulsory acquisition could not be exercised. The land could not be used except with the consent of the owners. The Palestine Land Development Company should be ordered, Riley said, to cease work until an 'agreement is reached between the govern-

[1] Article Two, paragraph one: '. . . . no military or political advantage should be gained under the truce'.

ments of Syria and Israel with respect to the work now being conducted in the Demilitarized Zone'.[1]

Subsequently, after a heated argument in the MAC and some shooting in the DZ, the Israelis decided to handle the dispute properly. They reminded the Chairman that he, not the MAC, was the proper authority in civilian matters, and they asked him to arrange meetings between the Company and the Arab landowners to fix the terms of compensation. The Chairman agreed. At the next meeting of the MAC on the 19th Israel asked for all civilian complaints, since they were the sole responsibility of the Chairman, to be struck from the MAC agenda. The Syrians agreed but asked that work on the project should not begin again until the Chairman had settled the dispute between the landowners and the Company. The Israelis pointed out that the Chairman had already agreed that the work would start on 23rd March. The Chairman denied this.[2] After an inconclusive argument the meeting adjourned on the understanding that the Chairman would begin his investigations immediately.

This argument over dates, minor in itself, highlighted the fatal weakness in the system of administering the DZ. At one time the Chairman complained that the Israelis had initiated the project without seeking his permission, but did they have to do so if they worked on their own land? If *all* 'laws, regulations and ordinances' were 'held in abeyance' how would it be possible to restore 'normal civilian life'? Could the Chairman fix the terms and compensation against the wishes of the Arab landowners? Could the Chairman prevent the Israelis from recommencing work, even on their own land? The Chairman, the

[1] Later, after the damage had been done, Riley explained that in fact Syria had no standing in the dispute, and that it was a matter to be settled between the Chairman, the Israelis and the local Arabs. He had written of the necessity for an Israel–Syrian agreement only because he had assumed that this was the way the parties wanted the question handled. He also withdrew his comments on sovereignty; although he never explained why he had brought them up in the first place since by his own admission he had no competence to decide on this issue.

After writing the memo Riley left for hospital treatment in New York. Thus during the following crucial weeks the only person enjoying the confidence of both sides was absent.

[2] The arguments related to an 'exchange of letters' written jointly by the Israelis and the Chairman: *op. cit.*, 6th mtg., 19th March 1951, pp. 16 *et seq.*

Israelis, the local Arabs all claimed to have certain powers and rights. Who was to decide which claims were justified? By 24th March the question was unavoidable: the Arabs refused to sell or to lease their land.

On the 25th the Company, acting on the orders of its Government, overrode the protests of the MAC Chairman and began work again on the project. During the next two days workers were fired upon. At a meeting of the Israel and Syrian Deputy Chiefs of Staff the rift steadily widened. The Israeli claimed that the project was civilian in nature and based upon duly acquired private rights. The Chairman could order only a temporary cessation while the matter of compensation, which Israel had agreed to pay, was settled. The Syrian demanded that all work be stopped pending a settlement of the 'overall Huleh project'. The Israeli stated that the work would go on. The Syrian replied that he could not answer for the consequences. The Israelis took warning and sent military patrols into the DZ: later they were replaced by armed police. On the 31st the Israelis evacuated 630 Arabs from the central sector and destroyed their villages. The Israelis claimed that the Arabs had asked to be removed because of the dangerous situation. But more likely is the explanation that they were thought to be assisting the Syrians. At the MAC meeting on 3rd April the possibility emerged that matters might be settled by high-level talks, and a beginning was made to a draft resolution to be taken back to the two governments for consideration.

At the next meeting, on 4th April, the Israelis complained that Syrian troops had entered the Arab village of El Hamma in the eastern tip of the southern sector. El Hamma had been a trouble spot from the beginning. Syrian police and troops often crossed into the village and once the Syrian Deputy Chief of Staff had made a speech there assuring the people that his country would maintain its position there.[1] The Israeli delegate said that an Israeli police patrol had been sent to the village to investigate, ostensibly to examine Jewish-owned land within the village confines. While the MAC was discussing the draft resolution, news arrived that the Israeli patrol had been fired on from the village and from a Syrian outpost just across the

[1] *I–SMAC*, 28th mtg., 19th April 1950, p. 1; 57th mtg., 14th February 1951, p. 13.

border. Seven Israeli policemen were killed. The Syrians agreed to an emergency meeting at El Hamma, but asked that the drafting of the resolution should be completed first as that would help to prevent future incidents. The Chairman, however, objected to a night meeting, to which the Israelis replied that they had lost confidence in the Chairman and would no longer deal with him. Later they told de Ridder, Acting UNTSO Chief of Staff, that they would attend no more meetings with the Chairman, Colonel Bossavy,[1] and until all Syrian military and para-military troops had been withdrawn from the DZ.

Attempts to settle the Huleh dispute by peaceful methods had ended. It was April 1951. Those considerations which had persuaded the Israelis to take an increasingly tough line with Jordan were also influential here. The Arab League had previously forbidden any separate agreements with Israel. The negotiations with Adbullah had been ruined. Unexpectedly heavy immigration and world inflation had gravely impaired Israel's economy and seriously aggravated the food shortage: a shortage which the Huleh project would do much to alleviate. It was believed that Syria's opposition to the project was part of a coordinated Arab plan to destroy Israel economically: with Egypt blocking the Canal, and Jordan using infiltrators to wreck the existing agricultural economy. The pattern of events seemed to be obvious, and the Israelis were disinclined to treat Syrian opposition as constructive or helpful in intent. The UNTSO could not prevent infiltration into the DZ, or Syrian control over parts of it. It looked as if the Syrians were deliberately courting trouble. So the Israelis decided that, if they were to protect their rights and survive, it was up to them to act independently, for no one else would help them.

On 5th April El Hamma and the near-by Syrian outpost were bombed for an hour. This was the first time that the Israel government openly violated the cease-fire provisions of the armistice.[2] Whatever the justification for the retaliation, Israeli estimates of its probable effects were naïve. The intention

---

[1] This lack of confidence was shared by the Arabs: *SCOR*, S/2088, 13th April 1951, p. 56.

[2] Against the wishes of Sharett and other moderates: *Times*, TA Correspondent, 6th and 7th April 1951.

was to persuade the Syrians to cooperate. Yet it was generally agreed that much of Syria's troublemaking stemmed from Colonel Shishakli's desire to raise the prestige of his army and his régime. None the less here were the Israelis offering an unavoidable challenge to that prestige.

The situation in the southern sector of the DZ deteriorated rapidly. Incidents involving Israeli police and Syrian soldiers grew more frequent. Troops were massed on both sides of the DZ. The Syrian government began canvassing the other Arab States for support in the event of war. De Ridder tried in vain to establish a cease-fire and to get the MAC working again. UN Observers raced around checking old complaints and unable to prevent new incidents. On 27th April, the Security Council began to discuss the Huleh project and the El Hamma incident. On 2nd May, Syrian troops entered the central sector of the DZ and Israel proper at Tel el Mutilla on the north shore of Lake Tiberias. Heavy fighting, involving artillery, began in earnest. Six days later the Security Council ordered a cease-fire, but the Syrians refused to cease fire or withdraw from Israel until 14th May, twelve days after the fighting had begun.[1]

To the Israelis the implications of the past months seemed crystal clear. A legitimate civilian project had been held up by armed violence and by the incompetence and weakness of the UN. Syrians had infiltrated into the DZ;[2] Israelis had been attacked and killed; and the UNTSO had been unable to provide any kind of protection at all. When Syrian troops invaded Israel the UNTSO fell apart. The Security Council and the

---

[1] The Syrian government denied that its troops had been involved (and the Security Council did not press the matter). However, the Syrian *Official Gazette* of 19th July 1951 announced the award of medals to soldiers who had taken part in 'war operations' at Tel el Mutilla in May. Riley reported to the Council that he considered that this proved Israel's allegations. In reply the Syrian Minister of National Defence stated that Syria was free to print what she pleased in the *Official Gazette*: 'The names of certain military sectors mentioned in the *Official Gazette* do not constitute any evidence against Syria, since military security calls for the use of every means to deceive the enemy, and giving certain sectors the same names as enemy sectors is an elementary method which was often used for this purpose during the Second World War.' *Report of the Chief of Staff . . . SCOR*, S/2359, S/2360, 1st October 1951.

[2] UN Observers reported that there were no Syrian troops in El Hamma. But they did not mention that they had investigated three days after the complaint had been laid, and two days after the village had been bombed, and virtually deserted.

Tripartite Powers virtually ignored the invasion. The parallels with 1948 were obvious, and not a few Israelis noted that in both instances they had been left to their own resources. UN Observers did not visit the Israeli side of the battle until five days after it began. The Israelis were forced, in the interval, to bring the Western military attachés to the front. Even so the Tripartite Powers, who had guaranteed to act in exactly such circumstances as this, said and did nothing until several days after the fighting had stopped, when they protested that Iraqi aid to Syria was provocative. Even if the Israelis' interpretation of these events was somewhat tendentious, this in no way diminished its influence. The Israelis believed that nothing had been done, that the much-vaunted guarantees were worthless, and that, as before in 1948, only a strong army and an aggressive policy would protect them.

The situation was first brought to the Security Council's attention by Syria after the bombing of El Hamma. The Israelis immediately filed counter-complaints. Most of the time was spent discussing the Huleh project. Of Syria's six objections presented in the formal complaint she mentioned only two in the debate.[1] One was that as a signatory to the GAA Syria could not allow such important work to be carried out in the DZ without her consent (however, the Syrian delegate to the MAC had already agreed that his country had no say in civilian affairs in the DZ). The other was that Syria claimed the area where the DZ existed as hers and could not allow a foreign company to work there until it had been returned to her at the final peace settlement. This claim came as a surprise to the Israelis who insisted that there had been no hint of it during the armistice negotiations. Certainly in the MAC the Syrians had behaved as if they had no claim to the DZ. The Syrians did not mention the one relevant objection to the Huleh project—that it impinged upon the rights of certain Arab landowners.

The Israelis were in a stronger position. It was relatively easy to show that Syria had no say in civilian affairs in the DZ, and that her consent was not necessary for the project. The difficulty lay in trying to show that the Israeli concession should prevail over Arab land rights, and this brought them back to Riley's

[1] *SCOR*, 541st mtg., 17th April 1951.

memo on sovereignty. The essence of their argument[1] was that the Government of Israel inherited all the powers and duties of the Mandatory government. It was sovereign everywhere within the former boundaries of Palestine except where there was explicit agreement to the limitation of that sovereignty. Thus, in the DZ, Israel's sovereignty was limited in respect of demilitarization and certain aspects of local administration because this was specifically provided for in the GAA. Where no such provision existed Israel's sovereignty must be considered complete. The Israelis also argued that the 'restoration of normal civilian life' meant the application of those laws, regulations and ordinances which had been in effect prior to 1948 under the Mandatory government. This included the ordinance granting the Huleh concession and the right of compulsory acquisition to the Palestine Land Development Company. Consequently the Company was acting within its rights and within the meaning of 'restoration of normal civilian life'.

In reply, Riley stated that there was nothing in the GAA to empower him to decide on who was sovereign in the area. He had to act solely within the framework set forth in Article Five, without going into the question of sovereignty. The Company was entitled to do what it wished so long as it worked on its own land. He agreed with Eban that there was nothing in the GAA which invalidated any provision of the Huleh concession. But, at the same time, Riley said, the Arab refugees who had returned to the DZ had a perfect right to stay there until there was a final settlement. He did not see that the Huleh concession could change that. The crux of the issue, in his opinion, was the necessity to reconcile the rights of the landowners with those of the Company.[2] From this the Israelis surmised that Riley, for other than legal considerations, considered Arab property rights to be more important than those of the Company, and that he would stop the project. Thus, they fought bitterly to persuade the Council not to hand the matter back to him for settlement.

The Council members said very little, although it was clear that they favoured Israel. There was little, however, that could be done, apart from re-emphasizing the disputants' obligations

[1] *SCOR*, 542nd mtg.
[2] *ibid*, 544th mtg., 2nd May 1951, pp. 3 *et seq.*

to use the armistice machinery and to obey the armistice provisions. The resolution[1] contained no mention of the Huleh project. Israel was ordered to return the evacuated Arabs to the
DZ; to permit UN Observers free access to all places in the
DZ; and to comply with the Chairman's requests, i.e. stop
work on Arab lands. Although the resolution was relatively innocuous, the intention of the sponsors (Britain, France, Turkey
and the USA) was plain. They announced themselves as entirely in favour of the Huleh project and expressed the hope
that it be completed as soon as possible. But everything had to
be done in its proper order. First, Israel should stop work on
Arab land. If the Company could not come to terms with the
owners then the matter should be placed in the hands of the
Chairman. If the Chairman was unable to satisfy 'all reasonable claims' and the MAC decided that he did not have the
authority to fix compensation and allow compulsory acquisition, then it was expected that Israel would invoke Article Eight
of the GAA, which provides for the revision of the armistice provisions by a conference, so as to provide the Chairman with the
necessary power. If the conference failed to reach an agreement
(and probably the sponsors felt that it would) then Israel could
bring the matter back to the Council. This time, all the necessary steps having been taken, the Council would have the
authority under the GAA to arrange for the implementation of
the project, and great care was taken to assure the Israelis that
this authority would be used.[2] This procedure was the only one
which would allow the Council to take concrete measures to
settle the dispute. Neither the Israelis nor the Syrians concerned
themselves with this. The former were angry because they, and
not the Syrians, had been censured; because there was no reference to the need for peace negotiations; and because they were
sure that Riley would accept the landowners' refusal to sell as
final and hold the project up. For similar reasons the Syrians
welcomed the resolution adopted on 18th May.

In fact the resolution did not improve matters much. The
Syrians insisted that it meant that the Israelis would have
to stop all work on the project until the dispute with the

[1] *SCOR*, S/2157, 18th May 1951.
[2] See esp. British delegate, *ibid*, 547th mtg., 18th May 1951.

landowners was settled. Riley, now acting as MAC Chairman, agreed with the Israelis that only work affecting Arab lands had to be stopped. The project went on while Riley tried to persuade the Arab landowners to agree to compensation. He failed. At this point the MAC should have been brought in to decide whether or not the Chairman had the authority necessary to order compulsory acquisition. The Syrians, however, would not discuss this unless other questions, for example the return of the evacuated Arabs, were also put on the agenda. Israel refused, claiming that these other questions concerned civilian matters and were not the responsibility of the MAC. Syria replied that it was up to the MAC to decide whether or not they were civilian matters. But the Israelis were in no mood to allow more inspection of their affairs in the DZ than was absolutely necessary. So the MAC did not meet to discuss the Chairman's authority. Once again the machinery for negotiating disputes had broken down. The deadlock persisted for months. However, the Israelis managed to devise a means of completing the drainage canal without using Arab land and so the matter passed off fairly peaceably.

Syrian control over the El Hamma area was consolidated, but the rest of the DZ passed under Israeli influence. The MAC met only occasionally in emergency session; however, informal meetings took place regularly and were most useful in settling minor disputes before they assumed a serious character. In January 1953, the canal was completed and the drainage of the swamps began.

The Israelis then turned to the next job on the list. This was the construction of a hydro-electric power plant, at B'nat Ya'acov Bridge, just north of Lake Tiberias, which involved building a water diversion canal from the plant to the north of the lake. Thus, not only was it necessary to work in the DZ, but also to divert a portion of the water from the Jordan River between Lake Huleh and Lake Tiberias. Although the River lies entirely outside of Syria, she did have traditional rights to sufficient water for livestock and irrigation in the vicinity. The concession for the project had been granted to the Palestine Electric Corporation on 5th March 1926 by the Palestine Government. It involved issues paralleling those raised earlier in the Huleh controversy: the struggle for power in the DZ, Syrian hostility to Israel's economic development, conflicting private rights, and military advantage. In addition some interesting new questions came up, centring around the use of an international waterway.

In the beginning the Israelis had visualized the project as only part of a comprehensive scheme for the exploitation of the Jordan River to be carried out on a regional basis in cooperation with the Arab states. (Cf. next chapter.) For months they had petitioned the U.S. State Department for support. Plans and proposals were submitted, emissaries sent, but there was no hint of encouragement from the Americans. A few days after work on the project had started, Foreign Minister Sharett repeated Israel's willingness to undertake the development of local water resources in cooperation with Syria and Lebanon. There was still no response from the State Department. Syria protested against the project and began mobilizing troops.

It was now October of 1953 and those considerations which were pushing the Israelis to commit mass murder at Qibya, regardless of international opinion, were influential here. The State Department's refusal to say anything about the Israelis' requests for support in the creation of a regional water development scheme only served to strengthen their feelings of isolation and danger. Had they not felt this way it is unlikely that they would have gone so far as the Qibya Raid or provoked the Americans into cutting off aid.[1] Had they restrained themselves it is just possible that a number of beneficial developments might have taken place.

On 2nd October, despairing of any cooperation from the Americans, the Israelis began work at B'nat Ya'acov.[2] The Acting MAC Chairman was informed of the project, but not of its full extent. He gave conditional consent. Later, when he discovered what was involved, he withdrew it pending Bennike's return from New York. On the basis of subsequent investigations Bennike asked the Israelis to stop work. They refused. The

[1] An account of Israeli complaints against the US is given by Hal Lehrman, in *Commentary*, April 1954.

[2] References to the B'nat Ya'acov dispute are drawn from, *Reports of the Chief of Staff, UNTSO . . .*, beginning with *SCOR*, S/3122, 23rd October 1953. UNTSO Chief of Staff was now General Vagn Bennike.

Syrians began to mobilize troops, and the Americans threatened to suspend aid. The Israelis rejected Bennike's insistence upon an unconditional work stoppage and negotiations broke down. The Israelis installed floodlights at the dam and work went on day and night. On 20th October American aid was suspended: B'nat Ya'acov on top of Qibya was too much. On the 27th the Council met and Israel offered to cease work. Work stopped on the 28th and aid was resumed.

Bennike's order had been based upon three considerations: the work was interfering with normal civilian life; the project when complete would interfere with normal civilian life; and the function of the DZ—the separation of armed forces—would be affected by the diversion from it of a considerable amount of water.

Bennike claimed that in each case he was basing himself solely upon Article Five. He was not questioning the rights of the Palestine Electric Corporation, but whether these rights could be implemented while the armistice provisions were in force. Israeli workmen were using Arab-owned land, some lands would be permanently flooded, some mills would lose their waterpower, and some Syrian farms dependent on the river for irrigation would be adversely affected during the dry season. On this last point Bennike agreed with the Israelis that Article Five related only to the DZ, and not to Syrian farms outside it. However, he argued, the Anglo–French agreement of 7th March 1923 guaranteed that existing Syrian water rights would not be impaired. The Israelis replied that this agreement was not necessarily binding on them, but even so they were willing to undertake an obligation to guarantee the Syrians the necessary water as an *ex gratia* act, 'motivated by considerations of equity and future good neighbourliness'. Bennike replied that this should have been done before the project began.

The merits of these arguments are obscure. In particular there has never been a ruling as to whether Bennike had the authority to deal with the claims of various riparian states to the use of an international waterway, a matter for which no provision is made in the GAA. His arguments concerning the question of military advantage were plainly dubious. In 1951 Riley had made it clear that it was not a valid question to raise either inside or outside the DZ. Furthermore, he had plainly stated that the DZ had not been created because of the peculiar topography of the area, or because fighting was likelier there than anywhere else. Despite this precedent, set by a man who had been involved in the armistice negotiations, Bennike insisted on the validity of his objection that the canal would provide Israel with a military advantage, and that this was expressly forbidden in Article Two of GAA.[1] The Security Council members did not fall in with Bennike's interpretation. The French delegate summed up the general consensus of the Council when he remarked that to him 'the main characteristic of a demilitarized zone was precisely its demilitarization'.[2]

The Council's debate lasted off and on for eight weeks. The Council members were divided not by the merits of the case but by their controversies with each other. The Lebanese and Pakistani delegates supported Syria. So did the Russian delegate, using a number of arguments that had been discredited in 1951. The Western Powers were inclined to support Israel, but they were handicapped by Israel's previous treatment of Bennike. Also they had no desire to antagonize the Arabs at a time when Middle Eastern defence plans were in such a delicate state and Eric Johnston was in the region. Furthermore, it was essential to avoid a Russian veto. On the other hand, a strong resolution in favour of the project, barring a Russian veto, might provide just the impetus necessary to get Johnston's plan accepted. The result of these considerations was a joint Anglo–French–American draft resolution[2] which satisfied no one but its sponsors. Along with the usual emphasis on compliance with the armistice provisions, there were expressions of approval for development projects which did not infringe on established rights and obligations. Syria was criticized for attempting to wield a unilateral 'veto power

---

[1] Article Two contains an injunction against gaining a military or political advantage under the truce. All the signatories agreed that this referred only to the truce period and not to the armistice; otherwise even something like building a road near the border would have been a violation of the GAA. After his retirement Bennike made several speeches strongly criticizing Israel for her violations (*sic*) of Article Two.

[2] *SCOR*, 655th mtg., 21st January 1954, p. 10.

[3] *ibid*, S/3151, 16th December 1953.

over legitimate projects in the zone'. Israel was criticized for not obeying Bennike, which meant that the Council could not discuss the validity of his decision, but only Israel's disregard of it. It was proposed therefore that the dispute be handed back to Bennike to be handled properly by him with 'the best guidance and all the help' the Council could give, and this was set forth in paragraph eight of the draft resolution. It read:

> The Security Council . . . *Requests and authorizes* the Chief of Staff to explore possibilities of reconciling the interests involved in the dispute, including rights in the demilitarized zone and full satisfaction of existing irrigation rights at all seasons, and to take such steps as he may deem appropriate to effect a reconciliation, having in view the development of the natural resources affected in a just and orderly manner for the general welfare.

The Pakistani delegate described this paragraph as full of dangerous ambiguities, a masterpiece of obfuscation: the function of the Council, he said, was to uphold the GAA, not to promote economic development; in any case the whole resolution was irrelevant because it made no reference to Syria's complaints that Israel had disobeyed Bennike, which was after all the reason for the Council meeting. The Lebanese delegate suggested that the paragraph be omitted, and in turn he submitted an amendment which simply called upon Bennike to bring about a settlement between the parties concerned. This was at least as obscure as its predecessor but had the advantage of brevity.

The Russian delegate insisted that Syria's consent was necessary for any project taking place in the DZ, and that the Council should take no action until the two countries had had time to reach an agreement. He made it clear that unless the draft resolution were altered he would veto it. At the time the Russian's statement was generally considered to be part of a plan to win over the Arabs by supporting them against Israel and the West. This probably is an over-simplification. The year 1953 marked a high point in Israel–Russian relations: diplomatic relations had been resumed, and trade between the two countries had begun to increase in leaps and bounds.[1] Rather,

---

[1] A new trade agreement was signed, involving large shipments of oil to Israel. Israel exports to Russia in 1954 were forty times greater than in 1950–1. In 1955 fuel purchases were doubled and Israel's trade with Eastern Europe expanded.

the Russians were reacting against the growth of the Ankara–Karachi axis, and the Johnston mission, both of which they regarded as signs of the steady spread of imperialism along their most vulnerable frontier.

The sponsors were now faced with the necessity of clarifying their resolution, when this was obviously the last thing they wanted to do. A new paragraph was added affirming that nothing in the resolution 'shall be deemed to supersede the Armistice Agreement or to change the legal status of the demilitarized zone therein'. The American delegate hoped that this 'concise formula' would remove all doubts and criticisms. The contradictions here are so patent that they must have been intentional. In paragraph eight Bennike was ordered to reconcile all interests, that is to say interests both within and outside the purview of the GAA. Now, according to the additional paragraph, this was to be done without going beyond the GAA or altering the status of the DZ. Intensive negotiations began behind the scenes, continuing right through Christmas and New Year's day, with the Israelis excluded and watching nervously from the sidelines. All the issues had been narrowed down to one point: whether Syria had the right to veto Israel development projects in the DZ. The Western Powers said no, not as long as land and water rights were protected. Lebanon and Pakistan said yes.

The Council finally voted on 22nd January. Pakistan had been replaced by Turkey, but Lebanon—and Russia—remained. The draft resolution had, in the meantime, been 'polished, amended and, let us hope, illuminated'. But its inherent contradiction was summed up in the British delegate's remark that it was designed to meet the views of both Israel and Syria. The Russians vetoed it. At this point the Secretary-General told the Council that time was 'a very pressing factor'. Two things were 'urgently' required: a confirmation of Bennike's original policy; and a directive referring the problem back to the MAC so that Bennike could proceed to a solution. The Secretary General pressed the Council for a 'speedy positive decision'. The meeting adjourned while the delegates sought further instructions from their governments. It did not meet again to discuss the matter. Technically, it still has it under 'urgent consideration'.

The Israelis yielded to American pressure and agreed not to renew work on the project. In 1955, after it was obvious that Johnston had failed, they insisted on starting again, but agreed that nothing would be done in the DZ itself. The Israelis controlled most of the DZ, except for the area around El Hamma which had been sealed off by the Syrians and which not even the UNTSO visited. Both sides found this division tolerable, and preferable to the probable effects of trying to change it.

The dispute over Lake Tiberias was explosive. Lake Tiberias lies entirely within Israel. When Palestine's boundaries had been laid down in 1923 the British had taken great pains to ensure that the Syrian frontier did not touch the Lake at any point.[1] Consequently, in some places the border lies only ten metres east of the Lake. Only a small number of Syrians live in the area, and they have water rights and fishing rights, granted in the Anglo–French Agreement of 1923. Originally the Israelis had offered to renew the arrangements for fishing rights by negotiations with the Syrian government. But it had declined to enter into talks with the Israeli government, and had done little to prevent Syrian fishermen from going out on to the Lake: in some instances there seems to have been positive encouragement to do so. Also Israeli fishing boats going to the richest banks along the north-eastern shore, where the Syrians lived, were often fired upon, as were the police boats which went to their aid.

In August 1951, Israel agreed that in order to reduce the tension, particularly high after Tel el Mutilla, she would send no boats in closer than 250 metres from the shore. In December 1951, the Israelis went back to their former fishing grounds and two men were shot at and killed about 100 metres from the shore. Syria refused to accept responsibility, on the grounds that the men were in closer than 250 metres. The Israelis replied that that agreement related only to the conditions obtaining in August. They insisted that the Lake lay entirely within their borders, and that they had a perfect right to go anywhere on it they pleased. Syria then insisted that Israeli boats must not

[1] See H. Frischwasser-Ra'anan, *Frontiers of a Nation.*

come closer than 400 metres from the shore. The Israelis refused with the result that the incidents continued, and on several occasions Syrian troops shelled boats on the Lake.

In 1954 Syria once again brought up the question of fishing rights. The Israelis offered to negotiate. Syria refused because it would have implied political recognition.[1] Israel then suggested that individual Syrians be granted special fishing permits upon application to the Israel authorities. The Syrians refused all direct contact and demanded that all applications be handled through the UNTSO. Deadlock obtained.

In December 1954, five Israeli soldiers were captured inside Syria while they were repairing a wire tap. Israel was censured by the MAC, which then asked for the release of the prisoners (one of whom had committed suicide in jail). Syria refused, and all efforts by the UNTSO failed. On 22nd October, two Israeli platoons crossed the line, destroyed a military convoy and took five soldiers as hostages, to no avail. By this time the Syrians had begun to reinforce their positions around the Lake. Artillery had been brought up, some positions had been set up inside Israel, and there was good reason to believe that they intended to impose their control over a 250-metre area.[2] Determined not to be dominated on Lake Tiberias, Israel launched a large raid in December 1955 destroying Syrian positions in the north-eastern area of the Lake.[3] This was the last important action on the Syrian border for some years.

[1] *I–SMAC*, 70th mtg., pp. 6 *et seq.*

[2] This was verified from captured documents: vd. *SCOR*, S/3516 Add. 1, 20th December 1955, and S/3518, 22nd December 1955, Annexes I–IV.

[3] In his *Report* (S/3516 and Add. 1) General Burns pointed out that the disparity between the provocation and the size of the raid indicated that trouble with Syria was not the main cause of the attack.

The Czech arms deal had been signed in September; Egypt and Syria had signed a Mutual Defence Pact a few days previously; and *fedayeen* had begun to operate out of Syria.

Chapter Eight

THE ARAB REFUGEES (1947–53)

MORE than half a million Arabs fled Palestine in 1947–8.[1] They represent the tragedy of Israel, that disaster which is the other face of triumph. A great deal has been written about them; in almost every case the writer felt it necessary to distribute blame, to place the onus on one man or another. But so far not enough is known about why things happened as they did to justify obstinacy on the subject. Lack of space does not permit a detailed examination of the various explanations usually put forward to explain the exodus, and for our purposes it is more important to study the effects of the refugee problem upon the shape and trend of events. Accordingly we shall confine ourselves to a brief outline of the major developments.[2]

The Arab exodus from Palestine can be divided into four major phases: from 30th November 1947 to 12th April 1948; from 12th April until June; the ten days' fighting in July; and finally the period between September 1948 and January 1949.

The General Assembly's resolution of partition on 29th

[1] The actual number of refugees has always been disputed. UNRWA accepted the figure of 726,000 as a reasonable, but probably inaccurate, estimate. A more recent study by Walter Pinner, *How Many Arab Refugees?*, based upon a close analysis of available statistics, places the total at 539,000 and I have accepted this as the most likely approximation.

[2] Two conflicting accounts can be found in Kimches', *Both Sides of the Hill*; and Childers' 'The Other Exodus', in the *Spectator*, 12th May 1961.

November was followed immediately by disturbances, in particular a mob attack on Jewish shops in Jerusalem, which was followed by an exodus of the more well-to-do Arabs. At this time few people thought that the British really intended to leave, and a short visit to one's family in Beirut was simply a convenient way of avoiding temporary unpleasantness. As conditions worsened, more and more Arabs left. Invariably the first to leave a potential trouble spot were the Arabs' leaders: the doctors, lawyers, politicians, teachers, and union officials. The British, as they retired, simply closed down the government offices necessary for the maintenance of law, order and public welfare. The Arab community, always badly organized, had relied upon the British for all its services. Now with the British gone, and their own leaders off in Damascus or Beirut busy issuing fighting statements, the Arabs fell apart, the community dissolved, rumour and panic created havoc. By the beginning of April perhaps over 200,000 had fled the country. Almost no Jews left. Their community was comparatively well organized and disciplined. They already had their own quasi-government which worked fairly effectively and had considerable authority. Many Jews, of course, felt that there was no suitable alternative to staying and fighting. No Jewish community leader abdicated.

This difference between the two communities was the *sine qua non* of the Israeli victory. The contest lay between the two populations and success would go to that which stood firmer, that which engaged itself more actively in the struggle. Those Arabs who did stay behind, willingly or no, were deserted by the men who claimed to be their leaders, and their will and means to fight was diminished accordingly.

Yet every circumstance favoured the Arabs. If they had stood steadfast to face the danger it is unlikely that the Jews could have held out, and certainly they would have been far less successful than they were. In the early months of 1948 their settlements were cut off and besieged, their convoys attacked and destroyed. The Arab Liberation Army moved freely about the north. The British Army was under instructions to hand their police stations, forts, and installations over to the Arabs;

the UN was prevented from moving into the country to try to restore order; and the British were arming the Arabs and maintaining a blockade against the Jews. The resources of the Jewish forces were scarce and inadequate to meet the potential danger. Only in the area around Tel Aviv was the position satisfactory, elsewhere the odds against them were overwhelming. It was this early, largely spontaneous flight which saved the Jews.

There is little concrete evidence to support the contention that during this first phase the Jews had decided upon a policy of expelling the Arabs. There is even less evidence to show that such a policy, if it existed, was carried out with the kind of consistency one would expect in these circumstances. Such evidence as does exist must be considered within the context of the times. The fighting was, to a considerable extent, a struggle between civilians: everyone was a potential if not an actual enemy. Both sides used the same sort of tactics against each other: a psychological blitz designed to weaken the nerve of the other side, attacks on all likely points of resistance and so forth. There is no evidence to show that the Jews acted any differently in this respect than did the Arabs. Whatever the thinking of the Jewish leaders on the subject, in practice the responsibility for dealing with the Arabs was left in the hands of the civilian and military authorities directly concerned. The fate of the Arabs in Haifa seems to have been typical of this period. About 25,000 out of the city's 70,000 Arabs had left by March. Almost all the city's 70–80,000 Jews remained. During the first three weeks in April another 25,000 Arabs left. When the British announced their withdrawal from the city and fighting actually broke out, the Arab community was weak, badly divided and poorly led. Fighting began on the 20th. On the 21st, with the outcome still in doubt, the Arab commander left the city, and the Arabs conceded surrender on the 22nd. The Jewish civic leaders made great efforts to persuade the Arabs to stay. Among their various reasons was the fear that if all the Arabs left the port would have to close down for lack of labour. The terms offered were generous, especially considering that the battle was mounting throughout the rest of the country. The Arabs after some deliberation, and for reasons which have never been fully explained, decided to leave, and those still in the city were evacuated by the British.

The massacre at Deir Yassin marks the great psychological turning point in the battle. On 12th April, members of the Jewish terrorist organization *Irgun Zvei Leumi* entered the reasonably friendly village of Deir Yassin and massacred over two hundred of its inhabitants, men, women, and children, and threw the bodies into a well.[1] The effect was to more than double the flood of emigration. In the month following Deir Yassin another 200,000 people left the country. Those Arabs who remained showed little inclination to continue the struggle. As soon as the battle approached they fled, leaving the fighting to the irregular and later the regular Arab armies. This was undoubtedly one of the reasons for the evacuation of Haifa. And possibly it also explains why, in the north where the Jews were outnumbered thirty to one and the Arabs received all the fortified positions from the British, many Arabs fled at the first sign of trouble. In Safad, for example, the Jews were outnumbered three to one, and by virtue of their Orthodox leanings were mostly unsuited and untrained for fighting. The local Arabs were strengthened by a large force from Syria under the command of the future President of Syria, Colonel Adib Shishakli. First victory went to the Syrians, but none the less large numbers of the local Arabs fled, and when the Jews finally won the remaining Arabs left. There is no evidence that these people were actually expelled. All one can say is that in the course of the battle the Jews used the ordinary methods of psychological warfare, as did the Arabs, and that theirs were more successful, at least partially because of Deir Yassin. It also seems true that the Jews were no longer interested, as they had been in Haifa, in persuading the Arabs to remain. The military advantages of the flight were too obvious to be ignored.

---

[1] The Jews too had their calamities. In the weeks before statehood an entire hospital convoy was wiped out just a few hundred yards from a British military camp which had orders not to intervene. Over eighty people were killed. In the Etzion *bloc*, except for three people, an entire settlement was massacred by Arab villagers, after it had surrendered but before the Arab Legion could gain control of the situation. When they did fight the local Arabs gave no quarter and took no prisoners. After the regular Arab armies moved in the rules of war were applied with the expected consistency.

But this is quite different from saying that those Arabs who had not fled before the fighting was over were later ejected from their homes and driven across the lines.

During the ten days of fighting in July the situation changed entirely. Then the Israelis undertook a clear-cut policy of expulsion. It is difficult to estimate the numbers involved, particularly since so many people had already left before the Israelis moved in. Expulsion seems to have been applied mainly in the central sector, in order to establish a thick defensive belt around Tel Aviv. The Army had not the means to ensure the good behaviour of a large potential fifth column and it was considered safer to remove any possible danger. It is not known if the decision was taken by the military or had the consent of the Cabinet as well. But the results indicate that in the north there was no policy of expulsion, or if there were it was not implemented with any recognizable consistency. The same is true for the south. In the fourth phase there does not seem to have been any special policy adopted. Fighting took place in the north and the south. In the north those who did not flee were allowed to remain, and most of Israel's Arab population lives there. In the south the fighting involved mostly Egyptians : the local Arabs were beduin and seem to have stayed clear of both sides.

The refugee problem became a political issue with the publication of the Bernadotte Report in which it was proposed that all the refugees be allowed to return to their homes. In its resolution of 11th December 1948 the General Assembly recommended that 'the refugees wishing to return to their homes and live at peace with their neighbours should be permitted to do so at the earliest practicable date, and that compensation should be paid for the property of those choosing not to return . . .' Not unnaturally, the Israelis refused to consider repatriation except as part of an overall peace settlement with the Arab States. Without peace treaties there could be no effective guarantee that the repatriated Arabs would live at peace in Israel and not act as a fifth column.

Security has always been the decisive consideration for the Israelis. At no time have they ever felt sufficiently sure of their neighbours' intentions to accept large-scale repatriation. The offer to the CCP in August 1949 to repatriate 100,000 was made under considerable pressure from the State Department, and its rejection gratefully received. On occasion the offer has been renewed but always as part of a peace settlement.

Another compelling reason for the Israelis' stubbornness, one seldom acknowledged, was the economic value of the exodus. The Arabs left behind them houses, shops and land, lying ready for the hundreds of thousands of Jewish immigrants flooding into the country. Four million dunams of land were abandoned, more than two and a half times the amount owned by the Jews in May 1948. By 1954 nearly 400 former Arab villages and towns were occupied by immigrants. Of the 370 new settlements established by January 1953, 350 were on former Arab property. In sum, military and economic developments precluded repatriation except in the most favourable of circumstances.

The Israelis argued continually in favour of resettlement in the Arab countries where the refugees could be more easily assimilated than in a Jewish country. At the same time they began divesting themselves of their obligations to the refugees. The 'reunion of families' scheme was implemented and about 37,000 people were repatriated. Arab funds blocked in Israeli banks were released, and the Israelis agreed in principle to the payment of compensation. The effect of these actions, and of the undeniable facts of Israel's economic and military position, was that UN pressure for repatriation fell off steadily as the years passed.

During the early years the refugee problem was thought to hold the key to peace: that is to say, if the problem was resolved there would be no reason for the Arab States not to make peace with Israel. The Americans, who concerned themselves most closely with the question, faced opposition from two directions. The Israelis would not accept large-scale repatriation; and the Arabs refused to accept resettlement because it weakened their political argument against Israel with whom they would not make peace in any case. Consequently they were suspicious of the various American offers of aid for economic development because invariably refugee resettlement was involved. After several schemes had been turned down, the Americans went to the General Assembly which duly set up a Reintegration Fund of two hundred million dollars to which any government in the Middle East could apply for money for development projects which involved 'the permanent re-establishment of refugees and their removal from relief'.[1] The Arabs refused to accept this kind of economic assistance and only a minute fraction of the money was used. By 1954 only 3,000 refugees had been 'reintegrated'. The resolution establishing the Reintegration Fund indicated the Assembly's definite shift away from its earlier recommendation for repatriation. Although it contained a restatement of the refugees' right to repatriation, it also said in effect that the problem could be solved without repatriation and that, lacking a peace settlement—the only circumstances in which repatriation was feasible—it would be. The Arabs thought otherwise, but as time passed their rigid refusal to implement measures to resolve the problem lost them much sympathy and support, and strengthened Israel's position.

The attitudes of the Arabs were inconsistent, paradoxical and contradictory. The policy of the Arab League, the official policy, was laid down at the Beirut Conference in 1949: a just solution to the refugee problem was repatriation; and without repatriation there could be no peace. This remained unchanged from 1949 onwards. The inconsistencies lay in the actions of the individual governments. There were too many different pressures at work, the needs of the various countries too diverse for it to be otherwise.

There were two influential factors: the distribution of the refugees, and their impact upon the host countries. Most of the refugees were concentrated where their presence had the greatest influence: Jordan and Lebanon. Jordan, by spreading itself over both banks of the river, had to absorb about 700,000 Palestinians into its original population of 420,000. Better educated and organized, more sophisticated and forceful than the original Transjordanians, they looked to Cairo rather than Amman for the redress of their grievances. The differences between the two sections of the population were never resolved, and Jordan's policy towards the refugees was confused and inconsistent. Lebanon had received only about ninety thousand refugees, but this meant a ten per cent rise in

[1] *GAOR*, 393 (V), 2nd December 1950.

the population. To a country painfully maintaining a balance between Christian and Moslem a sudden increase in the Moslem population had its attendant dangers. Those Lebanese, Christian and Moslem, who thought first of national stability, considered the refugees to be a menace and tried to segregate them from the mainstream of national life. They were opposed by those Lebanese, and these seem to have been in the majority, who looked to Cairo and Al Azhar for their future, and thought of the refugees as a living symbol of Arab aspirations and set-backs, far too valuable a weapon to be shut off and isolated.

The refugees in Jordan and Lebanon came under the in-fluence of Cairo, and through them Egypt exerted considerable influence on their host governments. The refugees had almost no impact in Egypt. They were bottled up in the Gaza Strip with almost no access to and little influence in Egypt proper. The government could act as it wished without concerning it-self with the refugees' reactions. The Syrians were in a similar position. They had about 75,000 refugees who were kept away from the borders to lessen the danger of border violence. The attitude of these refugees toward Israel were hardly more violent than those of the Syrians themselves, and, in any case, after 1950 the Syrian government swung more and more closely to the side of Egypt. Thus the two countries which had the least unwilling-ness to make peace with Israel and the most trouble with the refugees were largely influenced by the two countries with the least desire for peace, and the least trouble with the refugees. This helps to explain much of what went on between the Arab countries and with Israel, but offers no more than a clue to the Arab governments' actual attitudes toward the refugees.

In 1949, Jordan and Lebanon both agreed to settle the boundary question without dealing with the refugees. In 1950, Abdullah's draft Treaty made no mention of the refugees. Later that year President Shishakli of Syria agreed tentatively to re-settle his refugees, under UNRWA auspices, without a peace settlement. In that same year Egypt began to investigate the possibility of refugee resettlement in the El Arish area, near Gaza, and serious investigations to this end continued right up through 1955. Charges that the Arab governments used the refugees to suit their own political ends are justified. But at the same time there were Arabs concerned about the long-term social, economic and, ultimately, political effects of the problem. Their influence was never decisive but at certain times, particularly during the negotiations over the Johnston Plan, it seems to have been considerable.

The attitude of the refugees themselves was straightforward: they were determined to return home. It was estimated in 1955 that only about ten per cent would have agreed to resettlement in the Arab countries.[1] The significance of this consistency was weakened however by the refugees' misunderstanding of their true position. All their information came from the Arab governments. All UNRWA's field officers were refugees and themselves in sympathy with the desire for repatriation. UNRWA's policy was never properly related or understood, nor was that of the General Assembly, nor, indeed, that of the Arab governments. The refugees were told that the Assembly had given them the right to repatriation, that repatriation was entirely possible, and that resettlement would mean the loss of that right. According to this not unreasonable line of argument, if refugees were resettled in farming communities in, say, northern Syria, and prospered moderately they would not be able to, would not want to, press their claims for repatriation with the appropriate vigour and effectiveness. Consequently it was far better to remain in the camps and thereby sustain the need for repatriation. There is no indication that the refugees were told of or understood the extent of the Arabs' defeat in 1948–9, or of the difficulties involved in repatriation, or of those which would follow after repatriation.

The refugees did not think that repatriation meant living in a Jewish state. Repatriation meant returning in a conquering army, or as part of a vast fifth column, or in some other way involving the restoration of the Arab homeland. There was no thought of loyalty to a government of Jews, of submitting to the heavy demands of planned development in Israel, or of considering Israel as their country. To them Israel was something ephemeral, something which they had no intention of accept-

---

[1] F. C. Bruhns, in *Middle East Journal*, Spring 1955, p. 132. Other material on the refugees can be found in the *UNRWA, Annual Reports*; Peretz, *Israel and the Palestine Arabs*.

ing. Nothing was ever done which succeeded in educating the refugees to a more realistic appraisal of the situation. They remained committed to repatriation while it became less of a possibility and more of a dangerous dream. This was largely the handiwork of the Arab governments. They were the ones who controlled the sources of the refugees' information, who encouraged the belief in repatriation in Palestine, who provided the main opposition to resettlement, and who did so much to foster the refugees' unrest and frustration. Yet they were also willing to negotiate with Eric Johnston over a plan for resettling the refugees in the Arab countries.

Chapter Nine

THE JOHNSTON PLAN (1953–6)

T HE dispute with Syria over B'nat Ya'acov in the Jordan Valley mirrored the larger arguments over the exploitation of the waters of the Jordan River and the fate of the Arab refugees. Nowhere is the connexion between people and water more obvious than in the Middle East. In a land where rain is sparse and infrequent, a man cannot move without thinking first of water. Where it is not he cannot live. To find it can take months of exhausting, discouraging work. Then it must be husbanded carefully, every drop measured out. When the rain is too infrequent the land cracks, the wells dry up, the crops die, and the people sit about aimlessly, helplessly, passively. To move a home, to move a family, to move a village from one place to another is impossible unless there is water. To move over half a million people out of Palestine, and replace them with a million immigrants imposes an intolerable strain on the limited water available to everyone. Clearly the water resources had to be expanded. Such expansion would have two unavoidable effects. Israel's economic development would be encouraged; and the resettlement of the Arab] refugees would be facilitated.

The Americans had accepted the burden of refugee relief willingly. Realizing that they had had some share in the creation of the problem and that they were the only ones who could afford to do so, they paid close to seventy per cent of UNRWA's budget. But they had their own ideas of how the money should be spent, ideas represented by the Reintegration Fund. Ordinary relief was not sufficient. It had to be paralleled by rehabilitation, reintegration and resettlement; schemes which would in time remove the refugees from the charity rolls. For this kind of integrated programme the Americans were willing to pay out tens of millions, but the idea of paying out huge sums yearly with no sign of the burden alleviating was unacceptable.[1] In 1953, the new American Secretary of State, John Foster Dulles, went to the Middle East and among the various ideas he brought back with him was one for a Jordan Valley Authority, along the lines of the Tennessee Valley Authority. The idea was not a new one. The Tennessee Valley Authority had already been commissioned by UNRWA to investigate the possibilities. But it was the State Department's interest which gave the idea the necessary impetus. UNRWA agreed to let the State Department handle the negotiations and Eric Johnston was sent out as Special Ambassador.

The circumstances were hardly propitious. This was the time of Qibya and B'nat Ya'acov. Antagonism ran high. None the less negotiations began, and continued to make steady progress even though Arab–Israeli relations inexorably went from bad to worse. Concern for the fate of the refugees, and, in the case of Jordan and Lebanon, a fear of refugee influence upon national stability, were undoubtedly factors contributing to this anomalous development. But they do not explain why the Arabs were willing to consider a plan to benefit Israel while at the same time they were intensifying their campaign against her. Nor do they explain why, for example, Egypt should so strongly support a plan for resettling the refugees in Jordan, which would be of enormous economic and political benefit to the Jordan government, and at the same time should try to use the refugees to bring down that government. The course of Johnston's mission is very difficult to explain, and it seems best simply to put down what is known and let the reader draw his own conclusions.

[1] See U.S. Senate, *Palestine Refugee Problem*, 83rd Congress, 1st session (Washington, Government Printing Office, 1953); and House of Representatives, Committee on Foreign Affairs, *The Arab Refugees and Other Problems* . . . , 83rd Congress, 2nd session (Washington, Government Printing Office, 1954).

The Johnston Plan: 1953–6

The purpose of the Johnston Plan was to establish a Jordan Valley Authority composed of Israel, Jordan and Syria for the joint exploitation of the resources of the Jordan River, thereby providing newly irrigated land for the resettlement of a large number of refugees.[1] An underlying motive shared by the Americans and the Israelis was to establish a durable, effective basis for cooperation which in time might be extended to include matters of a more political nature.

As rivers go, the Jordan is unimpressive. Those who are unmindful of its historical associations and who know a river when they see one might call it a stream or even a brook. It flows its short length from its headwaters in Lebanon, Syria and Israel, lying narrow and overgrown with bush, down past Lakes Huleh and Tiberias, through the Jordan Valley, gradually broadening out into a wide, shallow, sluggish crawl ending in the Dead Sea. The river's course lies in a great crack in the earth's surface, and at the Dead Sea lies thirteen hundred feet below sea level. The greatest part of the drop, one thousand feet, takes place between the two lakes.

The Jordan Valley begins south of Lake Tiberias and has two levels or terraces; irrigation schemes include the upper terrace only. In the Valley, the river is fed by a number of small streams, and its largest tributary, the Yarmuk River, which flows through Jordan into the river near the Syrian border.

North of the Jordan lies the Litani River. This runs south through Lebanon to near the Israel border, then parallel to it and empties into the sea. Unlike the Jordan it lies entirely within Lebanon. Its volume is somewhat more than half that of the Jordan River. In the early 1900's, when the Zionists were considering the possible boundaries of Palestine, they concluded that if the country's agricultural potential was to be exploited fully the waters of the Litani would be needed. Diversion and conservation schemes based on its use were formulated, and at the Anglo-French negotiations in the early twenties the

[1] UN, *The Unified Development of the Water Resources of the Jordan Valley Region* (1953). The plan was drawn up by Charles T. Main Inc., and is often referred to as the Main Plan. See map p. 304.

Accounts of the negotiations can be found in G. Stevens, in *International Conciliation*, January 1956; Peretz, in *Middle East Journal*, Spring 1953; Eric Johnston, *NYT* 16th February 1954.

The Johnston Plan: 1953–6

Zionists pressed for all of what is now Lebanon up to Sidon, that is the whole of the Jordan River catchment area. Their claims went unfulfilled and in the end they found themselves without the Litani, and with only about twenty-three per cent of the Jordan watershed.[1] For better or worse the key to Israel's growth lay within the Arab countries.

The Israelis were naturally in favour of whittling down the refugee problem. More important was their pressing need to exploit all available water resources. It was estimated that even with all of the Jordan's waters they would be unable to meet their future requirements. Without any of the water they had no chance of surviving.[2] The implementation of a scheme for the drawing of at least part of the river's water was essential. Many schemes had been drawn up, but because eastern Palestine was now in Arab hands the most feasible was that at B'nat Ya'acov. Johnston's difficulty was to persuade the Israelis to hold off work until all possible avenues of cooperation with the Arabs had been thoroughly explored. They did not like the actual details of his Plan; and the more militant elements in the government insisted that the only way to persuade the Arabs to cooperate was to press on alone, using force if necessary. Eventually the moderates won on the argument that patience would have greater long-term political benefits. It was agreed that the Israelis would study the Plan and suggest modifications.

It was much more difficult with the Arabs. Qibya and B'nat Ya'acov had left them in no mood for cooperating with Israel.[3] Johnston refrained from discussing the Plan itself, and concentrated only on persuading the Arabs to agree to read it and make suggestions. He promised that the Plan did not involve an alteration in their political relations with Israel. He warned that the United States would not support the refugees indefinitely, and that unless the Arabs cooperated Israel would probably go it alone. The Arabs consented to consider the Plan. Adding to this substantial success Johnston stopped off in Cairo, and there he received assurances of strong support for his

[1] See Frischwasser-Ra'anan, *loc. cit.*, *passim.*
[2] UN Economic Survey Mission, *Final Report*, A/AC. 25/6, 26th December 1951. Part One, p. 2.
[3] 'In the Arab countries there was a general disposition to throw out not only the plan but Johnston as well.' Peretz, *Development. . . . loc. cit.*, p. 401.

mission.[1] Why the new and untried Egyptian government should have agreed to support what was after all a dangerous policy is unknown. But for the first year or two it seems to have carried out its promise despite steadily worsening relations with Israel and with Jordan, who stood to gain most from the Plan, and despite the growing opposition of Syria and Lebanon.

The Johnston Plan for the establishment of a Jordan Valley Authority was a straightforward scheme for the efficient and economical use of the Jordan Valley water resources to increase irrigation and hydro-electric power, so as to settle 200,000 refugees. It was based on the principle that the water must be used within the river's basin. Irrigation would extend to both sides of the Jordan Valley, the Yarmuk Plateau (between Syria and Jordan), the Huleh region, and eastern Galilee. Lake Tiberias would be the main storage reservoir, and hydro-electric power generators would be set up at appropriate spots. Israel would get thirty-five per cent of the available water; Syria and Jordan would divide the rest between them.

The Israelis responded with the Cotton Plan[2] which was a modification of earlier Zionist plans. It provided for the diversion of one-third of the Litani River into the Jordan River. Israel would get one-half of the total amount of water and this would be piped to the Negev. The Jordan Valley itself would be irrigated by a system of canals originating on the Yarmuk River. This would leave Jordan's water supplies entirely within her own territory. Hydro-electric power would be generated from B'nat Ya'acov, and part of it would be sent north to Lebanon in payment for the water from the Litani.

The Arabs submitted a plan which was most encouraging.[3] First and foremost, it provided for the sharing of water with

[1] The Egyptians set up a Technical Committee and provided experts to assist the Arabs in their deliberations: CSM, Ellis, 26th October 1953; Times, 27th October 1953; NYT, 7th July 1954; Le Commerce du Levant..., Abi-Zeyd, 29th January 1955.

[2] The Cotton Plan for the Development... of the Jordan and Litani River Basins, Israel Information Office, (New York, June 1954); vd. also W. Lowdermilk, Palestine: Land of Promise (London, 1946); and J. B. Hays and J. L. Savage, TVA on the Jordan (Washington, 1948).

[3] Arab League Technical Committee, The Arabs' Plan for Development... of the Jordan Valley (March 1954); also Arab Palestine Office, Comment on Water Development in the Jordan Valley Region (Beirut, June 1954).

Israel. In effect, the Arabs agreed in principle to cooperative efforts in the field of economic and social development. A joint scheme meant breaching the economic boycott, and consenting to continued immigration into Israel. Details apart, the Arab Plan augured well for the future. Its provisions were similar in principle to those of the other two plans, but different in emphasis. Irrigation would take place only in the Jordan catchment area. For military and political reasons Lake Tiberias was rejected as the main storage site. Instead it was proposed to build a high dam at Maqarin on the Yarmuk River and to use it to supply the irrigation system and hydro-electric power.

In principle the three Plans were at one.[1] Broadly speaking, there were five main points at issue: (1) the inclusion of the Litani River; (2) the site of the main storage reservoir; (3) the division of the water; (4) Israel's pipeline to the south; (5) and the form of supervision.

On the first point the Israelis insisted that there could not be a fully effective regional plan which did not use the Litani River.

---

[1] The *Johnston Plan* would irrigate a total of 936,000 dunams as follows:

Lebanon	zero
Syria	30,000
Jordan	490,000
Israel	416,000

210 million kwh would be generated annually (excluding the Dead Sea project) *
and the total cost would be 121 million dollars (excluding the Dead Sea project).

The *Cotton Plan* would irrigate 2,600,000 dunams as follows:

Lebanon	350,000
Syria	30,000
Jordan	430,000
Israel	1,790,000

These estimates include the use of the Litani and other small streams. The smaller figure for Jordan is because the *Cotton Plan* is more conservative about the irrigable potential of Jordan—1,400 million kwh would be generated annually (including the Dead Sea project) and the total cost would be 470 million dollars.

The *Arab Plan* would irrigate 878,000 dunams as follows:

Lebanon	35,000
Syria	119,000
Jordan	490,000
Israel	234,000

No estimates of electric output or of cost included. See *Jerusalem Post*, E. Mayer-Bentov, 25th June 1954; and UNRWA, *Bulletin of Economic Development*, No. 14, *Special Report on Jordan* (Beirut, July 1956).

* Sea water would be brought in from the Mediterranean to replace the river water lost through irrigation.

Johnston replied that it was a wholly Lebanese river, and the United States had no grounds for asking Lebanon to share its waters with non-riparian states. Development projects were already under way on it, and any attempt to include it in the JVA would probably be futile. He went on to argue that once the JVA was implemented the Lebanese might be willing to consider integration. The Israelis reluctantly accepted this argument because it meant weakening their claim to a larger allocation of water.[1]

The dispute over siting the main storage reservoir revolved around political and military considerations. The Israelis were of two minds. Lake Tiberias had obvious advantages, but if it were used the Arabs might insist on its being internationalized or on shifting the Syrian demarcation line to the middle of the Lake. Yet again, the Yarmuk lay wholly within Arab territory, and Maqarin was far removed from the border. Eventually the matter was settled out of hand. The Israelis discovered that they would have to use Lake Tiberias themselves as a local reservoir, which meant that the Arabs would get the high dam and storage site at Maqarin.

The argument over water allocations tied in with the question of the pipeline to the south. According to the Johnston Plan Israel would get about thirty-five per cent of the water; according to the Arab Plan about twenty per cent; and according to the Cotton Plan about fifty per cent (this presupposed the use of the Litani River). The Israelis had reckoned that to support an estimated population in 1960 of two million people they would need an extra 400 million cubic metres of water. In order to provide for post-1960 needs they asked for 550 mcm. The Johnston Plan allowed them only 394 mcm. A new survey indicated that Jordan had more irrigable land than had been thought but needed less water to irrigate it. It was agreed that the difference would go to Israel.

The dispute over the coastal pipeline reflected a serious difference of opinion over the purpose of the JVA. The Israelis had always thought of developing the Jordan Valley in terms of their own benefit. Survival, however slim the chances,

[1] Israel and Lebanon have held numerous talks on water development and apparently Lebanese development projects can be fitted into a regional scheme.

depended upon bringing the maximum amount of water south to irrigate the Negev. This meant taking the water right away from the river basin. This was contrary not only to international practice but to the principles of the Johnston Plan. The purpose of that Plan, and of the Arab Plan, was to settle the maximum number of refugees by irrigating the Jordan Valley and the immediate surrounding area. Israel was to be the 'residuary legatee', not the Arabs.

The question of the supervisory body caused some difficulty because of its obvious political implications. The Israelis thought in terms of a joint commission composed of themselves and the Arabs, something along the lines of the American–Canadian water commission. This 'political' approach was indicative of the spirit in which they considered the JVA. The Arabs wanted an international supervisory body set up, possibly by the UN, in which there would be no direct contact with the Israelis. Any other arrangement, they felt, would compromise the political *status quo*. The Israelis objected to UN participation on the ground that it was an unsatisfactory organization to work with. In any case, political considerations apart, they were convinced that things would work much more smoothly if there were normal contact between the various parties.

Negotiations lasted from 1953 to 1955. By August of that year all but complete agreement had been reached on a final plan. It was a modified version of the Arab Plan, although it embodied important concessions on both sides. The total cost was estimated at about two hundred million dollars, of which the US would pay two-thirds. UNRWA would supervise construction. The Litani River was not included. The main storage site was to be at Maqarin on the Yarmuk River. Israel accepted forty per cent of the water (400 mcm), agreeing to overlook her post-1960 requirements in the hope of an improvement in the political situation.[1] The Arabs agreed to let Israel use her share of the water in the south. This was a radical concession for them, particularly Egypt, who was by that time actively engaged in discouraging Israeli settlement in the Negev. The question of supervision remained unsettled. Agreement was reached, before the talks ended, that on the technical level there

[1] Syria would receive 132 mcm, Lebanon 35 mcm, and Jordan 480 mcm.

would be a joint commission of three including a neutral chairman from outside. This, it was hoped, would provide the Arabs with an adequate buffer against Israel, and Israel with the desired minimum of direct contact.

That the negotiations should have gone so far was an extraordinary achievement, completely out of keeping with the tenor of Arab–Israeli affairs, and of the Middle East situation generally.[1] From 1953 Israeli's relations with Jordan had got no better, and those with Egypt steadily worse. In the early months of 1955 the prestige and authority of the Egyptian government were badly shaken when Israeli troops attacked Gaza, and Iraq defied President Nasser's neutralist policies and joined with Turkey and the West in what was later called the Baghdad Pact. Old wounds were reopened, tensions built up. It was hardly the time for conciliation and compromise. The negotiations had not been made public in the Arab world until June 1954, and not widely so until the summer of 1955 when there was considerable opposition, which increased each day as the general situation worsened.

In August, Dulles tied the JVA to his peace proposals, thereby giving the lie to Johnston's promise that there were no political strings attached.[2] In Cairo the ex-Mufti of Jerusalem and the Moslem Brotherhood opposed the Plan. In Syria and Lebanon it was felt that the JVA would lead to a relaxation of the economic boycott, and that Jordan would resume her use of Haifa. This would have meant a substantial loss of income to the Syrian and Lebanese railway companies, to the Port of Beirut, to the two governments, and to the numerous individuals and groups who profited from a boycott which forced Jordan and UNRWA to use the long, roundabout route to the sea.[3]

The Arab League met in October to decide whether or not to

[1] The Arab governments had been represented at the negotiations by a technical committee, headed by Egyptian experts, which had no political authority or responsibility. This perhaps explains why, at this level, agreement had been possible.
The Israeli government had agreed to accept the JVA and signed a document to this effect.
[2] See below, Chapter Thirteen: resettlement was tied up with 'boundary adjustments' and 'formal treaty arrangements'.
[3] See G. Stevens, *loc. cit.*, also *Observer*, Partner, 18th September 1955; *NYT* 5th October 1955; *CSM*, Ellis, 18th October 1955; *NYT*, Schmidt, 21st October 1955 and *Scotsman*, Stephens, 15th November 1955.

accept the Plan. The issue was simple and straightforward: would the Arabs agree to what could be in effect the first step in Israel's economic integration into the Middle East—and the likely political consequences? Considering the existing state of Arab–Israeli relations and the general circumstances of that time there could be no doubt of the decision. Syria argued for an outright rejection of the Plan. But the Egyptians were able to persuade the meeting to put the Plan aside 'pending further study'. In this way the Plan was effectively shelved without risking the possible repercussions of an outright rejection.[1]

Johnston's failure was by no means final. That he could have brought matters as far as he did, despite attendant circumstances, indicated not just his ability but the compelling considerations of his mission. The need for water increased daily with each refugee child born, with each new immigrant, with each new house, with each new factory, with each new farm. In Israel the population reached two million in 1958, not 1960 as expected. Wells on the coastal plain dry up with accelerating frequency. Inexpensive conversion of sea water cannot for the next few years begin to fill the gap.

After the League's decision was announced Johnston said that for the time being there was no point in his returning to resume negotiations. The Israelis agreed to American arguments not to go ahead with the work at B'nat Ya'acov. But they continued work on the water diversion project. Instead of using B'nat Ya'acov as the take-off point they switched construction to Topha, outside the DZ, at the southern end of Lake Tiberias. Construction here was more expensive because equipment had to be installed to pump the water up from the low-lying lake, but it had the advantage of lying outside the complications of the DZ.

Jordan began work on her own water plan, based on the Yarmuk. Added to what Israel was doing, it bears a striking resemblance to the Johnston Plan as amended and agreed upon. There has been no official acknowledgement in the Arab countries that what is being done is part of the Plan previously rejected. The Arabs have still to decide whether or not they will cooperate in the exploitation and use of the waters, or fight.

[1] *Times*, Cairo Correspondent, 18th October 1955.

Chapter Ten

BOYCOTT AND BLOCKADE
(1949–56)

T HE purpose of the Arab boycott and blockade was to isolate Israel politically and economically, to drive her into economic and then political bankruptcy, and so into the hands of the Arabs. There were several advantages to this method: it was an acceptable substitute for force until the Arabs overcame their military inferiority; and it was an effective defence against the alleged economic power of Israel.

Because the Arab governments used the boycott and blockade as a substitute for military invasion it was essential to make it appear that these were in fact effective means of weakening and destroying Israel. Consequently, in the Arab Press and radio, one finds every sign of dissension in Israel, political instability, economic weakness and social tension, seized upon as evidence of the boycott's effects and of the steady deterioration of Israel. Understandably no effort was made to analyse these troubles in terms of Israel's aggregate difficulties, or to balance them by accounts of her positive achievements. (Israeli analyses of Arab affairs were slightly more objective.)

The principles of the political boycott were simple.[1] No Arab

---

[1] For pro-Israeli accounts of the boycott vd, Eytan, *loc. cit.*, pp. 83 *et seq.*; *Evidence of the Arab War in Peacetime Against Israel*, World Jewish Congress (New York, London, Jerusalem, 1957) pp. 50 *et seq.* MEM, LaB. *Egypt.*, and *Egyptian Economic and Political Review* contain considerable information about the Arab side of the boycott.

State would recognize Israel or make peace with her or meet with her representatives anywhere except in the MAC. The frontiers were closed and crossings allowed only in special cases. In the spheres of international organization and cooperation, no Arab would sit with Israel (except in the major organs of the UN where it was unavoidable). Israel was denied access to the regional offices of UN organizations, WHO, FAO, UNESCO, and ICAO, located in Arab countries. In order to accommodate Israel these organizations had either to take Israel into the European group or set up a separate office in Cyprus. This sort of activity was probably equally disadvantageous to the Arabs, since the Israelis were fairly advanced in these fields and, while undoubtedly an inconvenience, it could not be described as a danger to Israel.

As part of the political boycott the Arabs tried to persuade other countries, particularly those newly independent, not to recognize Israel. Despite some notable failures (Turkey, Ethiopia, Burma, Japan, the Philippines, Ceylon, Laos and Thailand) these efforts were largely successful. Neither Pakistan nor Indonesia, both Islamic powers, would recognize Israel. Those Asian states which recognized her, like India, approached the question of closer relations with considerable caution. The Arabs had the advantage, which the Israelis could not match, of the newly-formed Arab–Asian bloc. (The more amenable Afro–Asian bloc did not emerge until Ghana's independence in 1957.)

The Arabs' success amongst the Asians was watched with considerable anxiety by the Israelis. They had consistently hoped that through the medium of their own socialism and technology they would find much in common with the Asian countries, much support and much trade. This had been one of the main considerations behind the drive to Akaba in 1949. Now it all seemed to be for nothing. The Bandung Conference of Arab–Asian countries in the spring of 1955 stands as the high point of Arab efforts to isolate Israel from the rapidly growing bloc of newly-independent, neutral nations. The decision not to invite Israel was taken after much argument amongst the sponsors and after the Arabs had threatened to walk out. Since they composed one-third of the conference Israel's supporters backed down. Even so the Arabs' victory was not complete. Despite vigorous lobbying the Conference would agree only to a joint communiqué calling for the settlement of the Palestine question by peaceful means and on the basis of the UN resolutions.

The Bandung Conference marked the beginning of the end of the Arabs' ability to cut Israel off from Asia. Most Asian states, while willing to give audible signs of support for the Arabs, were unwilling to give up the practical benefits to be gained from friendly but discreet relations with Israel. After Bandung, Burmese Prime Minister U Nu visited Israel, and later Israeli technicians and experts went to some Asian countries. But in 1956 these were only small signs, insufficient to relieve the Israelis of that sense of oppression and isolation which so weighed them down during these years.

The economic effects of the boycott were more concrete and effective. There were two sides to the economic boycott. On the one hand it was a straightforward attempt to bankrupt Israel by cutting her off from all aid and trade from other countries. On the other it was a defensive manœuvre. The Arabs believed that Israel posed a serious economic threat to them and that she intended to dominate the entire Middle East commercially and financially. It was (and still is) thought that Israel had vast financial resources which would be instantly mobilized as soon as the boycott was removed in order to take over commercial and industrial development in the Arab countries, to control regional financing, and to establish Israel as *the* industrial centre of the Middle East. The Arabs believed that they could not stand against the supposed great economic potential of Israel and that they would become 'economic colonies' of Israel.[1] This belief, however unfounded on Israel's probable potential it may seem, was basic to the Arabs' reluctance to drop the boycott.

The boycott was first initiated in 1945 and directed unsuccessfully against all products of Palestine Jewry. After 1948 and the closing of the borders, it became somewhat more effective, but apparently many Arabs were unwilling to abide by its restrictions if it involved them in any personal financial loss.

[1] Examples of this trend of thinking abound: for example see Faris and Husayn, *loc. cit., passim.*

Kuweit and Bahrein sold oil to the Israelis. Cotton and other raw materials were often shipped to Israel *via* Italy, Greece and Cyprus. Egyptian sources claim that exports from Egypt to Israel increased from £E970,000 in 1949 to £E2,000,000 in 1951.[1] In this year, however, a Central Boycott Office was set up in Damascus with local offices in each Arab country to coordinate the work of the boycott.[2] Egypt and Iraq took the lead by establishing a series of strict controls to prevent direct or indirect trade with Israel; to prevent unintentional re-export to Israel; and to prevent unintentional import of Israel goods through 'front' companies abroad. Failure to comply with the regulations was punishable by up to ten years' hard labour. Similar controls were set up in the other Arab League countries, and by 1956 had been extended to Kuweit, Bahrein, the Sudan, Tunisia, Morocco, the Persian Gulf emirates, Libya and the Yemen.

Having set their own affairs in order the Arabs turned to the outside world. Most air and maritime companies refused to stop servicing Israel, and finally a compromise was reached whereby on any one voyage only Arab or Israeli ports would be visited. Both Lod and Haifa were transformed from important international transit points to local termini. Airlines diverted their eastern flights through Beirut or Cairo, and some stopped serving Israel entirely. There was no direct flight east from Israel until 1956 when *Air France* introduced a flight from Lod to Teheran *via* Turkey.

Attempts to prevent other countries from entering into trade relations with Israel were only partially successful. Hypothetically the Arabs could use their oil as a kind of economic bludgeon but in practice they could not for a number of reasons. The countries which did agree to have no or little trade with Israel were mostly Asian and some smaller European countries like Greece. But the United States supplied Israel with most of her aid, and Britain bought most of her citrus. Trade with Russia also increased rapidly, and substantial progress was made with

---

[1] *Al Misri*, quoted in *LaB. Egypt.*, 21st March 1952.
[2] Arab League Council Resolutions 468 and 482, 23rd September 1952: *Egypt and the United Nations, loc. cit.*, pp. 176–7; see also *MEM*, 17th January 1953, p. 11; *LaB. Egypt.*, 9th January 1953, 13th and 14th March 1953, 25th June 1953, and 4th July 1953.

other European countries. But such trade, aid and charitable assistance which Israel did receive in her first years were inadequate to her needs. This was due in part to the effects of the boycott, but more important were the heavy demands of nation-building, immigrant settlement, and defence. By 1952 Israel stood on the edge of bankruptcy. The government's New Economic Policy was described frankly as a last-ditch stand.

At this point the dispute over German Reparations came to the forefront.[1] For some time Israel and a representative Jewish body had been negotiating with West Germany for compensation for war crimes against the Jews. It was expected that part of the compensation would go to the Israel government, which stood as a kind of moral heir to the millions killed. Arab delegations were sent to Bonn to forestall the successful conclusion of the negotiations, and then to persuade the Bundestag not to ratify it. The Germans were threatened with complete boycott and, at one stage, the breach of diplomatic relations.[2] Political parties, the Press, commercial interests and industrialists were all approached. But the German government, supported by the Americans, stood firm, and the Agreement was signed and ratified. To sweeten the pill the Arabs were offered large long-term credits and technical aid. There was no boycott and no breach with Germany. German exports to the Arab countries increased fivefold between 1950 and 1956. It remains only to add that Israel got $715,000,000 in the form of goods over the next fourteen years; and that German reparations was the one single factor which saved Israel from economic ruin in 1952–3.

Unable to prevent countries from entering into trade agreements with Israel the Arabs tried to persuade particular companies not to sell to or buy from Israel. Companies doing business in the Arab countries and in Israel were given their choice of closing down in one or the other. In this way it was hoped to deprive Israel of her sources of raw and semi-finished materials, and of her commercial outlets. Without the necessary imports and exports Israeli commerce and industry would not be able to pay

---

[1] See Eytan, *loc. cit.*, pp. 90–1; Peretz, *loc. cit.*, p. 217; *JOMER*, 19th September 1952, p. 1; *MEM*, 22nd November 1952 and 17th January 1953, p. 8.

[2] But cf. *MEM*, 21st February 1953, p. 8, and 28th March 1953, p. 14, on the dangers of opposing German reparations to Israel.

their way. Over the years figures have been published of firms which have been boycotted by the Arabs or have left Israel but it is difficult to know what to make of these statistics since we do not know, for example, how many firms have continued business in Israel under different names. None the less, it is probable that the Arabs had considerable success. An elaborate espionage system was set up to discover who was doing business in Israel, and whether they were connected in any way with companies active in the Arab countries. If so, pressure could be brought to bear on the latter to stop the former. It was a cat-and-mouse game with the Israelis setting up front companies and the Arabs uncovering them, and new ones being set up. To this day it is not certain that the Boycott Office has succeeded in completely stopping even Arab exports to Israel through devious means.[1] Even so, despite their minor successes in circumventing the boycott, it cost the Israelis dearly.

The most unpleasant and reminiscent aspect of the boycott was its anti-Jewish bias. This was first manifested against Jews living in the Arab countries. From 1917 their position had not been easy, and soon the growing anti-Israel campaign included them as well. Reports from all the Arab countries indicate that the Jews there were subjected to increasingly heavy pressure designed to undermine their economic position, and to reduce them to second-class citizens.[2] In some Arab countries Jews were denied access to positions in the government, the Army (although this is understandable), banks, insurance companies and so on. At the same time there was an expanding campaign against Jews from other countries. Saudi Arabia, Iraq, Jordan and Syria refused entry to Jews regardless of nationality. The Arabs began to discriminate not only against firms dealing with Israel, but with 'Jewish firms' regardless of whether or not they

[1] In 1956 the writer saw Syrian goods on sale in Jerusalem shops.
[2] For example vd. *Radio Damascus*, 14th January and 16th February 1953, to the effect that Jews everywhere are traitors to the countries in which they live. (All references to radio broadcasts are taken from the BBC, *Summary of World Broadcasts*, Part 4)
In June 1953 the Arab Chambers of Commerces made a number of recommendations to their governments designed to drive Arab Jews out of finance and commerce; see *JAD*, 26th June 1953, p. 947; also *MEM*, 18th October 1953, p. 19; *JAD*, 4th June 1954, p. 487, and 3rd February 1956, pp. 634–5, quoting *Al Difa*, 26th January 1956.

had any trade with Israel. By 1955, this policy had become widespread and highly organized. Firms seeking contacts in the Arab countries and firms already there were questioned closely as to the religious affiliations of the owners, directors, managers and workers. At one point a questionnaire was circulated abroad amongst business firms,[1] but protests from the various Chambers of Commerce led to its withdrawal, and the usual methods of private investigation continued.

This kind of anti-Jewish activity could not harm Israel. It would, on the contrary, serve to strengthen, particularly amongst the numerous non-Zionist Jews, the feeling of the Jew's distinctiveness and his vulnerability even where he personally bore no responsibility for what had been done. From such a feeling Israel stood only to gain. Given the futility of this kind of boycott and the persistence and publicity with which it was implemented, one can only assume that it was motivated by other than economic or political considerations. Whether or not he was right, the ordinary Jew could be excused for believing that he knew what these other considerations were.

In the early years the Israelis showed little concern over the boycott. They seldom mentioned it and then only to argue that it had failed because of US grants-in-aid; or that the Arabs would have to drop it because it hurt them more than Israel; or that the Haifa Refinery was too valuable to Iraq for her to continue not to supply it. When the Arabs refused to cooperate in these illusions, emphasis was switched to the benefits of the boycott: for example, it forced Israel to develop independently of the economically unstable Arab countries. Inexorably, how-

---

[1] Questions one to four pertained to business relations with Israel. The remainder were as follows:

5. Do you have any Jewish employees in your company; if yes, how many and what are the positions held by them?
6. Are there any Jews on your board of directors as members?
7. Is any one of your managers or branch managers a Jew; if yes, please give the name of the department headed by such a man.
8. Is any one of the persons authorized to sign on behalf of your Company a Jew?
9. What is the number of Jewish workers in your factories and offices?

NYHT, Coblenz, 9th February 1956; *JAD*, 6th July 1956, pp. 1,345–8. See also *NYT*, 2nd December 1955, and 26th January 1956; *Times*, NY Correspondent, 29th December 1955, also 26th January 1956.

ever, with the growing awareness of Israel's extremely difficult economic position, the effects of the boycott could no longer be passsed off so lightly.

Rather than just talking about the boycott as a part of the plan to destroy them, the Israelis began to feel it as such.[1] By 1953, it was sincerely believed to be a potent weapon in the hands of the Arabs, a weapon which had to be destroyed before it destroyed Israel. This idea rapidly took hold and by 1956 was an article of faith. This corresponded with the deepening mood of isolation and insecurity throughout Israel generally, and was probably as much an effect of that mood as a cause. There was, however, little the Israelis could do. The boycott lay entirely outside the competence of the armistice machinery and of international law.

The concrete effects of the boycott are difficult to assess. The Israelis were right in saying that, over the short period anyway, it hurt the Arabs more than it did them. Before 1948 Palestine was the Arab States' best customer. She imported about five times more from them than did Egypt and seven times more than Iraq. She took about thirty per cent of Syria's exports and over ninety per cent of Jordan's. To make up Palestine's trade deficit about one-third of Zionist funds sent there went to the Arab countries. But even if the boycott hurt the Arabs it also deprived Israel of readily accessible, cheap material and goods. The losses were considerable. Some Israelis claim that the boycott plus the blockade cost them up to a hundred million dollars a year; others take a more conservative figure of fifty million dollars.[2]

These figures, however, do not tell the whole story. In 1949, Israel had a trade deficit of over two hundred million dollars; in 1951, it was over three hundred million dollars; and in 1954, it

[1] For example see *Israel Economist*, April 1953, p. 73: a case of propagandist turned prophet.

[2] Another estimate places the loss by 1954 at $120,000,000, i.e. the value of Arab property abandoned in 1948: *JAD*, December 1954, p. 310. Useful analyses can be found in *Commentary*, 1952, August 1953, September 1958; *Foreign Affairs*, January 1954; *Journal of International Affairs* No. 2, 1952; *Middle Eastern Affairs*, October 1955; and Israel Central Bureau of Statistics and Economic Research, esp. October 1955; *Israel's Foreign Trade* (Jerusalem 1954), special series No. 23.

was two hundred million dollars. Clearly the boycott was not the main reason for Israel's economic difficulties. The end of the boycott would have meant immediate large savings in transportation costs, fuel and bread grains : possibly as much as thirty million dollars. It is almost impossible to assess what might have been gained from the consequent expanded tourist industry and regional development plans such as the Jordan Valley Authority, and from new markets for commerce and industry. Whatever the first two might have brought in, Israel's long-term prosperity depended on the last. But, as the figures quoted above show, whatever the possibilities abroad, Arab markets for Israeli goods were limited, despite Arab fears. First of all, the lifting of the boycott would not necessarily be followed by trade agreements or by low tariffs. Secondly, the kind of goods Israel would export to the Arab countries—for example pharmaceuticals, cosmetics, diamonds, fertilizers, expensive clothing and leather goods—would not find much of a market amongst a largely poor population. At the same time Israel would have to admit Arab goods.

This brings us to one of the distinct advantages of the boycott. Although it caused the Israelis to suffer severe food shortages in the first few years, it did provide the incentive for the development of Israeli agriculture. Possibly, had the Arabs' cheap agricultural produce not been excluded, Israel's own more expensive agricultural economy would have been wrecked. The boycott also forced the Israelis to develop their own resources at a rate which otherwise would have seemed impracticable. The boycott served to stimulate heavy Jewish investment—as distinct from Zionist charity—in Israel, and thereby to strengthen Israel's connexions with the Diaspora. It is also possible to argue that Israeli industry benefited from having to sell in the highly competitive European and American markets. One wonders what would have happened to Israeli economic development had not the incentive of the boycott been there.

Israel's economic problems derived ultimately from the nature of the land and the very high rate of immigration. These same factors had existed during Mandatory days when there was trade with the Arabs, and there is little reason to suppose that a resumption of that trade would have led to any radical improvement. To take this reasoning a step farther: the losses caused by the boycott were substantial, but a much greater loss was sustained through the expenses of national conscription, buying arms, reserve training, para-military organizations; the millions of work days lost in call-ups during emergencies, in maintaining and expanding border defences, and in the losses suffered through sabotage, theft and murder. As we know from our own experience, good trade relations and frequent statements of peaceful intentions do not always alleviate the need to maintain a high degree of military preparedness.

One aspect of the boycott—the almost complete absence of communication between the Israelis and the Arabs—which deserves mention is, its effect upon thinking in Israel. The Israelis were, for all practical purposes, completely isolated from their neighbours, their enemies. Ordinarily this condition obtains only in wartime when relations between countries have so deteriorated that they see each other only on the battlefield. The isolation of the Israelis, the pressures put upon them in the way of propaganda and border raids—considering the conditions under which he lived, the ordinary Israeli did not see much difference between the effects of haphazard border marauding and the *fedayeen*—would naturally encourage a wartime atmosphere. But in this case there was no satisfactory way to strike back. At best retaliation raids were only a palliative. Obviously this atmosphere did much to help weld the diverse sections of a rapidly expanding population into a united, cohesive nation. At the same time it fostered the growth of a kind of morbid introversion and hysterical rationality engendered by the whole ethos of modern Jewish history. The consequence was not, as the Arabs hoped, to break the Israelis' spirit, but to make them more militant, to encourage extremism, to incite a sense of desperation which could find its only outlet in the use of force. This was not what the Arabs had been trying to achieve.

Chapter Eleven

THE BLOCKADE

THE dispute over the Suez Blockade[1] was in many ways a microcosm of the complexities and confusions of Arab–Israeli relations.

The Blockade began in December 1947 with the closure of the Suez Canal to all shipping destined for Zionist hands in Palestine, and from 1948 on affected all shipping proceeding to and from Israel. In May 1949 the Israelis complained to the MAC that the Blockade was a breach of Article Two, paragraph two, in which all hostile or warlike acts by military or para-military forces were forbidden. The Egyptians replied that the Article did not apply because only civilian authorities were involved; and that in any case the Blockade touched upon a 'political problem which is outside the competence of the MAC'.[2] The Chairman voted with Egypt but a month later in August he reversed his decision. Egypt appealed to the Special Committee.[3]

Subsequently the Blockade restrictions were relaxed, and in January 1950, for the first time since 1947, a ship carrying goods

---

[1] Although commonly used, the term 'blockade' is a misnomer because the Arabs never tried to seal off Israel's coastline. A proper blockade would have involved the use of military forces and not only would it have breached the GAA, but according to international law would have provided Israel with a *casus belli*.

[2] *E–IMAC*, 11th mtg., 31st May 1949; 12th mtg., 8th June 1949.

[3] *ibid*, 17th and 18th mtgs., 29th August and 3rd September 1949. The Special Committee exists in the Egyptian GAA only, and acts as a final court of appeal on 'questions of principle'.

for Israel was allowed through the Suez Canal. On 6th February, however, a Royal Decree was promulgated by the Egyptian government defining war contraband and the procedure of visit, search and seizure.[1] The stated purpose of the Royal Decree was to ensure that 'no arms, munitions, war materials or other articles considered as war contraband . . . [are] shipped directly or indirectly to institutions or persons on Palestinian Territory under Zionist control' (Article Two). Force could be used at all times against any ship attempting to avoid search (Article Three), and the cargo could be unloaded if it was considered necessary (Article Eight). Ships which had carried 'war contraband for the Zionists', shipowners or consignees associated with the Zionists or with close connexions with concerns situated on enemy territory, and consigners and consignees already on the blacklist, were all to be considered suspect. War contraband was defined as: military equipment and materials; chemicals, drugs, etc., capable of being used for chemical warfare; fuel; aircraft, ships, motorized vehicles, spare parts; all forms of money, metals, raw materials, planks, machinery and all other objects necessary for its manufacture or adaptable to that purpose (Article Ten). Ships found contravening these restrictions were to be blacklisted and their cargoes confiscated. Blacklisting meant denial of food, water, fuel and repair facilities at Egyptian ports. During the following months further provisions were passed to elucidate and consolidate these restrictions. During this time the Blockade itself was not applied with any consistency.

Finally, in January 1951, the Special Committee began to discuss the matter. The meetings went on for five months. It was during this time that Egypt explicitly enunciated the unexpected doctrine of juridical *status belli*, and consequently of belligerent rights. The Special Committee decided, Israel dissenting, that the Blockade did not fall within the compass of the GAA.

General Riley, UNTSO Chief of Staff, told the MAC that he had no doubt that Egyptian interference with goods destined for Israel was both a hostile and an aggressive action. But, he went on, because of the limitations imposed by the text of the GAA

[1] Quoted in *SCOR*, S/3179, 15th February 1954.

(Article Two, Paragraph Two) on the meaning of the term 'aggressive action', the Blockade was not necessarily a contravention of the GAA. So long as the Blockade was not being implemented by Egyptian military or para-military forces it was not a breach of the armistice provisions. Since he could base his decision only on the armistice provisions he was forced to accept Egypt's contention that the question lay outside the competence of the MAC. Riley went on, however, to emphasize strongly that the matter could not be allowed to rest there. To his way of thinking the Blockade was entirely contrary to the spirit of the GAA which was never meant to act as a cloak for hostile acts by either party. He warned in unmistakeable terms that the whole General Armistice Agreement was gravely jeopardized. If the situation was not to deteriorate either Egypt had to lift the Blockade, or the dispute had to be taken to a higher authority.[1]

Israel took her complaint to the Security Council where discussion began in July 1951, two years after the original complaint had been laid. The debate came at an inopportune time. The Middle East was more unsettled than usual. Abdullah had been assassinated just six days previously. There was trouble over oil in Iran. Egypt abounded with domestic difficulties and the position of the government was more than ordinarily insecure. The Americans argued that this was not the time to discuss the Blockade, because any well-publicized attempt to make the Egyptian government change its policy would only strengthen its determination not to. Furthermore, Western interference over Suez would harm the chances of establishing a Middle East Defence Organization. The Americans argued for either putting the debate off or else adopting an innocuous resolution not injurious to Egyptian sensibilities. The British disagreed. They wanted to resume oil shipments from Iraq to the Haifa Refinery which was badly needed to supply European post-war reconstruction. They argued that the diplomatic approach had been unsuccessful for two years and that there was no reason to assume that it would succeed now: strong, uncompromising action by the Council was necessary. In the end it was agreed to submit a strong joint draft resolution to the Council, but to hold

[1] *SCOR*, S/2194, 12th June 1951.

off voting while efforts were made to persuade the Egyptian government to moderate its policy of its own accord.

We have already discussed the central issues: the question of juridical or technical *status belli*, the main arguments pro and con, and the manner in which the Council avoided touching upon them. To recapitulate briefly: the Israelis argued that neither the UN Charter nor the GAA included any provision for a technical *status belli* or the exercise of belligerent rights, and that therefore Egypt was not justified in exercising them. They also argued that the Blockade violated the law of the freedom of the seas and the provisions of the Convention of Constantinople (1888) which guaranteed the right of free passage through the Canal to ships of all nations during times of war as well as of peace. By the exercise of visit, search and seizure Egypt was unlawfully encroaching on the sovereignty of the maritime nations concerned and of Israel. Speaking for the Israelis, Abba Eban admitted that the Special Committee had ruled against them but argued that the Council could not accept 'an unduly restrictive interpretation' of the armistice provisions which permitted hostile acts if committed by non-military authorities. He concluded by repeating Riley's warning that if the Council upheld Egypt the whole structure of the armistice might collapse.[1]

Speaking for Egypt, Mahmoud Fawzi replied that the issue had already been settled in the Special Committee, the decision of which was final. Consequently Eban's references to the Charter, the Convention of Constantinople and the GAA were irrelevant. After repeating the legal arguments in favour of Egypt's position he went on to point out that the exercise of visit, search and seizure was only the bare minimum of rights allowed to parties to an armistice agreement. Then he contended that the Royal Decree of February 1950 was the 'culmination, so far, of a continuous process of relaxing the measures imposed by Egypt'. As proof he cited the steady growth of traffic using the Canal (he did not say what proportion was destined for Israel). Subsidiary arguments were that Egypt was entitled, according to the terms of Article Fifty-one of the UN Charter and to various provisions of the Convention of Constantinople, to take measures necessary for self-defence against

[1] *SCOR*, 549th mtg., 26th July 1951, pp. 2–13.

the 'endlessness of the wild ambitions of world political Zionism, of which Israel is the spearhead'.[1]

Most Council members spoke of the unreasonableness of 'declaring war' two years after an armistice had been signed, and of the dangerous consequences this might have. The British delegate argued that 'the so-called' right of self-defence 'at any rate, to my delegation, seems to be a very vague conception'. According to the Charter it arose only in the instance of armed invasion, which was clearly not the case here; and its exercise could be continued only until the Security Council had taken the measures necessary to maintain international peace and security. He also referred to what was undoubtedly uppermost in his mind: Egypt's refusal to allow oil shipments through to the Haifa Refinery, and the subsequent loss of its refining capacity.[2] He did not find it necessary to add that most of the Council members were affected by this loss.

The Council adjourned for two weeks while unsuccessful efforts were made to persuade Egypt to moderate her policy.[3] A joint draft resolution was submitted calling upon Egypt to lift the Blockade. Both the Indian and the Chinese delegates made the obvious comment that the resolution paid insufficient attention to Egypt's legal rights in the matter. But the general opinion of the Council was that even if there were a *status belli* 'this would in itself afford no justification for the maintenance of the restrictions at the present time and in the light of the present situation'. There was another short delay while last-minute appeals were made to the Egyptian government. Eventually on 1st September the Council adopted the resolution (Russia abstained) calling for the lifting of the Blockade.[4]

Reactions to the resolution were mixed. The Israelis went away pleased. The British warned the Egyptians that so far they had been treated with 'extraordinary leniency'.[5] The Egyptians were naturally disappointed, particularly in Russia from whom

---

[1] *ibid, passim,* and 550th mtg., 1st August 1951.

[2] *ibid,* 550th mtg.

[3] *Times,* UN Correspondent, 18th and 21st August 1951, and Istanbul Correspondent, 28th August 1951; *CSM,* 21st August 1951; *JAD,* 27th July 1951, p. 1761; *NYT,* leader, 9th August 1951; *Times,* leader, 10th and 22nd August 1951.

[4] *SCOR,* S/2322, 1st September 1951.

[5] *Times,* leader, 3rd September 1951.

they had expected more positive assistance. They stated that they would ignore the resolution, and subsequently they announced that there would be the strictest application of the restrictions.[1]

Privately, the Egyptians hinted that these statements were only for domestic consumption and that blacklisted ships were being allowed through the Canal—although without access to port facilities. In 1952 an Italian ship did pass safely through the Canal on its way to Haifa; between October 1952 and November 1953 the Israelis complained of only six detentions. This, however, is only one side of the picture. It does not tell us how many shipowners refused to take Israeli cargoes through the Canal. The Israelis claim that in 1946–7 about 176,000 tons of goods, excluding oil, reached Haifa through the Canal. In 1953 there were only 15,000 tons, excluding oil, now a negligible quantity.[2] Thus, despite her increase in trade since 1947, Israeli trade through the Canal in 1953 was ninety per cent less than it had been then. In November 1953, two years after Egypt had told the Council about the progressive relaxation of blockade restrictions and in the middle of what was supposedly an Egyptian–Israel *rapprochement*, foodstuffs were put on the contraband list, along with 'all other commodities likely to strengthen Israel's war potential'. The new restrictions came at the same time as trade negotiations between Israel and India and Pakistan. The Israelis could hardly ignore the implications. The memorandum appended to the new restrictions left no doubt of their aim, despite the Egyptians' private assurance to the Israelis about peaceful relations.[3] The next month, December 1953, two more cargoes were confiscated; and in January a merchantman attempting to reach Eilat was fired on in the Straits of Tiran and forced to return. The blockade now applied to all Israeli trade passing through the Canal and through the Red Sea and the Straits of Tiran into the Gulf of Akaba.

The Gulf of Akaba is an indentation about 180 kilometres long running between the west coast of the Sinai Peninsula and the

[1] *NYT*, 3rd September 1951; *Times*, Cairo Correspondent, 4th and 5th September 1951; *LaB. Egypt.* 5th September 1951.

[2] Eban, *SCOR*, 661st mtg., 12th February 1954, p. 30.

[3] *MEM*, 17th January 1953, p. 11; *SCOR*, S/3168 and Add. 1, 29th January 1954.

east coast of Saudi Arabia. From east to west it impinges upon the territory of Saudi Arabia, Jordan, Israel and Egypt. At the head of the Gulf are the Straits of Tiran in which lie the islands of Senafir and Tiran. The only navigable channel lies between Tiran and the Egyptian coast, a distance of about three nautical miles. It was here that the blockade was established and the incidents took place.[1]

In 1949, with the consent of Saudi Arabia, Egypt set up military installations on the previously uninhabited islands of Senafir and Tiran. At that time official assurances were given that there would be no interference with the free passage of shipping. The promise was never kept. In July 1951, a British ship carrying arms for Jordan was fired on and prevented from entering the Gulf. In January and March 1953, a Danish ship headed for Eilat was detained and then released; in September 1953 a Greek ship *en route* to Eilat was detained and her cargo confiscated, on leaving Eilat part of her cargo was confiscated again; and in January 1954 an Italian ship headed for Eilat was fired on and prevented from entering the Gulf. In all instances the Egyptians stated that they had acted to prevent ships reaching Israel. The number of ships involved was not very large, but neither was the existing traffic through the Straits. At this time Eilat was still an unimportant port, even by Israeli standards. But it had great potential as an outlet to Asia and Africa, and without access through the Straits development in the southern Negev was stifled.

A few weeks after the last incident, the Egyptians set up new controls over traffic through the Straits. The effect was to prevent all shipping from reaching or leaving Eilat. Unlike the blockade at Suez where the occasional ship was let through, that at the Gulf was complete. Eilat was sealed off. The Egyptians claimed that the Straits lay within their territorial waters, and that belligerent rights entitled them to visit, search and seizure. The Israelis denied that Egypt could exercise belligerent rights. More important, they insisted that because four separate states lay along the Gulf, the Gulf and the entrance to it constituted, according to international law, an international waterway over

---

[1] A comprehensive, if tendentious account can be found in Bloomfield, *Egypt, Israel and the Gulf of Akaba.*

which none of the riparian states had sovereignty or special right.[1]

The Council began discussing the Blockade again in February 1954. This time the Western Powers were even less enthusiastic about sponsoring Israel's complaints because of difficulties in the Anglo–Egyptian negotiations over Suez. The Israelis, however, pressed on, anxious to obtain firm Council action before the British withdrew from the Canal Zone. This debate followed on the heels of the futile Council discussions on B'nat Ya'acov, and once again was marked by the ineffectuality of the Council in the face of a Russian veto. The arguments were the same as those put forward previously. Eban warned that Israel had reached 'a turning point in the security of our region'. Fawzi gave the Council a lesson in Charter law by pointing out that the previous resolution was formulated in such a way that it could only be a recommendation, not an order; and that, therefore, Egypt was entirely within her rights in refusing to implement it. After forty-six days of debate and private discussion a draft resolution was put forward by New Zealand.[2] The resolution was unremarkable, following the 'commonsense' approach of its predecessor. Russia vetoed it on the grounds that because the previous one had failed, the only way for the question to be settled was by direct negotiations between Egypt and Israel; however, the Russian delegate did not put forward any resolution to this effect.

Eban announced that his government would 'wish to examine with care the position created by the fact that no resolution recognizing Israel's fundamental rights under the GAA appears capable of adoption by the Security Council, even when the majority supports it'. Fawzi announced that Egypt, freed from outside interference, would 'of its own free will move towards tolerance'. From February to October 1954 shipping to and from Israel passed through the Canal without being stopped.[3] The Egyptians were anxious not to antagonize the Americans

---

[1] See *Revue Egyptienne du Droit International*, 1950; and Israel Foreign Ministry, *Background Paper on the Gulf of Akaba* (Jerusalem, May 1956).

[2] *SCOR*, S/3188/Corr. 1, 19th March 1954.

[3] Eighteen to and fifty-two from Israel. These figures illustrated the effectiveness of the blockade, since they were but ' a tiny fraction of what they would have been ordinarily': Eban, *ibid*, 683rd mtg., 3rd November 1954, p. 3.

or to give the British an excuse for not leaving the Canal by a tactless implementation of the Blockade restrictions.

Britain agreed to evacuate the Canal Zone without obtaining guarantees for Israel, and America subsequently decided to supply Egypt with arms. Assurances that Britain continued 'to desire a settlement in accordance with the Security Council resolutions', and that British policy was 'governed by the Tripartite Declaration'[1] were hardly reassuring to the Israelis, considering previous developments. With Russia supporting the Arabs, and the West anxious to repair the sins and omissions of previous centuries, the Israelis were exceedingly uneasy about their future prospects. For Israel as well as Egypt the summer of 1954 marked a decisive turning point, and a watershed of future developments.

On 28th September the Israeli ship *Bat Galim* was seized at Port Suez.[2] This was the first time the Israelis had attempted to send one of their own vessels through the Canal, determined that the Egyptians should declare themselves on the issue of free passage before the Anglo–Egyptian treaty or the American arms agreement were finalized. True to form, the *Bat Galim* case went before the Council for three months of fruitless debate and negotiation. Fearful of another Russian veto the Council members did not bring in a draft resolution. Instead the Council President summed up the 'general trend' of Council opinion: the 1951 resolution was still valid and in effect, and the crew, cargo and vessel should be released. Subsequently the crew was sent back to Israel, but the ship and the cargo were confiscated.

The Canal issue lay dormant. Few shipping companies would agree to try to run the Blockade for Israel. Attention turned to

[1] Letter from Anthony Eden to Eliahu Elath: Israel Foreign Ministry Press release (n.d.).

[2] The Egyptians claimed that the *Bat Galim* had opened fire and killed several people. The UNTSO found no substantiating evidence: the ship was armed with one unserviceable pistol. Despite the seriousness of the charge the Egyptians were most reluctant to discuss it in the MAC or anywhere else. After the longest session of filibustering any MAC had suffered, the Egyptians finally brought a draft resolution charging that the ship had entered Egyptian territorial waters, that this was a breach of the GAA, and that Israel should not do this again. The Israelis pointed out that this had nothing to do with Egypt's original complaint. The draft resolution was voted down, and the MAC found that Egypt's complaint was 'unfounded'. Later the Special Committee changed this to read 'unsubstantiated', as the former term reflected unfavourably on the Egyptians.

the Gulf of Akaba. By the beginning of 1955 the Egyptians had established a complete blockade of the Straits of Tiran: no ship was allowed through unless it had given prior notice; and no ships were allowed to proceed to Eilat. The Israeli port was completely cut off. The Israelis could do little about Suez. Distance, political boundaries, legalities and the international situation constituted virtually insurmountable obstacles. But their position in the Gulf was straightforward, their rights more clear-cut, and their ability to defend those rights much greater. In September 1955, Ben Gurion announced that he wanted another year in which to implement an emergency programme for settling strategic areas of the Negev, for building adequate lines of communication and for extending port facilities at Eilat. When this had been accomplished Israel would ask Egypt once more to lift the Blockade at Tiran—this time directly, and not through the Council or any other organization. If Nasser were as reasonable as some people said, then there would be no trouble. But, Ben Gurion said, if the Blockade were maintained Israel would use force. The Gulf of Akaba, he promised, would be open for Israeli shipping 'in one year or less', preferably as the result of negotiations, but if not, then by force.[1] (Thirteen months later Israel invaded Egypt.)

After Egypt nationalized the Suez Canal in July 1956 Israel tried to raise the issue of the Blockade once again, but with no success. Egypt stated that the Blockade would be maintained. The United States was unwilling to press Israel's claim in such unstable circumstances. From the American point of view this was undoubtedly the proper line to take; but one could hardly expect the Israelis to be satisfied.

In summation, the boycott did leave Israel with some benefits. The effect of the Blockade, however, was to prevent the economic exploitation of these benefits. There were always ways of circumventing the boycott, but if the Israelis could not get ships to and from the markets then it was all for nothing. It is impossible to determine the cost of the Blockade to Israel. In 1950 Eban told the Council that it ran to tens of millions of pounds in direct costs. Even assuming that he was exaggerating, it still must have been considerable. Furthermore it would have

[1] *NYT*, Love, 11th and 27th September 1955.

increased steadily as Israel's export potential developed but had to remain only partially exploited. By 1956, the losses, direct and indirect, must have been crippling. Even if she were not driven into bankruptcy, Israel faced reduction to a stagnant backwater of economic development, and an eventual easy prey for the rapidly developing Arab countries.

The Israelis' failure to obtain redress of their grievances through the armistice machinery, and the failure of the Security Council to deal with the problem effectively, whatever the reasons, threw the Israelis back on their own resources.

Chapter Twelve

ISRAEL AND EGYPT
PART ONE: TO GAZA (1949–55)

FOR the first few years the Egyptian General Armistice Agreement worked well. The political tensions which poisoned relations in the Jordan and Syrian MACs took much longer to seep in here. Both delegations had adequate authority to deal with most problems, and there was good faith, trust, and perhaps even friendship on both sides. Formal meetings of the MAC were held regularly once a month to discuss general problems, and no motions of censure or condemnation were presented. Most complaints were dealt with informally by sub-committees. During the first year, even though a number of people were killed, only one emergency meeting was held.

Reading the records of this first year or two, the general impression one receives is of a mutual desire to cooperate which was backed up by two governments. Why? (that one feels it necessary to ask the question is indicative of the ethos of Arab–Israeli relations). After all, there were fertile grounds for trouble. The Gaza Strip was five miles wide and twenty-five miles long. Into it were packed about 120,000 residents plus the same number of refugees, all living on sand dunes, semi-desert, and beach. There was a great deal of infiltration, with the attendant robberies, murders, and retaliation. The border situation was often serious, and not seldom grave. Neither singly nor in cooperation were the means available to control it.

But each side believed that the other was doing the best it

could to improve matters, and that nothing could be gained by acrimony. Egypt did not consider the dispute with Israel to be of primary importance. The Sinai desert separated Cairo from Israel, Gaza and the refugees. Cairo had its own problems. The Blockade could be applied with relative impunity, but an angry border was an unnecessary and dangerous luxury. Gaza itself was isolated and vulnerable, hemmed in by the sea, the desert and the Israelis. It was to Egypt's interest to cooperate in the MAC, whatever the difficulties. The Israelis wanted Egypt's friendship and believed that with patience and cooperation they could have it. So long as the Egyptians were doing what they could to control the refugees the Israelis were satisfied to accept the *status quo* on the border. Moreover, the sheer weight of events along the Syrian and Jordanian borders occupied those militants who otherwise might have demanded a more active policy. Thus, during the first year or so, a basis existed for a limited degree of cooperation and effective action.

But the pressures of the refugee problem could not be dispersed by the half-way measures of limited cooperation. The whole strip was seething with discontent. Infiltrators were increasingly active, and bloodshed increasingly common. Matters went from bad to worse in July 1950 when the Israelis, in one of their ruthless, ill-considered actions which did so much to anger the Arabs (and the UNTSO) and to stimulate violent infiltration, began to expel all the beduin living in the Majdal and El Auja districts.[1] All in all, about eight to nine thousand Arabs were expelled into Egypt and the Gaza Strip, often with great brutality. Planes and army personnel carried out the operation, driving the beduin before them. Tents, livestock, crops, and possessions were burnt. The Israelis claimed that these beduin were members of the Azazmeh tribe who had been in Egypt when the armistice lines were fixed, and therefore should not have been in Israel at all. Furthermore, the Israeli said, they had fought alongside the Egyptians in 1948-9, and since their return to Israel had been engaged in acts of theft and violence. The Egyptians and the beduin pointed out that the tribe had been based in the Negev for generations, and that their expul-

---

[1] Many Arabs were also expelled into Jordan under similar circumstances: see Peretz, *Israel and the Palestine Arabs* and Hutchison, *Violent Truce, passim.*

sion across the armistice lines was a violation of Article Five of the GAA.

The matter was taken to the Security Council and then returned to Riley and the MAC. Eventually the MAC decided, Israel dissenting, that the evictions were a breach of the armistice, and that the beduin should be allowed to return. The Israelis refused. The effect of the expulsions was to increase the rate of deterioration along the border. Between January and October 1951 over 166 complaints were submitted to the MAC, more than three-quarters of them coming from Israel. Armed attacks and mining incidents were frequent. Israeli settlers became more and more restless, and there was a corresponding rise in Egyptian complaints. The principle of unanimity in the MAC broke down. The end was in sight. Egyptian insistence on maintaining a *status belli* did not improve matters.

In October 1952, the MAC stopped meeting, and no further regular meetings were held for ten months, until after the Egyptian Revolution. During that time 314 new complaints were put on the agenda. After seven months, in May 1952, an emergency meeting was called to deal with the chaos along the border.[1] The situation was worse here than on any of the other borders.

The MAC Chairman sent a letter to Egypt pointing out, in strong terms, the probable results of her inadequate cooperation. The Israelis claimed that the local police were apathetic and had no authority. Furthermore, it was alleged that Egyptian military intelligence was involved in the recurrent incidents of robbery and sabotage. The Israelis pointed out that unless Egypt cooperated fully, force would be used against her. Subsequently, preventive measures, including mixed patrols, were agreed upon, and sent to sub-committee to work out the details. But the measures were never implemented, and the situation did not improve.

Then on 23rd July 1952 the 'Committee of Free Officers' overthrew the Egyptian government, and replaced it with a military junta. On 26th July King Farouk abdicated. The revolution was over; the Revolution had begun. Israel was part of that Revolution.

[1] *E–IMAC*, Emergency meeting, 4th May 1952.

To Israel, Egypt was 'the most important country'. Abdullah might drag the Arabs into a war with Israel, but only Egypt had the resources to carry it on. Abdullah might initial a draft treaty with Israel, but it could not be implemented without Egypt's consent. Egypt ran the Arab League; Egypt had the Suez Canal; Egypt had twenty million people. Without Egypt the Arabs' ability to oppose Israel would collapse. With Egypt it could continue. Only with Egypt could it be successful. The Israelis knew this, but they could not decide what to do about it. If the border situation was bad, striking at Gaza had little effect in Cairo. If the blockade at the Canal was onerous, appeals to the Security Council were futile. What then was Israel to do?

There was an influential group in Israel, including Prime Minister Ben Gurion, who, in the early years, believed that patience and placation would triumph; that in time Egypt's circumstances would lead her to seek a settlement with Israel. They believed that domestic unrest and the struggle against the British would force Egypt to ensure peace on her eastern frontier; and that there were no objective reasons for territorial disputes between the two countries. The Sinai Desert was a natural buffer zone, large and uninviting. The Gaza Strip itself was of negligible importance and, so far as the refugees there were concerned, the Israelis believed that there was substantial agreement on the various ways to deal with the problem. Similarly, in the economic and political spheres, it was unlikely that Israel would ever threaten Egypt's position. At the same time, these Israelis argued, the two countries had similar interests. Neither wished to see Abdullah's territories or influence extended; and both wished to see an end to British imperialism in the Middle East.

In sum, according to this line of reasoning, not only did Israel and Egypt have few interests which conflicted, but they had many in common; and these could form the basis of a conciliation. Naïve as this analysis was, unregarding of the 'objectivity' of psychological obstacles, it was not so wide of the mark. The Egyptian government did not feel compelled to make peace, but as its international position deteriorated—what with the disputes over the abrogation of the Anglo–Egyptian treaty, over the rejection of Western plans for a Middle East Defence Organization, and over the Sudan—it seemed wise to keep Israel friendly. Some contacts were made and by 1952 there was open talk by high officials in Cairo of the possibility of a peace settlement.[1] Talk, a few contacts between governments, and some newspaper articles do not make a peace movement, and it is hard to say just how far the Egyptian government was prepared to go, or even if there had been a decision to go anywhere. But the Israelis were quietly optimistic.

Prospects brightened out of all recognition when the revolution came. To understand how the Israelis felt at that time we must understand how closely the revolution fitted in with their notions of peace with the Arabs. The Israelis' fundamental doctrine was that the Arabs would seek Israel's cooperation: this was 'a moral, a political, an economic necessity'. The historical needs and conditions of the Arabs would not only encourage but compel them to work together with the Israelis. The two needed and complemented each other. If the Arabs did not 'learn from us and labour with us' then they would have to do it with 'strangers, potent and tyrannous', the imperialists.[2] The Israelis saw themselves as a bridge between the civilized West and the backward East, transmitting culture, knowledge and experience from one to the other. They would bring the social and economic revolution to the Arab world; they were the harbingers of the modern, progressive, and independent Middle East.

The Arabs' predictable lack of enthusiasm for this particular brand of messianism provoked the further analysis that anti-Israel sentiment was fostered by the reactionary elements in the Arab countries: the feudal landlords, the sheikhs, the old-time politicians, those groups which had the most to lose by Israeli-typified socialism. Just a few months before the Revolution, Ben Gurion had told the Knesset to be patient: there could be no peace so long as the Arabs were led by reactionaries; the prerequisite of peace was the establishment of 'liberal and democratic

[1] *Al Balagh, Al Ahram, Al Makattam* and *Rose el Yossuf*, referred to in *JP*, Diplomatic Correspondent, 3rd and 12th March 1952; *JOMER*, 5th April 1952, p. 1, and 25th April 1952, p. 12; also 29th February 1954; *NYT*, 4th March 1952; and *NYHT*, 10th March 1952.

[2] David Ben Gurion, *Rebirth and Destiny of Israel*, p. 219.

governments' in the Arab countries. The weaknesses of this line of reasoning did not at that time detract from its influence. With the failure of the CCP and the general consolidation of Arab hostility, the Israelis had nothing else to believe in. If it was invalid then there was little hope for the future.

The Israelis needed this revolution more than the Egyptians. The widely-trumpeted glories of Zionist state-creating had hidden from the outside world the harsh, hammering realities of state-building in the early 1950's. Each year had its own special hardship—1952 was the worst yet. The country was locked in the grip of rigid, deadening austerity, crippling taxes, and poverty. Outside aid and charitable support were falling off rapidly. Only German reparations had prevented bankruptcy and collapse. The border situation was murderous. The international position was one of growing isolation. The Republicans were now in power in the United States; Zionist influence had followed the Democrats into the wilderness. Russia's anti-Zionist, anti-Israel campaign continued to accelerate, culminating in the breaking off of diplomatic relations with Israel in February 1953. The penultimate stages of the Korean War had pointed out the hopelessness of the grand concept of collective security, in which the Israelis had placed much faith. The population, most of it new, untutored and untried, had lost its confidence, its sense of direction, its purposefulness. By 1952 the Israelis were beginning to grasp the full implications of the failure of the CCP's Lausanne Conference. Until now they had been too busy to stop and reflect. But, teetering on the edge of complete economic collapse, apparently friendless, and emotionally exhausted, they realized what it meant to have no peace.

The Revolution came, then, like the dawn after the darkest hours. The revolutionaries seemed to be just the men Israel was waiting for. Except for General Neguib, they were all young, *petit bourgeois* stock. Their behaviour was moderate, concerned with democratic feeling and a desire for continuity; the legal niceties were sustained; violence was avoided. The revolutionaries seemed to be governed by a sense of responsibility and of realism. Their interests were domestic: to purge the country of corruption, mismanagement and oppression, of social and economic injustice, and of Britain; 'to respect the constitution, and reform the Army and State'. The Israelis noted that there were few expressions of xenophobia, that they themselves were hardly mentioned. The Israelis were further reassured by their previous tenuous contacts with the 'Free Officers'. One Israeli,[1] Yeruham Cohen, who knew Colonel Nasser, then a lieutenant, fairly well from the days of the siege at Faluja, had been impressed by his belief that Egypt's real struggle lay within Egypt itself, and not in Palestine. Other officers participating in the armistice talks had maintained contact afterwards with far left-wing groups in Israel. The practical possibilities of this connexion were diminished somewhat by the Israeli government's subsequent suppression of these groups. But even so there were grounds for considerable optimism.

Three weeks after the revolution Ben Gurion extended the 'hand of friendship' to the new régime, declaring that Israel wished to see a 'free, independent and progressive Egypt'. He reiterated the argument that there were no valid grounds for conflict between the two countries, and he offered economic and political assistance, specifically Israel's assistance in ousting the British from the Suez Canal. As tangible proof of good will the Israel MAC delegates offered to drop their complaints from the agenda if Egypt would drop her, much fewer, complaints. General Neguib was informed that he could withdraw troops from Gaza to maintain order in Egypt proper and that Israel would not take advantage of the situation. Later, in November, at the General Assembly's debate on the peace resolution Eban set forth a detailed account of the concrete advantages the Arabs would gain from peace with Israel and plainly directed it towards Cairo.

The Junta responded to these overtures, and in March 1953 a set of Egyptian proposals was agreed upon as the basis for negotiations. Egypt asked for 120 million pounds sterling as refugee compensation plus massive Western economic aid for refugee resettlement; some adjustments of the border; the strengthening of the Tripartite Declaration; and a landlink to Jordan through the Southern Negev. The question of the future status of Jerusalem would be left aside until Jordan had been

[1] See Yeruham Cohen in *JOMER*, 13th February 1953, pp. 6–8.

consulted. The Israelis agreed to negotiate on these terms, on the understanding that her ability to pay compensation depended upon ending the boycott and blockade.[1] Contact between the two countries was through intermediaries, for example British M.P.s travelling from one country to the other. News of the arrangements leaked out, and the talks went underground. But relations seemed to improve slightly. In the summer of 1953 a *force majeure* shipping agreement was signed, and in December Ben Gurion resigned as Premier. Colonel Nasser spoke of his 'high hopes' and 'lively sympathy' for the more moderate Moshe Sharett.[2] The 'negotiations' continued through intermediaries but there was no progress. By the spring of 1954 relations between the two countries began to deteriorate and by August the border situation once again was serious.

The Israelis had been under considerable pressure from the Americans to make large unilateral concessions in order to create the right kind of atmosphere, but they had been unwilling to commit themselves until they were more certain of Egypt's intentions. Finally in August 1954 they made a number of small conciliatory moves. They reaffirmed their readiness to pay refugee compensation; to provide free port and transit facilities at Haifa; to provide a landlink between Egypt and Jordan; and to sign non-aggression pacts with all the Arab States. Also they announced that the remainder of refugee funds blocked in Israeli banks would be released.[3] But it was too late. The Egyptian government had already quietly renounced *rapprochement* and guerrilla squads were operating out of the Gaza Strip.

The immediate causes of the breakdown in the negotiations seem to have been the questions of a landlink and the Suez Blockade. What we know indicates that as time passed the Egyptians were less interested in a *rapprochement* than they were in renewing the struggle. The question of a landlink was a continuation of the old dispute over control of the Negev which was

---

[1] *JOMER*, 27th March 1953, pp. 1–2; *JP.* 27th and 28th May 1953; *NYT*, Sulzberger, 30th March 1953.

[2] Jean and Simonne Lacouture, *Egypt in Transition*, p. 233.

When Dulles visited Cairo General Neguib told him that, if the US helped him negotiate a favourable treaty over Suez with the British so as to disarm local critics, he would be willing to negotiate a settlement with Israel.

[3] *JOMER*, 22nd April 1955, p. 5; also see above, p. 15.

rapidly acquiring great symbolic importance in Arab eyes. The Israelis had always agreed that Egypt could have a landlink with the other Arab countries, and Ben Gurion had proposed a railway line. Sharett went farther and offered a corridor several kilometres wide. The Egyptians wanted more, something equivalent to a free zone encompassing most of the southern Negev. The Israelis considered that this claim far exceeded what was needed to establish a useful landlink and proved that the Egyptians were trying to cut them off from the Gulf of Akaba. This was substantiated by Egypt's refusal to give any promise to lift the blockade. As the Anglo-Egyptian agreement on the withdrawal of British troops from the Canal Zone drew closer the Israelis grew more insistent on this point. Many of them began to argue that Egypt was only pretending interest in a *rapprochement* in order to retain all the international favour possible, particularly from the United States, during this critical period, and that once the British had withdrawn she would turn against Israel again.

The Israelis decided, despite their announced support for Egypt against Britain, that they would try to persuade the British not to leave Suez until Egypt had given guarantees of free passage through the Canal. It was hopeless from the start. The Israelis had no status in the Anglo–Egyptian negotiations. If the British felt that they would have to leave an area so important to them as the Canal Zone it was unlikely that any consideration of Israel would persuade them to accept the cost of staying longer. In any case, the presence of British troops in the Canal Zone had not prevented Egypt from invading Israel in 1948 or from tightening the blockade. The attempt to use Britain's influence simply pointed up Israel's inability to carry her pro-Arab declarations through to their logical conclusions.

The abortive *rapprochement* is one of the most important and least considered episodes in Arab–Israeli relations. Finally the Israelis were meeting with the new, progressive Arab nationalism about which they had talked so much and of which they had held such high hopes. But instead of conciliation and eventually peace there was not only incompatibility but, as we shall see, growing hostility. The result was the Sinai campaign. What kept these two countries apart was not merely a disagreement over landlinks and free passage. This attempted *rapprochement* was not simply another of those 'peace moves', often initiated by well-meaning outsiders who trotted back and forth between capital cities, holding serious conversations with disenchanted officials, and issuing vague, pregnant hints to suitable members of the Press. The incident was small, played out over two years, submerged, scarcely noticeable in the rough, acrimonious hurly-burly of the period. But its implications were profound, touching the very heart of the relationship between the two countries. The failure to establish a *rapprochement* did not make war inevitable, but it convinced the Israelis that the 'new' Arab nationalism like the old had no place in it for them.

On the night of 28th February 1955 Israeli troops penetrated three miles into the Gaza Strip, blew up a water tower, attacked a military post, and wiped out a detachment of Egyptian reinforcements. Thirty-two Egyptian soldiers and two civilians were killed.

The Gaza Raid is often described as a decisive turning point in Middle Eastern affairs. Very briefly, it is said that it destroyed the substantial chances of a *rapprochement* and initiated another, vicious circle of border warfare; that it forced Nasser to obtain arms from Russia and thereby destroyed the fragile Western-sponsored stability of the Middle East; and that consequently it created a split between Egypt and the West which led eventually to the tragic events of 1956.

There seems to be a temptation to blame Israel for everything that goes wrong in the Middle East but the point is that, while the Gaza Raid was important, it did not create or initiate any trend of events. As we shall see from a more detailed examination of the evidence, relations between Egypt and Israel, and Egypt and the West, broke down before, not after, the Gaza Raid. The raid may have made Nasser more receptive to Russia's kindly offers of arms, but he was already looking to them to help him counteract Iraq's drift towards a military alliance with the West. The Egyptians had always told the British and the Americans publicly that even after the Anglo–Egyptian agreement over Suez was signed they would carry on their anti-imperialist campaign against Western influence in the Middle East. Egypt insisted on Arab neutrality, and this brought her into direct conflict with the West over plans for a Middle East defence pact. Egypt said no; Iraq and the West said yes. If Egypt was going to win the argument and maintain her claim to the leadership of the Arab world, she had to have help from Russia.

The Gaza Raid did not create a new pattern of events. It was part, an important part, of a trend which had begun months before.

The revolutionaries who came to power in Egypt, the 'Free Officers', were typical products of the vast social changes wrought in the Arab countries over the last few generations. They came to power with one aim: to restore to Egypt her honour and her greatness. Their stated objectives were to expel the British, and to prepare the way for thoroughgoing domestic reforms. The first of these, although difficult, was fairly straightforward. The second involved enormous problems and complications for which the Officers had no preparation and which they did not understand. They discovered that if there were to be thoroughgoing reforms they would have to retain power. There was no one else to take over the reins of government. But they had no plans, no training, not even a useful understanding of what the real problems were.

Despite this, various definite tendencies appeared amongst the new rulers, certain forms of thought and action took shape and became common features of the landscape. One was the growth of an authoritarian form of government with a definite leaning towards totalitarianism. Another was the attempt to provide a philosophic basis for the Revolution and its aims by scooping up a number of suitable ideas, by no means consistent with each other, from various sources into a bucket of social, economic and political egalitarianism.[1]

Then, in the early part of 1954, Colonel Nasser and his colleagues expanded considerably their interests and their aims. Up until this time the emphasis had been upon the Canal Zone and domestic difficulties. Now there was an unmistakeable growth of

---

[1] Even as late as 1957 Nasser was saying things like: 'The Social Democratic cooperative régime aims at curbing and eventually destroying opportunist exploitation meanwhile encouraging individual nationalism which is ever ready to cooperate for the benefit of society.'—*Egyptian Mail*, 7th December 1957.

militant, expansionist nationalist sentiment. Nasser declared that Egypt's place, thrust upon her by history, lay at the head of the Arab world, the Islamic world, the African world. This was her destiny; 'Fate is no Jester'.[1] Government propaganda became saturated with talk not only of liberating the Arab world, but of continuing the struggle against imperialism everywhere. There was a growing emphasis on xenophobia,[2] not only against the alien West but against 'foreign elements' within the Arab world itself. There was much talk of cleansing Arab society. The bedrock was Islam. Only the Arabs could restore Islam to its former greatness. There was talk of rebuilding 'our pure Arab–Islamic national character for the good of the Arabs and of Islam'.[3]

There were other symptoms. The Army was glorified and extolled as the nation's saviour, and stress was laid on the necessity for arming and strengthening it. It was proved that the defeat in Palestine was the fault of the corrupt Palace, politicians and businessmen, not the Army. None the less the shame of Palestine would be erased. This was an absolute imperative.[4]

This syndrome has a familiar pattern: authoritarian government, vague socialism, dynamism, intellectual fumblings, militarism, religiosity, and so on. It has been described, with some exaggeration, as the Egyptian version of Pan-Arab National Socialism.[5] We now know, at least we should know by now, that this kind of thing is not uncommon in countries which are under-developed, struggling for independence, material improvement and respect after years of exploitation, oppression and humiliation. (It is also not uncommon elsewhere.) In 1953–4 it had not yet become an accepted feature of the inter-

[1] Nasser, *Egypt's Liberation: The Philosophy of the Revolution*, p. 86.

[2] See *Voice of the Arabs*, 30th September and 3rd October 1954, for attacks against Christians and Jews.

[3] Saleh Salim, *Radio Cairo*, 29th May 1954. Arab, not just Egyptian, propaganda and writings were saturated with this kind of thinking.

[4] Especially noticeable after April 1954; vd. *Radio Cairo*, 13th April 1954; also Nasser, *Toute la Verité sur la Guerre de Palestine*; and his speech in *LaB. Egypt.*, 23rd July 1955.

[5] 'One has to see the distorted, hate-filled faces of those who gather around the radio sets listening to the inflammatory "Voice of the Arabs" to understand what is going on in this region'—Hans Tütsch, in Laqueur, *The Middle East in Transition*, p. 23. Tütsch was one of the few Western journalist if not the only one, who spoke Arabic.

national landscape but the Israelis could see clearly the dangers it held for them.

The 'Free Officers' took power assuming that they had only to clear away the old feudal, corrupt régime, so that the path would be clear for the young, uncorrupted, progressive forces to take over. They had not realized that Egypt's situation was not the handiwork of a few men, that the sickness went to the very vitals of society, and that they would have to stay in power. They had not realized the hard, interminable, heartbreaking nature of their task. They saw themselves as a new broom, and assumed that they could sweep the house clean right away. The first failures of their domestic policy, the subsequent disillusionment, anger and bitterness, the search for scapegoats, all had their effects. An activist foreign policy was one, a repressive police régime was another.

The Israelis had laboured under the same illusions as the 'Free Officers'. They too believed that the revolutionaries could make a clean sweep, that they could break with the past, reform their own house, and of course make peace with their socialist, progressive neighbours. That these hopes were completely unfounded, ignoring the pressing realities of Egypt, did not lessen the Israelis' disillusionment and bitterness. On the contrary, because the Israelis had hoped for so much and because they felt that these hopes had been exploited and contemptuously rejected they were doubly bitter. They struck back hard against the new Egyptian campaign against them. Their feud was now almost a personal one, with the one man who to them symbolized betrayal, Colonel Gamal Abdul Nasser.

In one sense the Israelis were being unrealistic. Certainly they expected far more from Nasser than he could possibly have given them. But at the same time their acrimonious reactions were rooted in an understanding of what was happening in Egypt. The Israelis knew that once the Suez issue was settled the Egyptians would turn to them with either peaceful or hostile intent. By mid-1954 the Junta's first attempts at domestic reform had ended in almost total failure, and the Israelis could see plainly that, planned or unplanned, the natural reaction would be to divert public attention by an anti-Israel campaign. Certainly there was no longer any possibility of a *rapprochement*.

This hypothesis was substantiated, not only by what was happening along the border, but by what the Egyptians themselves were saying.

The Egyptian Press worked under strict censorship, and almost all of it, including the most anti-Western, was run by selected army officers. The radio was state-owned, and under the direct control of the President's office. These organs hammered out the same message to the masses day in and day out. Whether or not they were aware of what they were doing Egypt's rulers were allowing an image of themselves to be created. Whether or not they knew what it was or agreed with it they were allowing a policy to be stated: aggressive, expansionist, anti-Western, anti-Israel, and, in its way, racist. Westerners who commented on these characteristics were told that they were only for public consumption, for the masses, necessary to maintain the people's confidence in the government, and that in fact the government was much more moderate and reasonable in its ambitions. An alternative explanation was that while some officials were undoubtedly extremist, for example those in the propaganda section, the real power lay with the moderates led by Colonel Nasser. There was some truth in these explanations. It must have been more than accidental that in his early speeches Nasser concentrated on domestic issues while Saleh Salim, Minister of National Guidance, emphasized the necessity of an activist foreign policy. Even so there was the indiscriminate propaganda machine hurling out its message daily, each word binding the government ever more closely to its creation. Propaganda has a life-force, a power of its own. It becomes policy, it makes policy. It forces the leaders to do what they now promised. The Israelis believed that even if President Nasser did not plan or even want to begin the campaign against them, he had promised that he would, at least his propagandists had said he would, which comes to the same thing, and he was committed to it if he wanted to stay in power.

If President Nasser announced, during the early stages of the *rapprochement*, that the lull with Israel was only temporary while the Government concentrated on getting the British out,[1] and this was constantly repeated and paraphrased on the radio and

[1] *Radio Cairo*, 28th December 1953; also Wheelock, *Nasser's New Egypt*, p. 210.

in the Press, then he was virtually committed. The reasons why he made that statement and why it was constantly repeated in one form or another are much less important than that he did make it, that his people believed him, and that the Israelis believed him.

By itself, Iraq's alliance with Turkey and Pakistan in the Western-sponsored Baghdad Pact would have been sufficient to prevent Nasser from carrying through a *rapprochement* with Israel.[1] But, in fact, the idea of *rapprochement* had been dropped before the Baghdad Pact took shape. During 1954, as agreement with the British over Suez drew closer, propaganda against Israel mounted. The *Voice of the Arabs* foretold the invasion that would destroy the Jews and restore Palestine to the Arabs.[2] The Anglo–Egyptian Agreement was initialled on 27th July 1954. On 1st August the *Voice of the Arabs* hinted that guerrilla contingents were being formed in Gaza. Just after this Israel restated her offers of refugee compensation and other proposals for a peace settlement. The Arabs rejected them contemptuously as an obvious effort to delude world opinion, and they renewed their promises of a second round against Israel.[3]

Between May and July 1954 Israel submitted almost 400 complaints to the MAC. In the weeks preceding the initialling of the Anglo–Egyptian Agreement Egyptian marauding let up and increased again afterwards. The pattern indicates that the Egyptians had a try-out during September, eased up during the first weeks in October and began in earnest toward the end of the month. The squads penetrated deep into Israel; roads, bridges, and water-pipes were sabotaged; large quantities of equipment and livestock were stolen. Between September and December 1954 the main pipeline to the Negev was dynamited four times. The whole programme of development in the south was threatened, and many of the settlers there were leaving.

[1] It was not until three days after his announcement of the Czech arms deal that Nasser pointed to the Gaza Raid as one of its causes. Prior to that the Baghdad Pact was designated the main culprit.

[2] For example, *Voice of the Arabs*, 10th and 15th May 1954. See Kimche in *JOMER*, 26th July 1957, for an interesting but tendentious account of the switch to an activist foreign policy.

[3] *Voice of the Arabs*, 30th August 1954, and 21st October 1954; see also Israel Foreign Ministry, *Arab Threats Against Israel*, Background Paper 6, 26th December 1954.

The Israelis were satisfied that the squads were being organized and trained by the Egytian Army. The Egyptians were warned continually that the raids must be stopped.[1] General Burns, the new Chief of Staff UNTSO, vainly proposed the establishment of more efficient border controls: joint patrols, local commanders' agreements, double-aproned barbed-wire obstacles along sections of the line, and the use of regular troops only for manning outposts.

The number of incidents continued to increase and as the infiltrators gained experience they penetrated farther into Israel. The Israelis alleged that in one period, 23rd to 25th February 1955, saboteurs reached the outskirts of Tel Aviv, roads were mined, government offices broken into, and one civilian killed. The Israelis claimed forty-five of these incidents during February alone. Ordinarily they would not have been inclined to pay too much attention to threats of a second round. But as the propaganda and sabotage attacks increased almost in direct proportion to each other it became difficult to ignore the reasonable assumption that the Egyptians might really mean what they said.

In December, after the main water pipeline had been dynamited for the fourth time, Saleh Salim, the Egyptian Ministe of National Guidance, stated on several occasions that Egyp would never make peace with Israel, not even if she implemented all the General Assembly resolutions on partition and refugees. He went on to dangle the carrot of an Arab anti communist military alliance in return for Western help ir destroying Israel.[2] Salim's statements, together with the stron; evidence of organized sabotage, painted too plain a picture fo the Israelis to ignore. The position of the moderates, particu

---

[1] 'The Israeli attack on Gaza surprised no one: Russia, the West and Egyp all knew that it was coming. . . . The only point in doubt was the manner of th attack: when, where and how would it be made'—Arslan Humbaraci, *Middle Ea Indictment*, p. 197–8. Humbaraci, a journalist, claims that he himself carried a Israeli warning to Cairo in the fall of 1954, and suggests that the West did nothir to stop the raid in the hope that it would frighten Egypt into a military allianc with the West.

A Syrian politician says that the British and the Americans told the Arabs tha they should join MEDO in order to obtain arms to deal with Israel: see Majd lany, in Laqueur, *The Middle East in Transition*.

[2] *ibid. Arab Threats Against Israel*, p. 1; also *MEM*, 1st January 1955, 9. 7.

larly Prime Minister Sharett, became increasingly difficult. On 17th February 1955 Ben Gurion returned from his retirement in the desert to become Minister of Defence.

Two events in the fall of 1954, which did much to stir up public indignation in Israel and to increase demands for action, were the capture of the *Bat Galim* and the Spy Trials. In the former instance not only were an Israeli ship and Israeli sailors involved, but there were reports that the men had been brutally treated during the early days of their captivity. The Spy Trials threw the country into an uproar. During the autumn of 1954 the Egyptians captured and tried a number of people, mostly Jews, for carrying out espionage and sabotage work for Israel. The defendants were tortured for confessions and found guilty. Jewish groups abroad managed to focus international attention on the case, and President Nasser promised that the death sentences would be commuted. But he had already executed half a dozen members of the Moslem Brotherhood for subversive activities and he could hardly excuse the Jews. Two of the defendants were hanged in secret. The Israelis took the executions like a national disaster. It was sincerely believed by practically everyone that the defendants had been framed, and that the trial was a plot against Egyptian Jews.[1] Grief and anger swept the country and there were widespread demands for retaliation.

Like the Egyptians, the Israelis also found that their relations with the Great Powers were pushing them toward an activist foreign policy. If 1953 saw the beginnings of a siege-like mentality in Israel, 1954 saw the beginning of that grimness of mind which arises only when the stark realities of survival-politics present themselves. 'We are,' Abba Eban told his countrymen, 'engaged in our most fateful political struggle since the establishment of the State . . . [the issues were] the security of Israel in the face of the hatred surrounding her . . . the relations of

[1] In fact the defendants were guilty. The ring had been set up by certain Israeli army officers with the knowledge of a few politicians. It is possible that these people were also responsible for the raid on Nahalin in Jordan and the voyage of the Bat Galim. At the time, Pinhas Lavon, the Minister of Defence, was held responsible and forced to resign to make room for Ben Gurion. Now it appears that Lavon was innocent. Ben Gurion's refusal to allow a complete public inquiry prevented a detailed assessment of responsibility in 'the Lavon Affair'. But there is a strong possibility that certain Israeli officers and politicians decided to facilitate Ben Gurion's return to public life by encouraging a national mood of activism.

Israel with the United States and Britain in view of their present policy. It is enough to define these issues to realize the severity of this struggle'. This 'present policy' of America and Britain was to persuade the Arabs into an anti-Russian alliance.

Western arms shipments to Iraq and to Egypt had been resumed in 1954 although on a small scale. The Israelis discounted arguments that the arms were few and would be used for defensive purposes only. They were concerned with the psychological consequences. They argued that by shipping arms to the Arabs, despite their avowed attitude towards Israel and without first obtaining formal guarantees, the Americans and the British were, willy-nilly, encouraging the anti-Israeli campaign, encouraging the assumption that Israel had been deserted or that Israel's interests might be sacrificed to win Arab favour. In an effort to allay Israeli fears the British, supported by the Americans and the French, offered their services as a mediator. The Israelis followed this up by renewing their peace offers. The Arabs vigorously declined and once again hinted that a pro-Western military alliance could be had at the expense of Israel.[1] Then, in January 1955, Iraq announced her intention of signing a mutual defence pact with Turkey. A month later, on 24th February, the Turco–Iraqi Pact was signed in Baghdad. A major turning point had been reached and passed. The Middle East's decline into chaos was almost assured.

The signing of the Pact came as a great shock to the Israelis. They saw immediately that they would have to bear much of the brunt of Egypt and Iraq's quarrel with each other over who was more loyal to the Arab cause: Egypt with her neutralism, or Iraq with her Western alliance. Also, Turkey was their best, their only friend in the Middle East; the only country to accord them full recognition, to support them in the Security Council, and to trade with them. Now she was entering into a military pact with Iraq, the one country that had refused to sign an armistice. What was worse Turkey agreed 'to work in close cooperation [with Iraq] for affecting the carrying out of the United Nations resolutions concerning Palestine'. It was

[1] The Assistant Secretary-General of the Arab League stated that the British were confusing two issues: the solution of the Palestine problem, which could be settled when Israel implemented the UN resolutions; and peace with Israel, which was impossible—*MEM*, 25th September 1954, p. 4.

only natural to wonder if this meant that Turkey would support moves to force Israel into giving up large slices of territory. The Israelis considered the 'hostile intent' so obvious that they found it 'difficult . . . to maintain a lofty philosophical detachment'.

The speed with which the United States and Britain expressed support for the pact only deepened the Israelis' sense of isolation and betrayal. Never since 1948 had their international position been grimmer. All sections of the population were bitter and disillusioned. Egyptian sabotage groups reached the outskirts of Tel Aviv at the same time as the Turco–Iraqi Pact was signed. Egypt had to be stopped and the West had to provide Israel with 'effective' security quarantees. Those Israelis who counselled patience and caution had few listeners. There were too many ordeals piled up in a great heap blocking the horizon, limiting the view.

Chapter Thirteen

ISRAEL AND EGYPT
PART TWO: FROM GAZA TO
NATIONALIZATION
(February 1955 – July 1956)

THE size and vigour of the Gaza Raid was a clear reflection
of Israel's disappointment in the new, revolutionary
Egypt. Unrealistic or not, that disappointment had a decisive effect upon policy over the next few years. Now that the
theories and hopes for peace had proved false the Israelis had
nothing to look forward to except hardship, danger, war and
perhaps extinction. It was a demoralizing prospect, not one to
foster the gentle art of diplomacy.

The Israelis had hoped that the raid would accomplish two
things: force a settlement of the border troubles with Egypt,
and persuade the Western Powers to provide them with useful
security guarantees. In neither were the Israelis successful, although the raid did have the effect of stating their case emphati-
cally. The debate in the Security Council took the usual course.
The Egyptians complained about the raid, and in turn the
Israelis brought out their old charges of infiltration and sabotage, the blockade, belligerent rights, propaganda, and so on.
In his report to the Council, General Burns pointed out that
the raid had to be considered within the perspective of prior
developments, and that, although infiltration from Gaza was
undoubtedly one of the main causes of tension, clearly the root

of the trouble was to be found elsewhere. Nothing else constructive was said. Everyone condemned the raid.

A motion of censure was adopted unanimously. Then, as a sop to Israeli charges of inaction, the Council moved on to a general discussion of the situation along the Gaza frontier. Even though the draft resolution was sponsored by the Western countries none of them seemed anxious to probe deeply into the sources of tension, although the French delegate did suggest that matters might be improved if the Egyptians restrained their language and stopped talking about extermination. The draft resolution took note of Burns's description of the situation; requested him to continue his negotiations for the implementation of practical proposals to stop infiltration; and called upon Egypt and Israel to cooperate with him. The resolution was passed unanimously.

Following the raid the border remained quiet for less than two weeks. In March, the mining of roads in Israel was resumed, and the sabotage squads began to operate again. There is no point in examining the worsening situation in any detail. Both sides were edgy and angry. Local commanders had a great deal of latitude. Neither side was willing to compromise or to trust the other. Nasser seems to have been often misinformed by subordinates about what was happening on the border. The Israelis called in the American, British, French and Russian ambassadors for talks. For the local situation they wanted strong action by the Council, at the very least a condemnation of Egypt. For the larger problem of security they wanted specific commitments from the West, at the very least arms but preferably a security pact. The Americans and the British stated flatly that they would not support any resolution condemning Egypt, and that if Israel went to the Council the Council would simply refer the matter to Burns. The Israelis went to the Council, and the Council referred the matter to Burns. The Israelis retorted that this left them with 'only one effective means' of checking Egyptian attacks. The request for arms and a security pact was also declined. The Americans told the Israelis that they would have to wait, but that they would not be deserted. There was a 'timetable' and it could not be wrecked for Israel; but if the Israelis suffered patiently they would get what they wanted eventually. The British spoke more plainly: if

Israel did not wait and suffer in silence, if she attempted to use force to alter the situation, then 'there will not be an Israel; or at least she will be back where she was twenty years earlier'.[1]

General Burns began travelling back and forth between Tel Aviv and Cairo discussing his proposals for improving border control. In April, both sides agreed to use regular troops only along the border and both accepted the principle of local commanders' agreements. Both also agreed to allow fixed UNTSO Observer Posts along the frontier (later the Egyptians objected and they were taken down: in August they were set up again). Israel favoured barbed-wire aprons but rejected joint patrols. The Israelis gave as the reason for their refusal considerations of national sovereignty (considerations which had not prevented the use of joint patrols along the Jordan border). Possibly a more weighty consideration was that, with a national election coming up in July and the border troublesome, the government did not consider it expedient to suggest that Israeli soldiers were not capable of guarding the frontiers properly. The Egyptians rejected the idea of barbed wire because of the political implications of enclosing the refugees. Instead they proposed a demilitarized belt one kilometre wide on each side of the line. The Israelis hesitated. Such a belt would have left most of their important southern settlements open to 'unofficial' infiltration which might or might not cease; and their previous experience with demilitarized zones was unhappy. In any case public opinion was against the proposal. As an alternative the Israelis suggested a mined strip one hundred metres wide, centred on the demarcation line and enclosed by barbed wire. This would be supplemented by meetings of the local commanders and direct telephone communications.

During his commuting Burns tried to persuade the Egyptians to agree to negotiate directly with the Israelis over these matters. He, the Israelis, and the Americans and British wanted fairly high-level talks involving political or diplomatic people as well

[1] This information is extracted from confidential reports by an Israeli journalist to the Foreign Ministry on a series of conversations he held with various officials from the American and British embassies in Tel Aviv in April 1954. The officials understood that their statements would be relayed to the Foreign Ministry. An American embassy official told me later that he did not believe that his government had ever had a 'timetable'.

as military. The Egyptians refused because of the political implications and asked for talks between the local military commanders. In mid-May border incidents began to recur in much the same pattern as before. Egyptian outposts fired on Israeli patrols, this led to return fire, and often to mortar and artillery duels. Mining incidents in Israel increased. The Negev pipeline was dynamited twice. At the same time Cairo announced, for the first time, that *fedayeen*, trained and supervised by the Army, were carrying out acts of sabotage in Israel. Finally, on 19th June, the Israelis compromised by agreeing to talks between officers at 'medium-level'.

Discussions began on 26th June at Kilometre 95. Border incidents stopped temporarily. The talks went badly from the beginning. Neither side was enthusiastic. The Egyptians made it plain that they were negotiating under pressure from the West, and that they were afraid they would be forced into peace negotiations. They would not agree to the direct meetings or to direct telephone lines between local commanders, customary on the Jordan and Lebanese borders. The Egyptians insisted that UN officials be present at all meetings, that all telephone communications be relayed indirectly through UN people, and that all written agreements be signed by the UN officials. With great reluctance, on 17th July, the Israelis agreed in principle to UN participation.

At this point the Egyptians announced that no Arab State would enter into any agreement with Israel until after there had been a meeting in Damascus to adopt a plan to prevent the Israelis from setting up bilateral agreements and by-passing the UNTSO. The Israelis concluded that the Egyptians were no longer interested in discussing border control and were looking for an excuse to break off the talks. The Israelis knew that Egypt had reached an agreement in principle with the Soviet Union that very month on the shipment of arms, and that she no longer need to court the favour of the West.

On 22nd August, a routine Israeli patrol along the Gaza Strip came under rifle and mortar fire from near-by Egyptian outposts. Reinforcements had to be brought up to extricate the patrol and the Israeli settlement of Nahal Oz was shelled by Egyptian mortars. On 24th August, Nasser told General Burns that Israel had started the incident and that Egypt would not continue with the negotiations. This statement was followed immediately by 'an organized series of attacks on vehicles, installations and persons' in Israel, carried out by gangs of marauders. 'The number and nature of these acts of sabotage perpetrated well within Israel territory, are such as to suggest that they are the work of organized and well-trained groups. Investigations so far completed by United Nations military observers tend to support this view. *The sudden resumption of this type of incident after they had practically ceased for three months is significant*.[1] The Israelis found themselves subjected to a series of attacks unparalleled since 1949. Military patrols and civilian traffic were fired on, settlements attacked, wells and pipelines blown up, roads mined. The raiders penetrated as far as Tel Aviv where they dynamited a radio transmitter and attacked houses. In the period 22nd to 29th August an estimated seventeen Israelis were killed. The *Voice of the Arabs* announced that the *fedayeen* had found their way to Tel Aviv and would persist in their attacks until Israel was destroyed.[2] Clearly the Egyptians were no longer interested in border control. The Israeli Government was under unprecedented pressure from the populace for action. Caught between terror and rage the people shouted for war. To add insult to injury the Egyptian attacks coincided with the ventilation of the Dulles Peace Plan.

For some time the Eisenhower Administration had been heavily criticized by the opposition for being anti-Israel and pro-Arab; and for doing nothing to give the Johnston Plan a sorely-needed boost. Also something had to be done to forestall the completion of Egypt's secret arms negotiations with Russia. This last seems to have determined the timing of Dulles's proposals for a peace settlement.[3] The Dulles Peace Plan contained nothing new or surprising except that it took the Arabs and Israelis unawares. Very briefly, the United States offered to provide substantial aid toward a settlement of the Palestine ques-

[1] Italics added. *Report of the Chief of Staff UNTSO. . . . SCOR*, S/3430, 6th September 1955, p. 8

[2] *Voice of the Arabs*, 31st August and 2nd September 1955.

[3] For text see *The Middle East: American Policy Statements* (USIS, London 1957), pp. 59–63. Both the Americans and the Israelis knew of the negotiations almost from the beginning.

tion, and security guarantees to maintain that settlement. Loans and grants would be provided to enable Israel to pay refugee compensation; to provide for refugee resettlement; and to assist in the repatriation of a 'feasible' number of refugees. Money would be provided for the realization of water development and irrigation projects which would facilitate resettlement. Any border settlement mutually agreed upon would be guaranteed. This was considered the most difficult problem of all, since 'even territory which is barren has acquired a sentimental significance'. Once all these issues had been settled, others such as the future status of Jerusalem could be resolved without too much trouble.

The Arabs did not reply until 11th October, two weeks after the Czech arms deal had been announced, and then they rejected the Plan. The Israelis described it as 'constructive, realistic and imaginative', and accepted it as a basis for negotiations. At the same time they saw in the Plan a denial of America's previous promises. The reference to American guarantees for an 'agreed frontier' implied that they could no longer expect the existing boundary lines to be guaranteed under the Tripartite Declaration. Also Dulles's reference to barren lands of sentimental value seemed to imply that Israel should cede all or part of the Negev. That Dulles should speak thus at a time when the Egyptians were sending in *fedayeen* to prevent settlement in the Negev seemed to the Israelis, in their despondency, more than just a coincidence: it was more important than ever to defend their southern territories.

On 28th August, General Burns warned the Egyptians that if the attacks continued they 'might provoke reactions which might lead to the gravest situation'. Immediately the number of attacks increased. The contempt implicit in this tacit rejoinder persuaded the Israelis to retaliate.[1] On the night of 31st August they attacked the police station at Khan Yunis, a centre of *fedayeen* operations. The station was destroyed and about thirty-six Egyptians were killed and thirteen wounded, mostly members of the police and military forces. The Israelis lost one

---

[1] Although this is not a point the Israelis were likely to appreciate, in fact once the *fedayeen* had entered Israel they could not be called back or in any way controlled by the Egyptian government.

killed and several wounded.[1] On 4th September a cease-fire was implemented—each party agreeing to maintain it so long as the other did. On the 8th, the Council met and unanimously passed a resolution ordering both countries 'forthwith' to restore peace and tranquillity to the area, and to continue negotiating with Burns on his proposals. Both the Egyptians and the Israelis seemed satisfied with the resolution although neither thought that the proposals would be adequate.

In the meantime conditions in and around the DZ at El Auja had been deteriorating steadily. In 1953, the Israelis had established a small settlement at Ketsiot in the DZ, killing a number of beduin in the process. The Egyptians had complained to the MAC, using the same arguments as the Syrians had done for the Northern DZ. The Chairman decided that although the Israelis had been wrong in using armed forces to clear the DZ of beduin, he was not competent to discuss the question of civilian settlement; the Egyptian GAA, unlike the Syrian, contained no reference at all to civilian activities in the DZ, and therefore the matter did not fall within the competence of the MAC.[2] In other words Israel had full authority in the DZ apart from the exclusion of military forces.

On the Egyptian side of the frontier, contiguous with the DZ in Israel, was another zone bounded by El Qouseima and Abou Aoueigila from which all Egyptian military forces were excluded: in effect, another demilitarized zone (Article VIII, paragraphs 3 and 4). The Egyptians were convinced that Ketsiot's settlers were in fact soldiers, and as a defensive move they brought up troops into their defensive zone. In September 1954 the MAC found that Ketsiot was organized as part of the Israeli Army. Israel appealed to the Special Committee, but no meetings could be arranged to clear the agenda, so the issue was never settled properly. In the DZ matters went from bad to worse. Neither side trusted the other, and senior officers on the spot acted as they wished, regardless of what assurances were given to Burns by their respective Ministries of Foreign Affairs.

[1] This was the most humiliating raid the Egyptians suffered. The Israelis simply drove up the main roads in the Strip, into the centre of Khan Yunis, blew up the station and drove back. The Egyptian Army seems to have been busy somewhere else.

[2] *E–IMAC*, Emergency mtgs., 2nd October 1953 and 27th May 1954.

After two minor clashes, the MAC decided upon a joint marking of the line between the two zones to eliminate unintentional crossing. Egypt then changed her mind. The Israelis decided to do it themselves, under UNTSO supervision. The Egyptians destroyed the boundary markers. At this time they had military posts several hundred yards inside Israel, within the DZ itself. The Israelis claimed that this annulled Egypt's promise to abide by the cease-fire of 4th September. An Israel military unit was sent into the DZ: Burns was assured that it would be withdrawn as soon as the Egyptians evacuated the Israeli DZ and promised not to interfere with the marking of the boundary. Later the Israelis added the condition that Egypt must also agree to withdraw her troops from the Egyptian defensive zone. After several days an agreement was reached whereby Israeli and Egyptian troops would be withdrawn on 2nd October from the El Auja DZ, the status of both zones would be reviewed, and the marking of the frontier would be discussed.

Then, a few days after President Nasser's announcement of the Czech arms deal, Israel charged that the Egyptians were still keeping troops in their zone. Egypt refused to allow the UNTSO to investigate and in reply claimed that the Israeli police sent to replace the troops guarding Ketsiot were also soldiers. Egyptian troops received orders to prevent 'by all means including the use of force if necessary' any marking of the boundary.[1] UNTSO surveyors on the job were forced at gun-point to leave, and once they were fired on by Egyptian troops. On 25th October an Israeli police checkpoint in the south-west corner of the El Auja DZ was attacked, one of its occupants killed, two wounded, and two kidnapped. Two days later Egyptian troops moved into Israel into this same corner of the DZ, and set up positions along a front about a mile long and just over half a mile inside Israel centred on El Sabbha. They refused to evacuate despite several requests by Burns. On the night of 28th October the Israelis retaliated by attacking and destroying the Egyptian military post at El Kuntilla, about

---

[1] Quoted from *Nasser's Pattern of Aggression*, Israel Office of Information, p. 13; see also *NYT*, 11th, 14th and 18th October 1955
The Egyptian claim was correct.

fifty miles south of the DZ. Simultaneously Israeli troops were sent into the DZ, once more with the assurance that they would be withdrawn when the Egyptians were. The Egyptians responded by strengthening their positions at El Sabbha and launching a few attacks against settlements along the Gaza Strip. There were also indications that the *fedayeen* were working out of Gaza again. They had been operating out of Syria, Lebanon and Jordan since the cease-fire on 4th September. On the night of 2nd November the Israelis attacked El Sabbha and drove the Egyptians out. The Israelis stated that in the prevailing circumstances they would remain in the DZ until Egypt withdrew her troops from her zone. And so the matter rested.[1]

On 27th September 1955, President Nasser had announced that his government would buy large quantities of arms from Czechoslovakia. The Czech arms deal stands as one of the most important single events in recent Arab history. Intended originally as a counterstroke to the Baghdad Pact and to the humiliation of the Gaza Raid, and as a means of strengthening Arab neutralism, it developed into a brilliant assertion of Egypt's independence and right to lead the Arab world. So far as Arab–Israeli relations were concerned it meant the West no longer held the balance between the antagonists. Arms shipments to the area could not be controlled. For the first time since 1948 an Arab country possessed, or would in the near future, the capacity to destroy Israel. This was no long-term prospect to be measured in generations, but in months and years; the time necessary to teach a man to fly a MIG, to drive a Stalin III tank, to fire a self-propelled gun. Possibly Nasser did not intend to use the arms against Israel. But the propaganda machine promised over and over again that when Egypt was ready Palestine would be liberated. Everything that happened along the border indicated that the pressure against Israel would continue to increase not diminish. Even if Nasser himself were reluctant to commit himself to a war policy it is unlikely that he would have been able to stand out against the very powerful activist influences which had received so much impetus from the Czech arms deal. This was the situation as the

[1] See Burns, *Between Arab and Israeli, passim* and *Times*, *NYT*, and *MG*, 1st, 2nd and 4th November 1955.

Israelis saw it; very little that had happened up until then or afterward indicated that they might be wrong.[1]

Almost coincident with the Czech arms deal was the renewal of *fedayeen* activity, this time from Syria, Jordan and Lebanon. Saudi Arabia put up some of the money. Syria helped with the organization. But the operations were set up and run by the Egyptian military attachés in the various countries. Evidently neither the Jordanian nor the Lebanese governments had any hand in these activities. Egypt held the key to stability on all of Israel's borders; a fact brought home forcibly with the eruption of violence along the Lebanese border—previously quiet—almost simultaneously with the signing of the Egyptian–Syrian mutual security pact.[2] Public opinion in Israel was solidly in favour of a 'tough' policy. The burdens and strain of the previous years had narrowed the horizon of the policy-makers, like that of the tired runner, to nothing except what was directly in front of them: the interest and security of Israel interpreted in the most restricted sense. The Czech arms deal had multiplied the dangers and given them an urgency and depth not experienced since 1948. There was a widespread, deep-seated distrust of American and British intentions; a fear that they would sell the Israelis down the river in order to persuade Egypt against defection to the East (hence the immediate importance of colonizing the Negev); and anger at the West's refusal to 'do something' about Arab hostility. The Israelis were now even less amenable to reason than previously.[3] The probable consequences of any further decline in their position were so frightening that they tended to ignore the limitations of the West's influence over the Arabs and the solid benefits of Western aid to themselves.

It is difficult to be precise about Israel's military position *vis-à-vis* the Arabs in the fall of 1955. But, according to one usually reliable source,[4] before the arms deal Egypt had a clear superiority over Israel in armaments: four times as many jets;

[1] On the basis of the documents contained in *Nasser's Pattern of Aggression* it would appear that Nasser intended to attack around April 1957.

[2] Signed on 20th October 1955; for text see *Middle East Journal* 1955, No. 1, pp. 77–9; also see *NYT*, 11th, 14th, 15th, 17th and 30th September and 8th October 1955.

[3] This is well summed up by Kimche: *JOMER*, 18th March 1955, pp. 5–6.

[4] *Times*, leader, 12th December 1955; see also Wheelock, *loc. cit.*, p. 241.

twice as much artillery; twice as many Sherman tanks, 300–150; and thirty-two Centurions of which Israel had none. Furthermore Israel's forces had to be rationed out along four frontiers. After the Czech arms deal Israel sent the U.S.A. a shopping list based on the assumption that Egypt was spending about $100,000,000 and getting the arms at bargain basement prices: 200 MIG 15s and twenty–thirty Ilyushin bombers (Israel had nothing to touch either type of plane); submarines, tanks and heavy artillery. The Israelis wanted forty F-86 Sabre jets, anti-submarine vessels, heavy tanks and anti-tank and anti-aircraft guns. These would cost somewhere around $50,000,000[1] The Israelis had sent another list to the French which we shall look at later, but even with the two lists added together Egypt still had arms superiority. The Israelis could not begin to absorb the amount of arms Egypt could, and they were counting on superior training to make up for the lack of quantity.

Now more than ever the Israelis wanted arms and, if possible, a security pact. The French were quietly encouraging but they had comparatively little influence in Western councils. The United States and Britain issued a joint declaration that they would not begin an arms race. Dulles told the Israelis that peace could not be kept by arms but by 'means of collective arrangements' which, if it meant anything at all, meant that Egypt would have to agree. The British announced that they were speeding up the shipment of arms and equipment to Iraq. Foreign Minister Sharett went to the meeting of the Western Foreign Ministers in Paris in October, and then on to the Geneva conference. In neither was he able to obtain anything more concrete than vague promises that Israel's interests would be taken into account. The West had no idea of how to counter this new Russian threat and the Israelis grew increasingly nervous that they might be offered up in part as a sacrifice.

These fears appeared justified by Prime Minister Eden's speech at Guildhall on 9th November. Eden proposed that the Arabs and the Israelis should reconcile their differences with each other, and negotiate a compromise between their various

---

[1] *NYT*, 18th November 1955; and *NYHT*, 11th December 1955.

Later, in 1956, the Israelis had to take into account that Syria too was receiving large quantities of Russian planes, tanks and guns.

territorial claims: that is to say, a compromise between Egypt's demand for negotiations on the basis of the 1947 Partition Plan, and Israel's demand for negotiations on the basis of the existing ADLs laid down in 1949. The Israeli response was instantaneous. They refused absolutely to consider any concessions based on the 1947 Partition Plan. They considered Eden's speech a crude attempt to gain Egyptian favour at their expense, and they would have nothing to do with it. Eden later admitted that November 1955 was hardly the time to discuss territorial concessions with Israel. *Fedayeen* were active all through the Negev, and the Israelis had just driven Egypt from El Sabbha. Israel's fears of British intentions were aggravated by Eden's comment several weeks later that there was nothing in the Tripartite Declaration about maintaining an arms balance, and by a report that Britain was shipping tanks to Egypt.

Eventually the uproar over the Guildhall speech died down and was forgotten. It stands, however, as a curious episode, largely unexplained, possibly of more significance than one has been accustomed to think. According to the most exhaustive study available of British policy during that period, the Guildhall speech was part of an Anglo-Egyptian, more correctly an Eden–Nasser, plan for the reconciliation of Arab–Israeli differences.[1] It is claimed that President Nasser was prepared to try to push through the Egyptian end of the reconciliation regardless of the likely opposition from his countrymen as well as from the other Arab countries on condition that Britain 'froze' the Baghdad Pact and did not try to extend it to include any more Arab countries. We know, however, that if the two leaders were in apparent agreement neither was acting in a manner calculated to further the implementation of that agreement.

November was Israel's worst month with the *fedayeen*. Their activities could not but so inflame the Israelis that they would refuse to consider any kind of concession to Egypt and regard Nasser's moderate statements with extreme suspicion. Also, at the same time as Eden was supposed to be promising Nasser that the Baghdad Pact would be 'frozen', the Jordan government was engaged, with Britain's encouragement, in talks with

[1] Childers, *Road to Suez*, pp. 140–4.

Turkey over entering the pact. One week after the Guildhall speech Jordan had submitted formal proposals for membership in the pact to the British government, and a few weeks later General Sir Gerald Templar arrived in Amman for direct talks. One can only conclude that, whatever the agreement between Eden and Nasser had been, neither was inclined, or perhaps able, to carry out his end of the bargain.

The matter becomes more and more curious. Exactly what kind of territorial settlement did Eden have in mind? Seven months before the Guildhall speech, the British were proposing to the Israelis that a territorial switch would provide an excellent basis for a settlement. Israel would give up the Negev, apparently to Egypt, and in return would obtain the West Bank from Jordan.[1] A few months after the Guildhall speech the British, at least Eden, were secretly discussing with Iraq the possibility of dividing Jordan, Britain's creation and faithful ally, so that Iraq took the East Bank and Israel the West (this was tied in with a plot to overthrow Nasser). Evidently this was all part of a plan for Iraq and Israel to make peace and thereby lay the groundwork for a general Arab–Israel conciliation, and the establishment of a pro-Western defence alliance for the Middle East. But if this is what Eden had in mind why was he risking the dangers involved in trying to bring Jordan into the Baghdad Pact, especially since Jordan was not going to be around for very long? Either Eden was playing a far deeper game than we can now guess or, more likely, the British were so disorganized at this time that several contradictory policies were being pursued at once. It remains only to add that the Israelis were unsympathetic to any suggestion that they give up the Negev. The West Bank may have had its attractions, but it had no empty spaces, no mineral resources, and most important of all no outlet to the eastern seas.

During all this, General Burns was still trying fruitlessly to negotiate an agreement between Cairo and Tel Aviv on his proposals for improved border controls. The border situation continued to deteriorate, particularly from early November on. Once again the Israelis found themselves subjected to an on-

---

[1] Extracted from the reports mentioned on p. 186 n.1; see also Kenneth Younger, in the *JP*, 9th December 1955; and Childers, *loc. cit.*

slaught unparalleled since 1948. In December, they announced their intention of calling a conference, under Article Twelve of the GAA, for the purpose of reviewing and revising the armistice arrangements. The idea seems to have found little support elsewhere and it was dropped.

When Eisenhower and Eden met in January 1956 to discuss the Middle East situation they found it impossible to reach any useful agreement. Eden was in favour of drastic steps, and for a time he argued that an unfavourable territorial settlement should be imposed upon Israel to stop Egypt's apparent leftward swing and to save Israel from herself. He also wanted, at the very least, to put some teeth into the Tripartite Declarations; and to create a joint military force which would move in immediately any fighting broke out. The Americans declined, pleading constitutional difficulties. All that emerged from the meetings was a clear picture of the many disagreements between the two countries. These persisted during the Tripartite talks with France in February. After weeks and weeks of discussions the only points of agreement were that Russia, along with Egypt and Israel, would object strongly if Western troops were sent to the trouble spots, and that the Tripartite Powers had no common policy. In lieu, it was decided to work through the Security Council.

In February 1956, Dulles accurately summed up the confusions in American thinking in a statement to the Senate Committee on Foreign Affairs. Arms for Israel was not the answer, he stated, and then forecast that within a few months Egypt would have military superiority. American policy, he affirmed, was based upon the firm implementation of the Tripartite Declaration. The United States was pledged to support 'UN action to save Israel'. But, he emphasized, should Israel be attacked no American aid would be sent without first obtaining the consent of Congress, and the United States would 'look to the UN to give the lead'.[1]

It would be too much to say that the Israelis were profoundly disappointed by the failure of the Anglo–American and the Tripartite talks. They had had little hope that the three Powers

---

[1] US Senate, *Hearings before the Committee on Foreign Relations*, 84th Congress, 2nd session, 24th February 1956, *passim* (G.P.O., Washington, 1956).

would work out a common policy. But they had counted on the Americans being willing to carry out their promises even if the British did not (France was a special case). Dulles's statement to the Senate committee indicated that the Americans had all but abandoned the Tripartite Declaration. Implicit in the Tripartite Declaration was the understanding that an arms balance meant that Israel would have sufficient to defend herself against another combined Arab attack. Evidently this was to go by the board. Also according to the terms of the Declaration the United States, as well as the other signatories, was committed to 'immediate' action against any aggression; 'action both within and outside the United Nations'. Dulles had now altered this: no aid would be given until Congress had approved and even then everything would have to be under the sponsorship of the UN. To the Israelis with memories of UN incompetence during 1947–8, of the effects of the Soviet vetoes in the Security Council, and of the strength of the Arab *bloc* in the Assembly, this was 'tantamount to abandoning Israel to its fate'.[1]

Border violence continued to increase. As always, the *fedayeen* attacks were just that much more intense than previously. Between 7th December 1955 and 9th March 1956 the Israelis claimed 180 separate acts of violence. General Burns was still unable to persuade the Egyptians to issue orders not to fire on Israeli patrols; roads were mined, traffic ambushed and civilians even in the outskirts of Tel Aviv were murdered. Toward the end of March border violence increased yet again, leading, as it had done previously, to a terrible massacre. On 4th April there were four attacks on Israeli patrols, and three soldiers were killed. On the 5th, three similar attacks took place in the morning, one in the presence of a UNTSO Observer. At noon another patrol was attacked, and the exchange of fire lasted for over two hours ending only after the Israelis shelled the Egyptian posts. Less than an hour later, at three, Egyptian batteries began to shell three Israeli settlements. The Israeli local commander seems to have taken the initiative in ordering an immediate retaliatory shelling of the market place in Gaza. About sixty Arabs were killed and a hundred wounded. The next day the *fedayeen* were sent back into Israel to exact revenge.

[1] Sharett to the Knesset, 1st March 1956: *NYT*, 2nd March 1956.

In the meantime, the United States had asked the Security Council to undertake a general discussion of 'the status of compliance given to the General Armistice Agreements'. A draft resolution was submitted authorizing the Secretary-General to undertake 'as a matter of urgent concern' a survey of the problems of enforcing the GAA's and the Council's resolutions; and to arrange with the parties and General Burns for the adoption of any measures necessary to reduce border tensions. Hammarskjold was to report to the Council within a month.

The Arabs argued that the draft resolution was an Israeli plot to force them into a peace settlement. They refused to cooperate unless assurances were given that Hammarskjold would confine himself only to the question of compliance with the GAAs, with the emphasis on the cease-fire provisions. The Russians supported this demand, and the necessary assurances were given. Before he left for the Middle East Hammarskjold promised he would concentrate on gaining agreement on practical means to reduce existing tensions along the frontiers. He pointed out that he did not want his trip 'muddled' by 'side issues'.[1] Later he referred indirectly to these 'side issues' when he explained that he had 'left aside those fundamental issues which so deeply influence the present situation'.[2]

The tour began inauspiciously, for it coincided with the launching of the *fedayeen* following the shelling of Gaza. Before leaving for Cairo Hammarskjold asked both sides to respect the provisions of Article Two of the GAA regarding the prohibition of the use of military or para-military forces. The Israelis agreed immediately but were obviously very annoyed. Since 6th April they had been subjected to a wave of *fedayeen* activity without precedent in scope and violence. On the 8th Ben Gurion announced that he would wait two more days before retaliating in order to give Hammarskjold time to get to Cairo and persuade the Egyptians to call off the raids. The Secretary-General reached Cairo but the raids continued. Ben Gurion repeated his warning on the 10th. On the 11th *Radio Cairo* announced that

[1] *Times*, UN Correspondent, 6th April 1956.

[2] *Report of the Secretary-General. . . . SCOR*, S/3596, 9th May 1956, p. 55. Other documents relevant to his tour are, beginning 12th April, S/3584, S/3586 and S/3587.

the raids in retaliation for the shelling of Gaza were now over. That same day the Egyptian government announced that it accepted Hammarskjold's request regarding the use of military and para-military forces. But the *fedayeen* already in Israel could not be recalled and that night five more people were killed and fifteen wounded.

In a sharp exchange of letters with Hammarskjold[1] Ben Gurion expressed his dissatisfaction with a situation in which the Egyptians ordered border violence whenever they wished; not even the presence in Cairo of the UN Secretary-General inhibited them. However, the bulk of the long correspondence between the two men centred on the controversy over the limits of Hammarskjold's terms of reference. Hammarskjold insisted that he had been sent out to discuss the armistice provisions with regard to the existing state of tension along the border. Other matters could be discussed only in so far as the various parties were willing to discuss them with him in his general capacity of UN Secretary-General. The Israelis persisted during his trip in their attempts to persuade Hammarskjold to widen the scope of his talks. They argued that Egypt's reaffirmation of Article Two could not be considered genuine and unconditional if she continued to ignore the Security Council's resolution on the Suez blockade. Similarly, Jordan could not be considered as implementing the GAA when she refused to carry out the provisions relating to the Special Committee, the Wailing Wall, Mount Scopus and so on. Hammarskjold, however, refused to be carried beyond what he considered to be his terms of reference.

He was largely successful in obtaining agreement in principle to most of the measures Burns had been proposing for the past eighteen months (although few of these were ever implemented). Also, all the governments agreed to an unconditional reaffirmation of the cease-fire provisions of the various GAAs, subject only to the right to the exercise of self-defence as defined in the UN Charter. In his Report, Hammarskjold explained that he had insisted on a reaffirmation of Article Two, comprising the cease-fire provisions, because it was based upon Charter commitments and the Council's resolution of July 15, 1948. Accordingly, the principle of reciprocity did not apply. He

[1] *Report of the Secretary-General . . . SCOR*, S/3596, 9th May 1956

pointed out that he had not obtained a general agreement to comply with all the provisions of the GAAs; this, he wrote, was the next vital step. Allied to this was the necessity for improving 'the general political relations between the parties . . .'; lacking this nothing of lasting value could be accomplished. The Israelis regarded the report as of 'first-class importance', but considered that everything depended upon what steps were taken next.

At the subsequent Council meeting Britain submitted a draft resolution in which the parties were ordered to implement the local arrangements already agreed to in principle; to adhere to the unconditional cease-fire; and to establish full compliance with the General Armistice Agreements, and with the Council's previous resolutions on the border situation. In the Preamble the Security Council expressed itself as 'conscious of the need to create conditions in which a peaceful settlement on a mutually acceptable basis of the dispute between the parties can be made'. This paragraph was almost word for word the same as that included in the text of the Anglo–Russian communiqué issued after Premier Khrushchev's visit to Britain in April, and the Russians had consented to its being included in the draft resolution. But the Arabs objected to this paragraph so the Russians insisted that it be withdrawn. The Arabs claimed that the paragraph was designed to force them into peace talks with Israel, and to circumvent the General Assembly's resolutions on borders and refugees. The British, making what was to be their last attempt to persuade the Arabs to accept some reasonable settlement, agreed to delete the paragraph in order to achieve the 'lowest common denominator of agreement'. The resolution was adopted in its truncated form on 4th June.

The Arabs hailed this as a great diplomatic victory.[1] They saw themselves as having forced the Council to accept their limitations on Hammarskjold's mission, and, what is more important, upon the GAAs as a whole. Only the cease-fire provisions of the GAAs had been restored. Nothing concrete had been done about the question of compliance with the general provisions of the GAAs—on which the Israelis placed such store—or about the implementation of the other provisions relating to local arrangements.

[1] See *MEM*, 9th June, 1956, pp. 2–6.

From Gaza to Nationalization : February 1955–July 1956

On 17th June 1956, Moshe Sharett resigned as Foreign Minister and was replaced by Golda Meir, a strong supporter of Ben Gurion. Moderation—at least the Israeli version of moderation—had failed. The activists were in full control. Since November 1955 Sharett had usually had his way. There had been no 'official' retaliation raids, not even during periods of great provocation. The one exception, Tiberias, had been undertaken without his knowledge when he was out of the country. Considerable effort—to the extent allowed by public opinion—had gone into cooperating with the Egyptians and Hammarskjold but there was nothing to show for it. Also, Sharett had been unable to obtain arms or a security pact with any of the Powers.[1] Every day Israel's position compared to that of the Arabs continued to deteriorate. Every day their capacity to destroy her increased.

A week after Sharett resigned, President Nasser, caught up in the web of his struggles with the British and the Americans, nationalized the Suez Canal Company. By a simple exercise of governmental authority, the application of a law recognized in every land, the unsuspecting President gave his enemies the opportunity and the excuse to destroy him.

[1] Ben Gurion and the Ministry of Defence made all the arrangements with the French.

Chapter Fourteen

ISRAEL AND EGYPT
PART THREE:
PRELUDE TO THE INVASION

THE nationalization of the Suez Canal Company, like the Czech arms deal, stands as one of the great advances in Egypt's struggle to free herself from the coils of psychological bondage. It also stands as a convenient mark of the rising tide of war. On this day, we are accustomed to say, Egypt made Britain and France into her enemies and brought them into alliance with Israel. The claim is exaggerated. The forces of war had been afoot for many months. The nationalization of the Suez Canal Company does not mark the beginning of the story but the final chapter. The story is a long and complicated one. To understand how it began we must go back to 1954. Since the subject of this study is Israel we shall begin with her. At the same time we should remember that she did not play a decisive role in creating the conditions which led to the invasion. She had her own game to play, but the only circumstances in which it could be played were set up for her by France, Britain—and Egypt.

In the summer of 1954 the Israelis were undecided about Egypt and her intentions. The *rapprochement* was obviously a failure, propaganda attacks had increased, and the blockade was slowly being tightened again. But it was still not certain which way the Egyptians would jump once their treaty with Britain had been safely negotiated. As soon as the Anglo-

Egyptian treaty was initialled, guerrillas were sent into Israel, pipelines dynamited, roads mined, and coincident with this were statements by high Egyptian officials in clear, unmistakeable terms to the effect that Egypt's next task was to liberate Palestine. The Israelis had their answer: the Egyptians were moving towards war. The Israelis reacted by asking for arms to balance those being sent to Egypt, and to Iraq, and for a security pact with the United States. To ensure that there was no mistake about Egypt's intentions Israel sent numerous messages to her through the medium of Britain, France and the US requesting her to stop guerrilla activities or risk retaliation. By February 1955 the Israelis were satisfied that President Nasser could have no doubt of what they would do if his border policy did not change. The Gaza Raid, large and fierce as it was, was similar to those launched against Jordan (except that the Israelis had learned to take care to avoid injuring civilians) and indicated that the Israelis, whatever their public demands for arms, felt capable of handling the Egyptian border in the same way as they had handled the Jordanian. Egypt, unlike Jordan, had the potential to defeat the Israelis, but this could not affect the Israelis' capacity to handle the situation as it existed then and as it was likely to develop over the next years.

One cannot be precise of course, but if one were to point to a time when the Israelis began to consider seriously the prospect of war with Egypt it was during these months between the summer of 1954 and February 1955. It was during this time that the Israelis began to believe that Egypt would go to war as soon as she believed that she could win. However disheartened the Israelis may have been by this knowledge they were still in control of the situation and they knew it. There was no immediate need to prepare for war. It is true that requests for arms were sent out to the Powers but this was part of the normal merry-go-round of 'arms balance'. What the Israelis did was raise their price for not considering war with Egypt. In 1953 or early 1954 they would have accepted a relatively quiet border, a modicum of cooperation between local commanders and some relaxation of the blockade as a satisfactory indication that Egypt did not intend to pursue an aggressive policy. By January 1955 they required more than this. As the months passed and the blockade was tightened, the Gulf of Akaba closed, the boycott extended, the *fedayeen* attacks increased, the propaganda intensified, it took more, for example, than a lull in the border attacks to persuade the Israelis that Egypt had ended her hostile policy. In June, news of Egypt's negotiations with Russia began to come through and the Israeli 'price' rose accordingly. It was then, in early September, that Ben Gurion warned Egypt that if she persisted in keeping the Straits closed Israel would use force to open them within the next twelve months.

It is interesting that Ben Gurion should still have considered the economic situation more pressing than the military. Evidently he felt that Israel could deal with the *fedayeen* on their own terms, and that Russian aid to Egypt did not present any immediate threat to the arms balance. The economic situation was much more serious; apparently so serious that it justified risking war to gain direct access to Asian and African markets. That he did not mention arms, although he knew of the arms negotiations with Russia, indicates that he underestimated the amounts involved. Had he known surely his price for peace would have been higher.

The Czech arms deal completely altered Israel's relations with Egypt and the rest of the Arab world. 'No man in his senses', Ben Gurion said, 'will believe that Nasser and his colleagues might use the Soviet arms for a war against the West, or the British arms for a war against the East.' Israel was the obvious target. All the major Egyptian leaders said so, the radio said so, the Press said so, the border situation implied as much. Who were the Israelis to disregard this mass of circumstantial evidence?

It is hard to say how set the Israeli activists were on war. Possibly, if Egypt had met their price by opening up the Gulf of Akaba they might have been persuaded to hold off, possibly not. Israeli strategy always had to start from several unpalatable bases. Israel had no hinterland into which she could withdraw and recover her strength. She had no manpower resources upon which to draw once the main armies were engaged. She had no natural resources by which to sustain and feed herself once she was at war, or once the sea-coast was blockaded. Her land area was attenuated, her lines of communication exposed, invading armies could split her asunder at any one of a dozen places. She always had to be prepared to fight on four fronts at once. Potentially she was far inferior to Egypt alone. She could not afford to cut her corners too finely. She had to strike while the calibre of her individual soldiers was still sufficient to outweigh the quantitative disadvantages. The decisive month seems to have been April 1956; it being then decided, barring unexpected changes in Egypt's attitude or in the international climate, to go to war as soon as all necessary preparations had been made.

April 1956 was a very bad month for the Israelis. The armistice régime was in ruins; the Security Council was useless; the Tripartite Declaration was virtually disowned; the Great Power conferences had achieved nothing. All the safeguards laboriously built up around the cease-fire in 1948 had disappeared. President Nasser was steadily extending his influence over the other Arab countries. No one seemed able to stand before him. *Fedayeen*, controlled by Egyptian military attachés, operated across all four of Israel's borders. General Glubb was expelled from Jordan along with most of the British officers in the Arab Legion (Nasser claimed that he had no hand in this—but the effect, which was what concerned the Israelis, was the same as if he had). It seemed that soon Nasser would be able to do as he wished in the Middle East. Along the border the Egyptians refused to cooperate. The bulk of their army was in the eastern Sinai near the Israeli border and April was the worst month to date for *fedayeen*.

Strategic considerations aside, the effect of all this upon public opinion in Israel was profound. The first and most important function of any government is to provide for the protection of its citizens. A government which cannot do that soon loses its position. By early 1956 the Israeli population was severely exercised by its lack of security and its grim future prospects. Public opinion is seldom rational, particularly in times of stress, and the Israeli population was not likely to heed comments that they had brought many of their troubles down on themselves, or that President Nasser was not the evil genius they made him out to be, or that the Arabs had strong justification for what they were doing. The people had fixed on the one central issue. Their security, present and future, was in serious danger, and they demanded that their government do something about it. No government dare ignore such a summons. The Czech arms deal had darkened Israel's future prospects as nothing else had done. But it was the *fedayeen* who brought that insecurity home to every Israeli, who created that great, swelling tide of public demands for action, which drowned the voice of the moderates, and gave the government no alternative but action sooner rather than later. It is true that the Israelis had suffered less from border marauders than the Arabs. In 1956 (before the Sinai Campaign), about fifty-eight Israelis were killed and one hundred and sixty wounded: the Arabs had about two hundred killed and two hundred wounded.[1] But while the moral implications of killing a man are the same whatever his nation, the political implications are not necessarily so.

In Egypt, only the Palestinians living in Gaza or soldiers and police stationed there or in the area were affected. In Syria, the only people affected were that small number living or stationed in the immediate vicinity of Lake Tiberias. In Lebanon, only those living right next to the border had anything to fear and that from accidental shots. Even in Jordan there were few instances of Israelis penetrating more than four or five miles, and that was mainly in the sparsely populated Hebron hills south of Jerusalem. In Cairo, Damascus, Amman and Beirut—everywhere in the Arab countries except the areas mentioned—the citizens moved about freely and without fear. One could walk in the fields on a lonely afternoon, or travel to see friends in the evening. When one drove from Homs to Aleppo at night, or from Cairo to Alexandria, one did not think of Israeli raiders. In the Arab countries the 'belt of fear' could be drawn by a red pencil running alongside the border. The destruction of Qibya was a terrible thing, but the citizen of Nablus a few miles away was safe. In Israel the 'belt of fear' ran from border to border, north to south, east to west. At night travel anywhere in the country was dangerous—during the day anywhere that was

---

[1] In 1954, the Israelis suffered 180 casualties from infiltration: 50 were caused by people from Gaza. In 1955, the Israelis suffered 258 casualties: 192 were caused by people from Gaza—Ben Gurion to the Knesset, 2nd January 1956: *JAD*, 13th January 1956, p. 529.

relatively isolated, a highway in the south, an orchard outside
Tel Aviv, a suburb of Jerusalem. The *fedayeen* roamed everywhere. A small group of three or four men in one busy night
could throw a whole district into panic for months. Parts of the
country, even in the fertile north, saw only the occasional military or police patrol; no civilian would go there because of the
fedayeen. No one felt secure, no place was considered safe.

In such circumstances a comparative analysis of casualty
statistics is meaningless. To kill an Israeli is no greater crime
than to kill an Arab, but the effect upon public opinion is something else again. Fifty-eight dead is perhaps not very many in
one year—more people than that might die in road accidents.
But it was the manner of death that was important. The Israelis
were not more easily frightened than other people, but when
each felt the peril to be so close he was bound to turn to his
government and demand his primary, fundamental right: protection. Furthermore, economic development in the whole of
the south was seriously hindered and development of the south
was one of the keystones of Israeli economic planning. Here was
another challenge no government could ignore. Taking the
fedayeen operation as a whole, the number of casualties, the
amount of machinery and goods stolen, the number of mining
incidents, the dynamited pipelines: all were less important than
their psychological impact. If the Egyptians' intentions were to
strike fear into the hearts of Israelis they succeeded. It is odd that
they did not consider that such acts would also arouse anger, and
that an angry population would demand an end to its fears.

In April it was finally decided by Ben Gurion and those
around him that Egypt meant war. Nothing that transpired in
the following months indicated that they might be wrong. Israel
had to attack first. But the Israelis were not strong enough to
attack Egypt and at the same time maintain an adequate defensive posture along the other borders. Arms had to be obtained. There had to be a favourable line-up of Great Powers;
but over this the Israelis had little control. They could only
wait and seize their opportunity when it arose. They did not
have long to wait.

The French were the central figures in the events of the next
months. Basically they were interested in maintaining their

position in North Africa, particularly Algeria, and in retaining such of their influence as still remained in Syria and Lebanon. They believed that the Baghdad Pact was 'a gigantic error' based as it was on the assumption that the security problem dominated everything. The French argued that the Soviet challenge had to be met where it was most dangerous, in the economic field. And it could be met only by a common policy between the Western Powers, a policy which was conspicuous by its absence. Attempts to drag the Arab States into security pacts would lead to trouble, perhaps disaster. The Arabs must be left to work out their security problems by themselves. Also, attempts to carve up Israel in order to appease the Arabs would solve nothing and only cause more instability and friction than already existed. The French were convinced that the Tripartite Declaration was the best weapon to hand for controlling the Arab–Israeli dispute, and that it should be redefined in clear, practicable terms, and the arms balance restored.[1]

For a short time it appeared that France's opposition to the Baghdad Pact might provide some basis for her cooperation with Egypt. But attempts in this direction failed because of Egyptian support for the FLN in Algeria. On 14th March, Foreign Minister Christian Pineau, one of the few people in France to support Nasser, met him in Cairo. He proposed that France would not support the Baghdad Pact or other Anglo–American attempts to build a Middle East military alliance on condition that Egypt ended her assistance to the FLN. Nasser refused, and thereby alienated his most influential ally in France. Two days previous, on 12th March, Premier Mollet had met with Prime Minister Eden to discuss their common interests on Egypt (this was just after General Glubb had been expelled from Jordan). In a way Pineau's offer was Nasser's last chance.

For some months now the French had been eyeing the Israelis with growing friendliness. Relations between the two countries had been fairly good ever since the 1940's when the Israelis forced the British out of Palestine. A succession of socialist

[1] From a French memorandum to Washington and London prior to the Eden–Eisenhower talks: *JAD*, 10th February 1956, p. 646; vd. also *NYT* and *Times*, 3rd March 1956.

governments in France had viewed Israeli achievements with approval, and French defence officials and army officers saw in Israel's army a means of defending their own interests. Israel was the only country capable of standing up to Nasser's Egypt. Also Israel had an effective stabilizing influence upon the general situation. So long as Israel remained sufficiently strong the borders of Syria were safe from Iraq. Similarly, the Israelis were in a position to prevent an Egyptian or an Iraqi takeover of Jordan. In these matters Franco–Israeli interests in containing Egyptian and Iraqi influence coincided perfectly.[1] By mid-1955 the French considered themselves Israel's allies and were ready to fight should she be attacked. This was a defensive, not an offensive alliance. The Israelis submitted a 'shopping list' to France and some planes, tanks and guns were sent,[2] but this seems to have been done within the framework of the arms balance described in the Tripartite Declaration, and left Israel still with inferior quantities of equipment.

France's eventual decision that Nasser must be destroyed coincided almost exactly with Israel's. The French took another look at Israel's 'shopping list' and in mid-April there was the first of several shipments of Mystère fighters to Israel. What had started out being an arrangement for Israel's defence was now evolving into an agreement for the invasion of Egypt. It seems likely that sometime in June or early in July, that is before the Suez Canal Company was nationalized, Ben Gurion went to France secretly to discuss arrangements with Premier Mollet, and immediately after the nationalization decree France began to ship large shipments of arms and equipment to Israel, this time with the utmost secrecy.[3]

In the meantime, independent of their growing alliance with Israel, the French were constructing another one with the

[1] In this context see Ben Gurion's statement that Israel would not stand by and see Syria's independence 'merged' with Iraq: *JOMER*, 6th April 1956, p. 5.

[2] The Arab League claimed that these included 30 Mystère jets, 15 Ouragan fighters and 33 Sherman tanks: *MEM*, 7th April 1956, p. 29. These estimates seem much too high.

[3] Childers, *Road to Suez*, although weak on Arab–Israeli relations, is the best detailed, comprehensive analysis of this period, and I have drawn on it extensively or this chapter. See also Elizabeth Monroe, *Britain's Moment in the Middle East*.

British, more accurately with Eden and some of his colleagues. Here too there was a happy coincidence of interests in March–April 1956. Like the French, the British were concerned over the growing influence in other lands of President Nasser and of his ideas of 'positive neutralism'. They had been especially watchful since January 1955 when he had wrathfully denounced the incipient Baghdad Pact and set himself up as the opponent of everything for which Iraqi Premier Nuri es-Said stood. In November 1955 there had been this strange interlude of promised cooperation between Eden and Nasser which had never materialized. In December of that year old hostilities were renewed. On 1st March 1956 General Glubb and most of the British officers in the Arab Legion were expelled from Jordan. The news reached Foreign Minister Selwyn Lloyd while he was talking with Nasser in Cairo. Nasser immediately denied any foreknowledge of or responsibility for the expulsions. Probably he was telling the truth, but his propaganda machine hailed it as a great victory for 'Nasserism' and a great blow to the imperialists. One can imagine Lloyd's humiliation and anger. It was an affront which he and his government would neither forget nor forgive. Even the calmer heads amongst them had to admit that even if Nasser were not connected with the expulsions in Jordan the effect was the same as if he had been.

Both Eden and Nuri saw the main issue clearly. The pro-British connexion of Jordan was threatened by an Egyptian takeover. Both leaders considered this eventuality incompatible with their respective national interests. For a year now the two men had been discussing the possibility of dividing Jordan up between Iraq and Israel, using this as a basis for an Arab–Israel settlement and going on from there to construct a general Middle East defence alliance. Nasser's 'positive neutrality' and the arms deal made haste necessary. If Nasser, or pro-Nasser groups, ever succeeded in gaining control of Jordan then Britain's influence in the country would be shattered, and Nuri would be hard put to defend himself against the ideas of such a successful enemy pressing so close on his borders. The two men were in agreement that Nasser must be removed; and in the subsequent confusion Jordan could be duly apportioned and the original plan proceeded with. It is difficult to say when this arrangement was finally decided upon, but it was sometime between March and July 1956.

This brings us to the Americans. They had been largely responsible for the early success of the Egyptian revolutionary government. But as time went on they grew increasingly disillusioned with these men who refused to tie themselves to Western defence alliances and to the anti-Russian, anti-Communist *bloc*. The man most responsible for American foreign policy was Secretary of State John Foster Dulles. Seldom has the international arena contained a figure of such high-mindedness, such rectitude. He conceived of foreign policy in moral terms. He did not like 'neutrals'. To Mr. Dulles one was either for the forces of good and against Russia and China, or one was against America. The choice was as simple as that. His views reflected the thinking of many Americans and were deeply rooted in the social history of the people. In the early '50's Prime Minister Nehru was deeply suspect, Marshal Tito was guilty. In April 1955 Nasser went to Bandung where he associated not only with these men but with others even worse, men like Chou En-Lai. Nasser came back a new man, a world figure, a major exponent of neutralism. Bandung marks a major expansion in Nasser's intellectual and political development, but it was the beginning of the end for him in America. However suitable and understandable neutralism was in the Middle East it had no place in the America of the middle '50's. Then came Nasser's violent opposition to the Baghdad Pact, the increasing antagonism of his propaganda machine towards the Americans, and the Czech arms deal in September 1955. Relations between the two countries went from bad to worse during the next months.

On both sides there were misunderstandings, fantasy, and always suspicion and anger. In May 1956, the Americans, who had always accepted that Israel must have a reasonable amount of arms, agreed to release France from some of her NATO obligations in order that she might divert Mystères to Israel (this was apart from the secret shipments about which apparently the Americans knew nothing). Similar permission was given to Canada to divert Sabre jets to Israel (these were never delivered). Because of this and for various other reasons, on 6th

May Nasser suddenly announced full diplomatic recognition of Red China. Nasser's own newspaper, *Al Goumhourya*, described recognition as a 'strong diplomatic blow to the West's very existence'.[1] A military mission was sent to Peking, the point of the trip being that even if, as Russia had suggested, the UN imposed an arms embargo on the Middle East, China would not be bound by it, and Egypt would still be able to obtain arms.

From this it was only a short step to Dulles's cancellation in July of the offer to finance the Aswan Dam. The decision was not entirely unexpected, except perhaps in Egypt. The British, French, Israelis, and Iraqis had been arguing for some months that the offer should be rescinded. There was strong domestic opposition to the granting of enormous sums of money to neutralists, left-wingers, and the like. There was an even more widespread aversion toward the kind of diplomatic blackmail Nasser seemed to be using. There were growing complaints from America's friends that neutrals like Nasser got more aid and attention than did her loyal allies.

It has been suggested that the Israelis were largely responsible for persuading Dulles to withdraw the proffered loan. There is no doubt that the Israelis were against the loan and worked vigorously in conjunction with the various Zionist and pro-Zionist organizations to have it rescinded. But in this instance the pro-Israeli groups were riding a groundswell of anti-Egyptian, anti-Nasser feeling. Furthermore, Dulles and President Eisenhower were almost immune to the pressures of pro-Israeli groups. They had proved this as early as October 1953 when because of the B'nat Ya'acov dispute they had halted aid to Israel despite the imminent state and municipal elections in which the Jewish vote was heavily involved.[2]

---

[1] Quoted in *MEM*, 19th May 1956, p. 8.

[2] They proved it again when they took decisive steps to halt the Israeli invasion of Egypt despite the protests of the local Zionists. Even so, the number of Jews voting the Republican ticket continued to increase. Lawrence H. Fuchs, *The Political Behavior of American Jews* (Glencoe, Ill. 1956) is informative, but humorist Allan Sherman is briefer: 'Harvey and Sheila moved to West L.A. They bought a house one day, financed by F.H.A. It had a swimming pool, full of H_2O, traded their used MG, for a new XKE, switched to the G.O.P. That's the way things go.' 1963 Warner Brothers Records Inc.

Dulles had, so he thought, good and sufficient reasons for cancelling the offer of a loan. There is no reason to believe that pro-Israeli pressure had any important influence upon his decision.

From the cancellation of the loan for the Aswan Dam it was only another step to the nationalization of the Suez Canal Company. Truth does not always have a noticeable effect upon events. Nasser did not nationalize the Suez Canal. He nationalized the company which was responsible for taking ships through the Canal, maintaining it properly, hiring pilots and so on. The Suez Canal belonged to Egypt. It had always been considered an integral part of Egyptian territory. The water, the bed, the banks, all were as Egyptian as the Thames is British. The Canal was 'international' because of explicit treaty arrangements between the Egyptian government and various contracting Powers which guaranteed free passage to ships of all nations. The Company was not responsible for enforcing free passage, or for not enforcing it. That was always the responsibility of the Egyptian government. Whether the Suez Canal Company was nationalized or privately owned had no bearing on the status of the Canal and the implementation of the international treaty arrangements regarding its use. For example, the argument that nationalization would mean that Egypt had a stranglehold over the Canal was meaningless. She had always had that 'stranglehold'. Israeli ships had been denied the use of the Canal since 1948. The status of the Canal Company had no bearing on the issue. But all of this, while of academic interest, was irrelevant to the affairs of the time. President Nasser had exercised, admittedly in an abrupt and rude manner, what was an undoubted right of his government, a right sanctioned by the law of every country. In the exercise of that right Nasser burnt his last bridge.

Nationalization marks not the beginning of the story of the invasion but the last chapter. Nasser had lost control of the situation. He could avert disaster only by offering peace to Israel on her terms and by rescinding the nationalization decree. Both were politically impossible. Consequently he could only struggle vainly to twist away from the men gathering round to destroy him.[1]

In a consecutive and apparently planned series of actions, Nasser persuaded the Israelis that he intended to invade them. He had said so, his Ministers had said so, the propaganda machine said so; the boycott, the blockade, the arms deal, the *fedayeen* implied as much. So the Israelis decided to strike before he was strong enough to destroy them. Similarly, he antagonized the British by carrying on the struggle against them in all parts of the Middle East, and, latterly, in Africa. He attempted to extend his influence throughout the Arab world to the detriment of King Husain, Nuri es-Said, British oil interests along the Persian Gulf, and the British government. He attemped to break up a pro-Western military alliance based on Turkey, Iraq and Pakistan. He took steps which resulted in increased Russian influence in the Middle East. He antagonized the French by assisting the FLN in Algeria, by attacking pro-French leaders like Bourguiba, by extending his and Russian influence into Syria and by threatening a takeover of the Fertile Crescent. He antagonized the Americans by his, or his propaganda machine's, rude comments about American imperialism, by his insistence upon neutralism, and by his heavy flirtations with the Russians and worse still the Chinese. He antagonized the more conservative elements in the Arab countries and he refused to compromise with Nuri es-Said, the most formidable of the old-time Arab leaders.

The list of condemnations is a long one. Whether they are justified or not is not entirely to the point. To drive the French out of Algeria, to release the Persian Gulf from British tutelage, to insist upon Arab neutrality, to restore Palestine to the Arabs, are to many people commendable objects, worthy of the most vigorous efforts. But the plain political fact is that, commendable or not, moral or immoral, President Nasser and his government managed to antagonize just about everyone who was in a position to do them harm. Inexperience, lack of tact,

---

[1] One of the themes of Childers' book is that the British and the French deliberately engineered the withdrawal of the Aswan loan knowing that in retaliation he would nationalize the Canal and thereby provide them with an opportunity to move in.

misunderstanding, unrealism, all played their part. The simple fact, pleasant or unpleasant, is that once the Suez Canal Company had been nationalized the Egyptians had widened the gulf between them and their adversaries beyond the capacities of bridge builders. Since the early part of 1956, Eden, Mollet, Nuri, Ben Gurion and others wanted to see Nasser brought down and the Egypt he was trying to build destroyed, in the belief that he represented only himself and that Egypt would be other than she was were he and his colleagues to disappear. It took only this last step to set the scene. There was nothing left to do now but work out the details of the act.[1]

---

[1] *Crisis: The Inside Story of the Suez Conspiracy*, by Terence Robertson (Toronto, 1964) was published while this book was being prepared for publication so that there was no time to assess and incorporate his research.

Robertson argues that Nasser began preparations for the Suez takeover immediately after the Anglo–Egyptian treaty was signed in October 1954 (p. 6), and also that Nasser was prepared for Dulles' cancellation of the Aswan loan offer weeks before it took place (p. 65). Nasser is said to have received a Soviet offer of a loan for the dam in mid-June (p. 62).

Also, see below p. 224 n.

Chapter Fifteen

ISRAEL AND EGYPT
PART FOUR:
THE FINAL PREPARATIONS
(July–October 1956)

FOLLOWING the nationalization decree, about half of Egypt's forces in Sinai were withdrawn back to the Canal as a precaution against the British and French military build-up in Cyprus. This was followed by a significant improvement in the border situation around Gaza. None the less it was still bad enough to be considered serious. There were frequent incidents between patrols, many mining incidents, a heavy increase in thefts and attempted break-ins and some *fedayeen* attacks. The Israeli border settlements suffered heavily and often retaliated with small raids. By the end of the summer when it appeared that the worst of the crisis over Suez had passed there was a slow but steady increase in activity from Gaza. Along the other borders the situation remained serious. Accidental and haphazard infiltration had virtually ended. Jordan in particular took strict measures to ensure that the border remained quiet. None the less *fedayeen* managed to expand their operations out of Jordan, and Syria, although here they were never very active. Throughout the summer the border situation remained tense, and in the autumn it grew uglier. The Israelis launched several very large raids against Jordan police and military posts during September and October in supposed retaliation for incidents committed by the *fedayeen* operating out of Jordan. Certainly the provocation was there, but in part at least the raids were a feint designed to keep attention focused on the Jordan border while preparations were made to attack Egypt.

The Israelis still had every reason to believe that the lull, such as it was, during the summer and autumn would end once the Egyptians were persuaded that the danger of an Anglo–French invasion had passed; and that they could expect the following months to be worse than ever before. Nothing happened during the summer or the autumn to convince them that the *fedayeen* would be stopped or that Egypt would not invade when she was ready.

During the summer and autumn Israel's plans for the invasion went ahead. The events of those months are complicated and obscured in shrouds of official secrecy, special pleadings, and propaganda. There is not the space to indulge in a detailed analysis of all the ifs and buts, nor is it necessary. The main lines of development are fairly clear, the motivations obvious; it remains only to fill in the outline.

The French were the central figures. Apparently they had two separate sets of secret arrangements: one with the Israelis; and the other with the British. In the week following nationalization they met with the Israelis and drew up a detailed agreement for large arms shipments. France also agreed to provide Israel with some naval support, air transport, and, at the very last moment, fighter squadrons to strengthen the defences of the Israeli metropolitan areas against attacks from Egyptian Ilyushins, or from the other Arab countries.[1] At the same time the French and the British were collecting an invasion force in Cyprus. The French were ready to attack immediately, but the British argued that it would take several months more to collect an adequate force, and so the invasion was postponed.

The British knew little about Franco–Israeli cooperation except that it existed. But they too were playing their own game, possibly without the knowledge of the French. Eden and Nuri

[1] Ironically, it was these which led to the first charges of collusion. The pilots had no time to change their uniforms for Israeli ones, and they were spotted by newspapermen.

were proceeding with their plan to occupy Jordan. The occupation was to take place before Jordan's elections on 22nd October, which the nationalist, pro-Egyptian party was almost certain to win. The plan involved sending in Iraqi troops, ostensibly to protect King Husain, but actually to take over the country. Jordan then would be divided between Iraq and Israel. The two countries would settle their differences with each other. This would provide the basis of a general Arab-Israeli reconciliation. During the chaos of the Iraqi takeover in Jordan, Egypt would be invaded and Nasser overthrown. This would leave Nuri free to lead the Arab world into a Western defence alliance. That the breadth of these plans and the naïve assumptions underlying them bore a striking resemblance to Britain's earlier plans, *circa* World War One, to 'biff' the French out of the Middle East and to establish her hegemony over the area between the Persian Gulf and the Mediterranean, was possibly an indication of how seriously Eden was influenced by obsolete, romantic ideas of Britain's role in the Arab world.

King Husain, however, refused to allow the Iraqis into the country. The Israelis threatened to attack the West Bank if the Iraqis did enter Jordan. Their threat was highlighted by their massive raids against Jordan during September and October. It is possible, of course, that the Israelis wanted to frighten Husain into allowing the Iraqis into Jordan and so facilitate the takeover. But this seems unlikely if only because of Britain and Israel's apparent ignorance of each other's intentions prior to 16th October. In any case, Israel's protests against the entrance of Iraqi troops were so loud and convincing as to strengthen Husain's determination not to have them. The elections were held without them, and they did not enter the country until early November, after the invasion of Egypt, when anti-British feeling in Jordan was so strong that a take-over was impossible.

The keystone of the Anglo–French plan was to ensure that Nasser did not settle the dispute over the nationalization of the Canal Company. Everything depended upon making it appear that he was obstinate and untrustworthy, and that the Canal must be taken away from him, by force if necessary. The original intention was to go to the Security Council with a strong resolution which the Egyptians would oppose and the Russians veto. Then it would be possible to claim that, since there was no possibility of peaceful redress of grievance, force would have to be used. The Americans forestalled this by insisting upon a conference of Canal users. The meetings held, the issues raised, are not of much importance (except that Egypt still refused to allow Israel free passage through the Canal). Anxious to make a peaceful settlement, Nasser went as far as he could in meeting the demands of the more reasonable, disinterested countries. What these countries wanted were assurances on various points, and over the weeks and months an agreement was gradually hammered out. This hastened the Anglo–French desire to bring matters to a head. It would not do to invade Egypt after the dispute had been settled.

To watch the British and French governments during those summer months was a depressing experience. It is easy to see why the Israelis thought it necessary to go to war. Whatever one might think about Israel's right to exist or the rectitude of its policies, it is reasonable that a country thinking itself threatened by invasion will do what it can to save itself. But what of the British and French? What did they have to lose that justified so dangerous a blow to the UN and world peace? Was it simply that millions of French and Englishmen could not bear to be bested by the Egyptians, the despised gypos of colonial days? During that summer, the carefully concealed prejudices, the hatreds and frustrations pent up over years of post-war decline and defeat, came spilling over the dam of manners and gentility in a fetid, mucky tide of jingoism.

The Americans, particularly Dulles, stuck by Egypt although they had no reason to like Nasser: neutrality was 'immoral', and nationalization created an awkward precedent for the future of the Panama Canal. None the less, Dulles kept Britain and France away from Egypt with exasperating diplomatic footwork. He persuaded them not to go to the Security Council right away, but instead to a maritime conference where a lot of time and dangerous energy could be dissipated in speechmaking and lobbying. He kept them wondering whether or not he favoured force: each week he said something different. It was a performance which drove them wild with vexation.

Finally, overriding Dulles's protests, Britain and France went to the Security Council on 23rd September. The invasion fleet was ready; all that was needed now was to complete the diplomatic preliminaries. In the Council, the Americans, Egyptians, Indians and Hammarskjold collaborated to draw up a compromise resolution to meet all reasonable demands. The British and French countered by tacking on riders which they knew the Egyptians would oppose and the Russians veto. Accordingly, the British and the French could leave the Council on 11th October claiming that peaceful negotiation had failed. On 16th October, Eden met with Mollet in Paris for long secret talks. Presumably at this time each told the other as much as he thought it expedient for him to know. At the very least a general agreement was reached on a coordinated tripartite invasion of Egypt.

As I have tried to make clear there is absolutely no substance to claims that there was no collusion between the three countries. For months now, the British and French, and the French and the Israelis, had been discussing and planning ways to deal with Egypt. The French and the British were agreed on invasion immediately after nationalization at the very latest— and probably months before then. The Israelis had started to think about it seriously after the Czech arms deal—and it is unlikely that they hid anything from their closest allies, the French. By April 1956 the two countries were in fairly close agreement over what was to be done. The evidence suggests that until the Eden–Mollet meeting on 16th October the British had not been told that the Israelis intended to attack within the next few weeks and that France was actively supporting them with arms. This may seem strange but no more so than many other things which were happening then.

The plans for attacks must have been based on two premises. One was that Israel alone had to inflict a clear, decisive victory over Egypt. There could be no shame for Nasser in being defeated by a tripartite invasion; but if he were defeated by Israel alone the humiliation could be ruinous. This would be true even if there were, as there would have to be, obvious evidence of large numbers of French arms: Egypt had her Czech arms,

Israel had French ones. Israel had to inflict her defeat upon Egypt before the Anglo–French invasion.

The second premise was that the British, and to a much lesser extent the French, must not be connected with the Israeli invasion. There had to be no signs of collusion. If there were, it would destroy British influence in the Middle East, and with it that of her allies there. Therefore the Anglo–French invasion would take place after the Israeli invasion, at the time when the Israelis had advanced so far westward that the fighting endangered the security of the Canal and international navigation. This would provide the necessary excuse for an allied landing to protect the Zone and, in the way of things, for the overthrow of Nasser and the establishment of a more amenable government in Egypt.

In the last two weeks of October final arrangements were completed. We do not know the exact timetable, but Childers' seems to be a reasonable estimate.

2nd November, Friday. Beginning of the weekend when everyone relaxes; the US election moving into its last frenzied week. Israel would attack in the morning and the fighting would continue until

5th November, when the fighting would be near the Canal, endangering free passage. The British and the French would then deliver their Ultimatum ordering both sides to withdraw ten miles from the Canal. It would be the day before the American elections and Eisenhower would be helpless. The Egyptians would reject the Ultimatum.

6th November, |US Election Day. The Ultimatum would expire and the bombing of Egypt would begin. Landing-craft would sail from Malta—three days to Port Said. Paratroops would land, great international confusion, and Iraqi troops would be in Jordan.

7th November, the UN meets but is not agreed on what action to take and unable to muster a majority to oppose the paratroop landings. Eden and Mollet argue persuasively that they are acting only to separate the combatants and to protect the Canal.

Bombing of Egypt would involve leaflet campaign to coincide with radio broadcasts calling upon the Egyptian people to overthrow Nasser who had led them into war with Israel and forced the Great Powers to intervene.

10th November, the full invasion force would arrive by sea. By this time Nasser would be gone, or captured by an expedition to Cairo.[1]

What actually happened was quite different. The Israelis moved off suddenly on 29th October. The Americans had become suspicious, particularly after the 26th, when the full mobilization orders were broadcast. Eisenhower told Ben Gurion plainly that he would act to prevent an attack regardless of the effects on American Jews and his party's prospects during the election.

Then came the totally unexpected Hungarian Revolution. The Israelis thought that while the revolution was on the United States, Russia and the UN would not have the time or the inclination to intervene against Israel. So the Israelis moved—after informing the French but not the British. The move was so sudden that not all the necessary equipment had arrived or been set up.

In the meantime Eden, who was a very sick man, was having increasing trouble with a vigilant public and the Americans. The French realized that he would probably cave in if they did not push him along. They alone had little to lose if collusion became known. Their main aim was to end Egyptian aid to the FLN, and one wonders if there were any limits to what they were prepared to do. In any case, Israel's early invasion came as a jolt to Eden. The Americans immediately asked the Security Council for an emergency meeting. That same day, the 30th, Mollet went to see Eden and told him that regardless of the consequences France would veto the US draft resolution in the Council; things had gone too far for them to back out now. Mollet also insisted that Britain and France must issue their Ultimatum immediately. At the rate the Americans were moving, in another day or two the UN would have the matter in hand and there would be no opportunity for an invasion. Eden agreed to the veto, and having no clear idea of Israel's military position also agreed to issuing the Ultimatum.

[1] Childers, *loc. cit.*, pp. 257–8. Cf. below p. 224 n.

Only an ill man, confused, possibly hysterical, could have agreed to either. There was no chance for success and yet he persisted.[1]

At six p.m., on 30th October, the Anglo–French Ultimatum was issued ordering a cease-fire, and forbidding the combatants to approach closer than ten miles to the Suez Canal. This was confusing because Israeli troops were still no closer than 120 miles from the Canal, except for 400 paratroopers at Mitla Pass. The Ultimatum would have made sense if it had been issued a few days later as originally planned; that is, when the Israelis reached the Canal. As it was, many people were understandably bewildered, not least the Egyptians who rejected the Ultimatum. Accordingly, Anglo–French forces bombed Cairo and invaded the Canal Zone.

Our narrative ends here.

[1] He attempted to create the illusion of neutrality by repeating his warning of 12th October to Israel that if Jordan were attacked Britain would go to her aid.

Robertson's account (pp. 132–74) of these final months differs considerably in detail but not substance from Childers'. Robertson offers evidence that Ben Gurion flew to France on 22nd October to meet with Pineau and with Premier Mollet who apparently was not aware of the full extent of Franco–Israeli agreement on the use of French planes and equipment to assist Israel. On the 23rd Selwyn Lloyd and Patrick Dean from the Foreign Office joined the meeting, and on the 24th Ben Gurion, Pineau and Dean signed a formal agreement setting out the arrangements for a tripartite invasion of Egypt (pp. 161–63).

Chapter Sixteen

CONCLUSION

___

IT is now 1965. Nine years have gone by since Israel's invasion of the Sinai Desert and Israel survives and flourishes. Her campaign against Egypt was a moderate success. Casualties on both sides were heavy enough to make both reluctant to suffer similar losses again. The Arabs drew off, the border warfare ended, relative peace reigned. The Israelis clearly illustrated their readiness to fight for their survival. The Arabs obtained a better idea of what victory might cost them. Each side was made more fully aware of the other's capacities. This led to increased mutual respect and, fortunately, caution. Eilat is open to shipping. This delineates the achievements of Israel's campaign.

If Israel still exists, so do the boycott and the blockade. The refugees are camped along the borders, restless, vengeful and rapidly increasing. The Arab radio and Press continue their campaign of incitement against Israel. The border is quiet, but basically the conditions of the 1950's which led to war continue. Neither propinquity nor time have succeeded in bringing the two sides any closer together. Each new generation is born to be schooled in the hates of their fathers and to add to these the fervour of youth and the sanctity of time.

What keeps the Arabs and the Israelis apart is not merely disagreements over the division of the Jordan waters or of the Negev. Each is convinced that the other is not to be trusted and is on the offensive.

The Arabs refuse to make peace with Israel because they see

it in their interests to destroy her or at the very least contain her. The Arab case is so simple, so straightforward, so obvious, and yet few Westerners, caught up in the historical complexities of Christian–Jewish history, ever think about it. The Arabs believe that the Zionists came and took Palestine away from the Arabs: the Jews were having trouble with the Christians, so they robbed the Muslims. This is the central issue. The Arab is on the defensive. To him the Israeli is the aggressor, the man to be feared. In refusing to make peace the Arab is acting in self-defence. He does not believe that the Israelis will be satisfied until they have conquered more land, until they have taken over economic control of the Arab world, and until they have subverted the Muslim way of life. In 1956 the Israelis claimed to have 'redeemed' the Sinai Desert; will they make another attempt at liberation?; will they invade the West Bank?: these are questions the Arabs ask themselves and, on the basis of the growth of Zionist claims since 1917, they find it reasonable to assume that the answer is yes.

The Israelis believe that they are in their homeland where they belong, and that the Arab is trying to destroy them. To the Israelis, the Arab is the aggressor: consequently they must be prepared to attack in self-defence at any time. Also, the more pressure the Arabs put upon the Israelis and the longer this pressure is maintained, the more the Israelis think in terms of expansion as a means to increased self-defence. This, of course, is seized upon by the Arabs as justification for their claim that the Israelis are expansionists. So the circle is complete and vicious. Each is convinced that the other is expansionist, and that no concessions can be offered because the appetites of the other are insatiable.

Unfortunately peace does not depend only upon persuading each side of the placid intentions of the other. Both the Arabs and the Israelis are passing through the most aggressive stages of their respective nationalisms. Implicit in every nationalist movement is militancy and expansion, and you cannot stifle either without endangering the momentum of the movement and consequently the health of the nation. To a degree, the fears of each about the intentions of the other are justified. The Israelis, perhaps, are slightly more advanced than the

226

Arabs in that while they are still very tough and aggressive they feel that their 'great days' are over and consequently they are readier to settle down peaceably with the comfortable feeling of a job well done. The Arabs, on the other hand, are just reaching their peak and they view with increasing eagerness the opportunity to swamp the Israelis and to revenge the last and greatest in a long series of Western-imposed humiliations.

The possibilities for a settlement are unlikely to improve for some considerable time. The older generation of Arab and Israeli politicians may have been aggressive, but by all accounts the new generation is even more extreme and uncompromising and it, in turn, is surpassed by the youngsters now coming up through the primary and secondary schools. Obviously peace must be a very long-range goal.

For better or for worse Israel is here and any attempt by the West or the UN to carve her up as a prelude to peace is likely to generate more difficulties than it resolves.

Nine years have gone by since the last Arab–Israel war. Israel has completed the final stages of her project to draw the waters of the Jordan River off to the Negev. This is the last source of water available to her, and she has made it clear that she will have it. Each year as her population increases she has that much less room for compromise and manœuvre. The Arabs have two choices. They can cooperate with Israel in the use of the river water, as was tacitly agreed upon with Eric Johnston in 1955, or they can carry through their plans to divert the river's headwaters and invite war.

The Arabs search for revenge and self-respect, the Israelis for survival. For both the stakes are high.

APPENDIX

Israeli–Lebanese General Armistice Agreement
Ras En Naqura, 23 March 1949

PREAMBLE

The Parties to the present Agreement,

Responding to the Security Council resolution of 16 November 1948, calling upon them, as a further provisional measure under Article 40 of the Charter of the United Nations and in order to facilitate the transition from the present truce to permanent peace in Palestine, to negotiate an armistice;

Having decided to enter into negotiations under United Nations Chairmanship concerning the implementation of the Security Council resolution of 16 November 1948; and having appointed representatives empowered to negotiate and conclude an Armistice Agreement;

The undersigned representatives, having exchanged their full powers found to be in good and proper form, have agreed upon the following provisions:

Article I

With a view to promoting the return of permanent peace in Palestine and in recognition of the importance in this regard of mutual assurances concerning the future military operations of the Parties, the following principles, which shall be fully observed by both Parties during the armistice, are hereby affirmed:

1. The injunction of the Security Council against resort to military force in the settlement of the Palestine question shall henceforth be scrupulously respected by both Parties.

2. No aggressive action by the armed forces—land, sea, or air—of either Party shall be undertaken, planned or threatened against the people or the armed forces of the other; it being understood that the

use of the term 'planned' in this context has no bearing on normal staff planning as generally practised in military organizations.

3. The right of each Party to its security and freedom from fear of attack by the armed forces of the other shall be fully respected.

4. The establishment of an armistice between the armed forces of the two Parties is accepted as an indispensable step toward the liquidation of armed conflict and the restoration of peace in Palestine.

Article II

With a specific view to the implementation of the resolution of the Security Council of 16 November 1948, the following principles and purposes are affirmed:

1. The principle that no military or political advantage should be gained under the truce ordered by the Security Council is recognized.

2. It is also recognized that no provision of this Agreement shall in any way prejudice the rights, claims and positions of either Party hereto in the ultimate peaceful settlement of the Palestine question, the provisions of this agreement being dictated exclusively by military considerations.

Article III

1. In pursuance of the foregoing principles and of the resolution of the Security Council of 16 November 1948, a general armistice between the armed forces of the two Parties—land, sea and air—is hereby established.

2. No element of the land, sea or air military or para-military forces of either Party, including non-regular forces, shall commit any warlike or hostile act against the military or para-military forces of the other Party, or against civilians in territory under the control of that Party; or shall advance beyond or pass over for any purpose whatsoever the Armistice Demarcation Line set forth in Article V of this Agreement; or enter into or pass through the air space of the other Party or through the waters within three miles of the coastline of the other Party.

3. No warlike act or act of hostility shall be conducted from territory controlled by one of the Parties to this Agreement against the other Party.

Article IV

1. The line described in Article V of this Agreement shall be designated as the Armistice Demarcation Line and is delineated in

pursuance of the purpose and intent of the resolutions of the Security Council of 16 November 1948.

2. The basic purpose of the Armistice Demarcation Line is to delineate the line beyond which the armed forces of the respective Parties shall not move.

3. Rules and regulations of the armed forces of the Parties, which prohibit civilians from crossing the fighting lines or entering the area between the lines, shall remain in effect after the signing of this Agreement with application to the Armistice Demarcation Line defined in Article V.

Article V

1. The Armistice Demarcation Line shall follow the international boundary between the Lebanon and Palestine.

2. In the region of the Armistice Demarcation Line the military forces of the Parties shall consist of defensive forces only as is defined in the Annex to this Agreement.

3. Withdrawal of forces to the Armistice Demarcation Line and their reduction to defensive strength in accordance with the preceding paragraph shall be completed within ten days of the signing of this Agreement. In the same way the removal of mines from mined roads and areas evacuated by either Party, and the transmission of plans showing the location of such minefields to the other Party shall be completed within the same period.

Article VI

All prisoners of war detained by either Party to this Agreement and belonging to the armed forces, regular or irregular, of the other Party, shall be exchanged as follows:

1. The exchange of prisoners of war shall be under United Nations supervision and control throughout. The exchange shall take place at Ras En Naqura within twenty-four hours of the signing of this Agreement.

2. Prisoners of war against whom a penal prosecution may be pending, as well as those sentenced for crime or other offence, shall be included in this exchange of prisoners.

3. All articles of personal use, valuables, letters, documents, identification marks, and other personal effects of whatever nature, belonging to prisoners of war who are being exchanged, shall be returned to them, or, if they have escaped or died, to the Party to whose armed forces they belonged.

4. All matters not specifically regulated in this Agreement shall be

Appendix

decided in accordance with the principles laid down in the International Convention relating to the Treatment of Prisoners of War, signed at Geneva on 27 July 1929.

5. The Mixed Armistice Commission established in Article VII of this Agreement shall assume responsibility for locating missing persons, whether military or civilian, within the areas controlled by each Party, to facilitate their expeditious exchange. Each Party undertakes to extend to the Commission full cooperation and assistance in the discharge of this function.

Article VII

1. The execution of the provisions of this Agreement shall be supervised by a Mixed Armistice Commission composed of five members, of whom each Party to this Agreement shall designate two, and whose Chairman shall be the United Nations Chief of Staff of the Truce Supervision Organization or a senior officer from the Observer personnel of that Organization designated by him following consultation with both Parties to this Agreement.

2. The Mixed Armistice Commission shall maintain its headquarters at the Frontier Post north of Metulla and at the Lebanese Frontier Post at Ras En Naqura, and shall hold its meetings at such places and at such times as it may deem necessary for the effective conduct of its work.

3. The Mixed Armistice Commission shall be convened in its first meeting by the United Nations Chief of Staff of the Truce Supervision Organization not later than one week following the signing of this Agreement.

4. Decisions of the Mixed Armistice Commission, to the extent possible, shall be based on the principle of unanimity. In the absence of unanimity, decisions shall be taken by majority vote of the members of the Commission present and voting.

5. The Mixed Armistice Commission shall formulate its own rules of procedure. Meetings shall be held only after due notice to the members by the Chairman. The quorum for its meetings shall be a majority of its members.

6. The Commission shall be empowered to employ Observers, who may be from among the military organizations of the Parties or from the military personnel of the United Nations Truce Supervision Organization, or from both, in such numbers as may be considered essential to the performance of its functions. In the event United Nations Observers should be so employed, they shall remain under the command of the United Nations Chief of Staff of the Truce

Supervision Organization. Assignments of a general or special nature given to United Nations Observers attached to the Mixed Armistice Commission shall be subject to approval by the United Nations Chief of Staff or his designated representative on the Commission, whichever is serving as Chairman.

7. Claims or complaints presented by either Party relating to the application of this Agreement shall be referred immediately to the Mixed Armistice Commission through its Chairman. The Commission shall take such action on all such claims or complaints by means of its observation and investigation machinery as it may deem appropriate, with a view to equitable and mutually satisfactory settlement.

8. Where interpretation of the meaning of a particular provision of this Agreement, other than the Preamble and Articles I and II, is at issue, the Commission's interpretation shall prevail. The Commission, in its discretion and as the need arises, may from time to time recommend to the Parties modifications in the provisions of this Agreement.

9. The Mixed Armistice Commission shall submit to both Parties reports on its activities as frequently as it may consider necessary. A copy of each such report shall be presented to the Secretary-General of the United Nations for transmission to the appropriate organ or agency of the United Nations.

10. Members of the Commission and its Observers shall be accorded such freedom of movement and access in the areas covered by this Agreement as the Commission may determine to be necessary, provided that when such decisions of the Commission are reached by a majority vote United Nations Observers only shall be employed.

11. The expenses of the Commission, other than those relating to United Nations Observers, shall be apportioned in equal shares between the two Parties to this Agreement.

Article VIII

1. The present Agreement is not subject to ratification and shall come into force immediately upon being signed.

2. This Agreement, having been negotiated and concluded in pursuance of the resolution of the Security Council of 16 November 1948 calling for the establishment of an armistice in order to eliminate the threat to the peace in Palestine and to facilitate the transition from the present truce to permanent peace in Palestine, shall remain in force until a peaceful settlement between the Parties is achieved, except as provided in paragraph 3 of this article.

3. The Parties to this Agreement may, by mutual consent, revise this Agreement or any of its provisions, or may suspend its application, other than Articles I and III, at any time. In the absence of mutual agreement and after this Agreement has been in effect for one year from the date of its signing, either of the Parties may call upon the Secretary-General of the United Nations to convoke a conference of representatives of the two Parties for the purpose of reviewing, revising, or suspending any of the provisions of this Agreement other than Articles I and III. Participation in such conference shall be obligatory upon the Parties.

4. If the conference provided for in paragraph 3 of this Article does not result in an agreed solution of a point in dispute, either Party may bring the matter before the Security Council of the United Nations for the relief sought on the grounds that this Agreement has been concluded in pursuance of Security Council action toward the end of achieving peace in Palestine.

5. This Agreement is signed in quintuplicate, of which one copy shall be retained by each Party, two copies communicated to the Secretary-General of the United Nations for transmission to the Security Council and to the United Nations Conciliation Commission on Palestine, and one copy to the Acting Mediator on Palestine.

Done at Ras En Naqura on the twenty-third of March nineteen forty-nine, in the presence of the Personal Deputy of the United Nations Acting Mediator on Palestine and the United Nations Chief of Staff of the Truce Supervision Organization.

For and on behalf of the Government of Israel	For and on behalf of the Government of the Lebanon
(Signed)	(Signed)

SELECTED BIBLIOGRAPHY

A list of all the sources relevant to Arab–Israeli relations would be too lengthy to include here. The list below is for the general reader who would like some idea of the more important works on the subject.

Documents

The most important are the unpublished *Records* of the Egyptian, Jordanian, Lebanese and Syrian Mixed Armistice Commissions which can be found only in the countries concerned and at the UN. References to the *Records* can be found in the *Security Council Official Records, Reports of the Chief of Staff, UNTSO.* . . .

The *SCOR* contain all documents, complaints, resolutions, etc., submitted to the Security Council, including *Reports of the UN Mediator*, and *Acting Mediator, Reports of the UN Secretary-General* . . . and *Reports of the Chief of Staff, UNTSO.* . . . The records of Council meetings are useful.

Also useful are the *General Assembly Official Records*, especially
Report of the UN Special Committee on Palestine (1947)
Report of the UN Mediator on Palestine (1948)
Reports of the UN Conciliation Commission for Palestine including the *Interim* and *Final Reports of the UN Economic Survey Mission for the Middle East* (1949)

For the refugee problem see *Annual Reports of the Director of UNRWA* (1950–56); *Interim Report of the Director of UNRWA* (1950); *Special Report of the Director of the Advisory Commission of UNRWA* (1950); *Special Reports of the Director of UNRWA* (1953–56)

Periodicals

Commentary
Economist
Egyptian Economic and Political Review

235

Selected Bibliography

Periodicals—(cont.)

Foreign Affairs
International Affairs (RIIA)
International Conciliation
International Organization
Israel Economic News
Israel Economist
Jewish Agency Digest of Press and Events
Jewish Observer and Middle East Review
Mideast Mirror
Middle Eastern Affairs
Middle East Forum
Middle East Journal
Midstream
Muslim World
Proceedings of the Academy of Political Science
Spectator
The World Today
Zionist Review

Detailed examinations of the legal aspects of the Suez Blockade can be found in *The American Journal of International Law, International and Comparative Law Quarterly, Revue du Droit International pour le Moyen Orient,* and *Revue Egyptienne du Droit International.*

Newspapers

Apart from the well-known American, British and French papers, others of interest are *La Bourse Egyptienne, Commerce du Levant-Beyrout Express, Egyptian Gazette, Egyptian Mail, Jerusalem Post,* and the *Jewish Chronicle.*

Pamphlets and Books

The Arabs and the Israelis both have their Offices of Information situated in New York and London, their own Government Information Services, their Ministries of Foreign Affairs, and their captive organizations, all of which publish unending streams of material, some of which is useful.

Most of the books on Arab–Israeli relations are heavily biased and this diminishes their value accordingly. I think that the most informative, despite the limited period it covers, is Lt.-Gen. E. L. M. Burns, *Between Arab and Israeli* (Toronto, 1962). Others are:

236

Selected Bibliography

Childers, E. *The Road to Suez* (London, 1962)

Eytan, W. *The First Ten Years* (London, 1958).

Gabbay, R. E. *A Political Study of the Arab–Jewish Conflict: The Arab Refugee Problem* (Geneva, 1959).

Glubb, Gen. John. *A Soldier with the Arabs* (London, 1957).

Hutchison, Cmdr. E. H. *Violent Truce* (London, 1956).

Kimche, Jon and David. *Both Sides of the Hill* (London, 1960).

Lehrman, Hal. *Israel: The Beginning and Tomorrow* (New York, 1952)

Lilienthal, Alfred. *What Price Israel?* (Chicago, 1953). *There Goes the Middle East* (New York, 1957).

Lorch, Natanel. *The Edge of the Sword* (New York, 1961).

McDonald, James. *My Mission in Israel* (London, 1951).

Rosenne, Shabtai, *Israel's Armistice Agreements with the Arab States* (Tel Aviv, 1951).

Sachar, Harry. *Israel: The Establishment of a State* (London, 1952).

Safran, Nadav. *The United States and Israel* (Cambridge, Mass., 1963).

Weizmann, C. *Trial and Error* (London, 1949).

Young, Lt.-Col. Peter. *Beduin Command* (London, 1956).

A periodical article worth attention is Moshe Brillant, 'Israel's Policy of Reprisals' in *Harper's*, March, 1955.

For events in Palestine prior to 1948 see:

Abcarius, M. F. *Palestine through the Fog of Propaganda* (London, 1946).

Barbour, Neville. *Nisi Dominus* (London, 1946).

Frischwasser-Ra'anan, H. *The Frontiers of a Nation* (London, 1955).

Hanna, Paul L. *British Policy in Palestine* (Washington. 1942).

Hurewitz, J. C. *The Struggle for Palestine* (New York, 1950).

Stein, Leonard. *The Balfour Declaration* (London, 1961).

Useful books on Zionist thought are:

Ben Gurion, David. *Rebirth and Destiny of Israel* (New York, 1954).

Halpern, Ben. *The Idea of a Jewish State* (Cambridge, Mass., 1961).

Hertzberg, Arthur (ed.). *The Zionist Idea* (New York, 1960).

There is a great deal of very good writing on Arab nationalism. The two best, I think, are:

Gibb, Sir Hamilton. *Modern Trends in Islam* (Chicago, 1947).

Selected Bibliography

Smith, Wildred C. *Islam in Modern History* (Mentor Books, New York, 1959).

The history of Arab nationalist thought is briefly summed up in H. Z. Nuseibh, *The Ideas of Arab Nationalism* (Ithaca, NY, 1956). Gamal Abdul Nasser's *Philosophy of the Revolution* (Washington, 1955) and Anwar el-Sadat's *Revolt on the Nile* (London, 1957) give interesting autobiographical details of a nationalist's development.

The following books contain a number of valuable articles on the Arab world, its problems and its development.

Frye, R. N. (ed.). *The Near East and the Great Powers* (Cambridge, Mass., 1951). *Islam and the West* (The Hague, 1957).

Haim, Sylvia G. (ed.). *Arab Nationalism: An Anthology* (Berkeley and Los Angeles, 1962).

Laqueur, Walter (ed.). *The Middle East in Transition* (London, 1958).

General Reading

Berger, M. *The Arab World Today* (London, 1962).

Campbell, John C. *Defense of the Middle East* (New York, 1958).

Carnegie Endowment for International Peace. *Egypt and the United Nations* (New York, 1957). *Israel and the United Nations* (New York, 1956).

Earle, E. M. *Turkey, the Great Powers and the Baghdad Railway* (London, 1923).

Eden, Sir Anthony. *Full Circle* (London, 1960).

Hollingworth, C. *The Arabs and the West* (London, 1952).

Ireland, P. W. (ed.). *The Near East: Problems and Prospects* (Chicago, 1942).

Kedourie, Elie. *England and the Middle East: 1914–21* (London, 1956).

Kirk, George. *A Short History of the Middle East* (London, 1957).

Laqueur, Walter. *Communism and Nationalism in the Middle East* (London, 1957). *The Soviet Union and the Middle East* (London, 1959).

Lenczowski, George. *Oil and State in the Middle East* (Ithaca, NY, 1960).

Monroe, Elizabeth. *Britain's Moment in the Middle East: 1914–1956* (London, 1963).

Parkes, James. *A History of Palestine from 135 AD to Modern Times* (London, 1949).

238

Peretz, Don. *Israel and the Palestine Arabs* (Washington, 1958).

Perowne, Stewart. *The One Remains* (London, 1954).

Pinner, Walter. *How Many Arab Refugees?* (London, 1959).

Robertson, Terence. *Crisis: The Inside Story of the Suez Conspiracy*, (Toronto, 1964).

Rondot, Pierre. *The Changing Patterns of the Middle East: 1919-58* (London, 1961).

Saint Anthony's Papers. *Middle Eastern Affairs, Number One* (London, 1958). *Middle Eastern Affairs, Number Two* (London, 1961). *Middle Eastern Affairs, Number Three* (London, 1963).

Shwadran, Benjamin. *The Middle East, Oil and the Great Powers* (New York, 1955).

Taylor, A. R. *Prelude to Israel: An Analysis of Zionist Diplomacy* (New York, 1959).

Tuchman, Barbara. *Bible and Sword: England and Palestine from The Bronze Age to Balfour* (New York, 1956).

Warriner, Doreen. *Land Reform and Development in the Middle East* (London, 1957).

The Middle East Institute (Washington) publishes the lectures delivered at its annual conferences, some of which are excellent.

The Royal Institute of International Affairs (London) and its Information Department have published a number of works on the Middle East, including:

The Middle East: A Political and Economic Survey, edited by Sir Reader Bullard, 3rd ed. (London, 1958).

Documents on the Suez Crisis, selected and introduced by D. C. Watt (London, February, 1957).

British Interests in the Mediterranean and the Middle East (London, 1958).

Also see Chatham House Memoranda:

The Western Powers and the Middle East, rev. ed., June 1959.

Britain and the Suez Canal, D. C. Watt, rev. ed., June 1957.

The Baghdad Pact: Origins and Political Setting, July 1956.

INDEX

Index